Too Relieved To Grieve

The Alternative Heartbreak Handbook

By

Karan Scott

To Clive,

Here's your bloody book, signed, sealed & delivered! Mission accomplished.

Seriously though, I am forever grateful. Thank you for everything!

Karan

xxx.

23.9.2019

Disclaimer

The following content is based on first-hand accounts of historical events. However, certain names, locations and events have been changed, composited or fictionalised with imaginative licence for dramatic purposes.

Identifying names, locations and characteristics of individuals mentioned have been changed to protect their privacy.

Whilst the author has made every effort to provide accurate information at the time of publication, neither the publisher nor the author assumes any responsibility for errors or changes that may occur after publication.

No responsibility for loss to any individual or organisation acting on or refraining from action as a result of the material in this publication can be accepted by the publisher or author.

Phoenix vector by mehibi

To my babies,

We made it my darlings, and I could not be prouder of who you are.

You are strong, brave, compassionate and kind.

I love you.

Damn this is gonna hurt. *Takes a deep breath*. Oh well, here goes.

The Gist, Part I

I was in love with him, once. I loved him with every fibre of my being. It pervaded every aspect of who I was: mentally, emotionally, physically and spiritually. I allowed him to become the centre of my universe. Had my toenail clippings been analysed, the DNA of my love for him would have been seen waving devotedly from the microscope slide. I had it bad. I was so in love with him... once.

Q: So, what happened?

Well, he dumped me. He dumped me after 24 years, two children, and one thriving family business together, that's what happened. His actions resulted in what felt like being evicted from my own life, and the children and I from our family home. He removed me from so much that had once been mine, and systematically dismantled everything we had built together; but it's not as cut and dried as that.

Whilst the hard-heartedness of those decisions and actions did occur, and were truly heart-breaking and terrifying to live through, I went on to discover this implosion of my life was ultimately an invitation to a new life. A fresh lease where I could live out *my* life's purpose, as opposed to merely serving as Operations Manager in his. I was now free to realise *my* dreams, rather than spending my finite life equity, facilitating his. Oh, how this was just the beginning.

Q: So, what's this all about Karan, what are you having me read here?

Essentially, I'm here to offer you hope, on a couple of fronts, and to help guide you through your own life implosion; but damn it's gonna hurt... *me*. As an intensely private and introverted INFJ kind of girl *[Google it]*, I'm about to feel the fear and do it anyway and chronicle the gradual degradation of my once sublime and happy relationship.

So private am I in fact, that there will be people I've known for years, decades even, who have no inkling of what's about to hit these pages. But I'm on a mission to help those in the same boat, who've had their hearts, minds and lives smashed and splattered as I have, so I must put on my big girl pants and get on with it.

You see, once you've stared down the barrel of penniless-single-parent-Christmas-homelessness, there's not a lot left to frighten you in quite the same way ever again, which is what's going to get me through this writing process. This is where my courage is going to come from; if I can get through living it, I can certainly get through writing about it. That being said, please do excuse my intermittent whimpering as I haul my vulnerabilities kicking and screaming into the light for the first time in my life. We all have to grow through what we go through, so let the soul sharing commence.

The Gist, Part II

Now I said *relationship* earlier because we were together from June 1989 until September 2013, but we were only married from September 2002. The sublime happiness bit came before we were married. We were deeply in love, devoted to each other and we did everything together. We were the archetypal star-crossed lovers no one ever believed could, should, or would split, but we did.

[6]

The marriage bit quickly oversteered out of control, like a sports car on an ice rink. Had we just taken our foot off the accelerator for a second, we could perhaps have straightened up and regained control, but neither of us did, so we didn't. Instead, we tried to power through, and we crashed.

It was gut-wrenchingly devastating at first, because I for one had truly believed he was The One, and we were forever. Now, years after the crash, and empowered with newly acquired wisdom, I have become too relieved to grieve. I can see clearly now why it was all so necessary and pricelessly valuable. I can't speak for him because we no longer speak, and I no longer have any insights into his soul, but from my perspective, I apparently needed us to crash. Evidently, the crash evolved into the best thing that could have happened. The alternative would have been more of the same, and I prefer where I am now thanks very much. I just didn't appreciate that immediately in 2013, when we were hurtling towards our brutal and catastrophic stop.

I will introduce us to you in a moment, so you'll be able to understand and feel our story more fully, but I want to say this to you before we really begin: it is my sincerest wish for you to be able to gain strength from my story, and to perhaps adopt a different way of looking at your own situation. Too many people panic and rush headlong into a self-harm or self-medication ritual to cope, and I want to show you there's a better, more empowering way. Please don't shrink down into bleak despair, because I'm here to help uplift your spirit and restore your hope.

Admittedly I have winced whenever the "*you should write a book*" subject has come up in conversation, because I felt it would be like prising open the slowly healing flesh of a machete wound; far too painful to contemplate. Why would I ever put myself through such a thing? How needlessly masochistic.

How terrifyingly public: *Me? Emote? In front of people?* I felt sure that was never going to happen.

Then it occurred to me there may be at least one person in the universe who'd be interested in what I have experienced, and how I have gradually mastered the existential threats to my heart and mind. There may be at least one heartbroken and grieving soul who could be inspired by a uniquely empowering perspective, which would help them to find the strength within to begin again. So, I stopped wincing and actively started musing. Then this happened.

My friend told me about a woman she'd known, who had two teenage children and whose husband had committed adultery, before abandoning his family altogether. The woman was at such a loss, and so completely overwhelmed by the depths of her husband's betrayal, that she committed suicide; completely unable to go on. When I learned of this woman's pain and despair - where not even the irrefutable love for her children was enough to sustain her fight – I realised this was the time I had to let my own darkness come into the light to help others. No one should ever feel so bereft. Certainly not on my watch, when I can at least offer my way as a means of some assistance and support. It was time to get over myself.

If you've been similarly hurt, not knowing what to do because you're disorientated, unable to think because your head is spinning, because you're barely able to breathe due to the Grief Elephant on your chest, then you are precisely the person I want to help. I want to give you another way of thinking, a pathway to coping, an emotional care package to help you through the most desperate nights of your life. I want you to know my story, so you can have faith that you will be okay too – if you just hold on.

I'm nothing special. I have no marketable superpowers. All I have is the wisdom and experience I've acquired during my life, which I'm sharing with you. I want to give you clarity; to help you think when you think you can't. To encourage you to feel your feelings, even though they probably terrify you and send you reeling. To embrace and reclaim your purpose in life, rather than ceding it to others as I have done. To help you understand you're within a process that *will* end, and that you are safe to live in your own head, by your own hand, and – eventually – thriving in your own once reluctant independence.

Don't doubt you have got this. You can absolutely master your situation. I know you probably don't believe me in this moment, but everything is cyclical, and it's just a matter of time before your life turns towards the light again. I too have been swallowed whole by the darkness, where the depths of my despair felt eternally endless, but it *does* get better. Please remember how you have survived 100% of the worst days of your life, which is how I know you can wake up and fight for every tomorrow.

You are stronger than you can possibly imagine. You have a steely core just begging to be acknowledged and activated. You have been dormant and small for far too long, and I want you to now acknowledge and trigger the unstoppable greatness within you. How do I know you're strong, resilient with greatness within? Because you're reading this book; you're proactively seeking solutions and ways to feel better and become stronger. You are not a quitter. You are <u>not</u> down and out. You just need a little help to get off the mat, so let's do this!

Life's platitude menu tells us that time heals all wounds. Now as much as my fingers drum when having to endure such incoming old chestnuts, there is always a kernel of truth within the platitude. What I can tell you from my own experience is, by respecting the process, by allowing enough time to pass, for my heart and mind to fully recover, I am now able to look back with a poignant respect for how my life has unfolded; exactly as it should, in perfect time. Your life will unfold this way too.

I can now visualise and appreciate how all the jigsaw pieces of my life were gradually being manoeuvred into place, for my greatest and highest good, when I felt entirely abandoned and forsaken by the universe. Granted, my jigsaw pieces now present an entirely different picture to the one I had before, but I can assure you my new picture is now more beautiful, vivid and vibrant than anything that came before it. I can testify to the perceived wisdom which states that if we lose anything, it will always be replaced with something of equal or greater value. Please have faith, you will be okay. You will be changed, but you will be okay.

There will be tears and snot bubbles [*mine!*] as I tell you my story, but they will be fuelled by the love and happiness attached to the memories I'll be evoking. It *is* sad my relationship had to end, but nothing lasts forever, and it is with this open acceptance of a fundamental truth that makes me now too relieved to grieve. I am choosing to be happy and thankful it happened at all, rather than grieving for its inevitable end. I'm not necessarily expecting you to have reached the same point on your journey just yet, but please remember progress is a process, not an event.

Please take whatever you can from anything between these two covers and discard the rest. Some things will resonate with you, and some things will not.

You may agree or disagree with the decisions and actions I have taken, but I have always endeavoured to be honourable; particularly from Act II onwards. You will not find a single proclamation within this book which says I did everything perfectly, because I didn't. I made mistakes. I have made enormous great errors in judgement which can still be seen from space, but I always sought to keep them to a minimum, and I continually strive to never repeat them. After all, when you make the same mistake more than once, it's a choice.

To reduce the number of mistakes I'm so clearly capable of making, or to mitigate the losses from those I stumbled into without looking, I have followed one simple mantra without fail. Every single critical choice, action or decision went through Oprah Winfrey's wisdom filter: **If you do your best in every situation, it puts you in the best possible position for the next situation**. I can say hand on heart – whether you agree with me or not – that I did my best. I now sleep like a log with a clear conscience and squeaky-clean karma. I have no regrets and I am simply too relieved to grieve.

A LITTLE HISTORY, FOR CONTEXT

The Gist, Part III

My younger brother, Paul, and I were born and raised on a brand-new and modern council estate in Average Town. Our parents divorced when we were very young, and Mum remarried to give us a stepfather, Noel. Always close to and nurtured by Mum, and where Noel was concerned, we were well looked after, materially speaking. We also had our health, and enjoyed a happy-*ish* family dynamic, which included Dad at weekends, birthdays and Christmas. But let's magnify this a little, so you can really see what happened, because everything has influenced me one way or another, and this will help you to understand my choices later.

Mum

In my lifetime, all was generally well until 1983. In 1983 Noel visited Canada to complete a long-term work project, and whilst there, optimised his time by having an affair with a woman called Joyce. This destroyed Mum. He eventually returned home to make amends and repent. After a lot of time and angst they reconciled. Noel then departed for Japan for more work where yep, you guessed it, he optimised his time again. This plunged Mum into an even deeper, darker spiral of despair and self-loathing, which essentially heralded the end of my childhood. I was 12.

With her now small, loving but fragmented family scattered throughout the British Isles, with no one living within one hundred miles, Mum had regrettably few people she felt she could turn to about this (as she was a private person too), so I stepped up. To the detriment of my middle school education, I tended to the manifestations of Mum's despair daily, working desperately to prevent her anorexia and heavy drinking from tightening their grip any further. It was during these dark, disorientating days, witnessing Mum's harrowing struggle with heartbreak, that I swore I would never allow a man to reduce and weaken me as Mum had done.

A seething sense of anger crept stealthily into my soul and took up residence beside my throbbing generic teenage angst. I eventually learned about the futility of misdirected anger, and duly learned to harness it correctly in later years, but for now I was perpetually furious with the world and everyone in it. Through his selfish and thoughtless actions, Noel had turned my world upside down, as well as destroying my beloved Mum. Paul was shielded from the vast majority of the fallout, due to his tender years and innocence, but that's not to say he was unaffected. He was affected alright, but Paul has always been a stoic, sensitive and introverted person, who doesn't always choose to share his thoughts and feelings. One thing is clear though, Noel successfully threw a grenade at our lives, as he revelled with wanton disregard in Canada and Japan.

You see, Mum's life had been far from a bed of roses until this point, so she was already carrying a huge burden of emotional turmoil, before Noel's multiple betrayals. Noel knew all of the gory details, but the swinging brick in his chest didn't seem to care. Maybe he was the product of his upbringing, but then aren't we all? Maybe he was just a bastard, who can say for sure? All I know is that he left us in his wake, scrambling to hold on to ourselves and survive.

It's fair for you to assume my relationship with Noel, upon his return and for evermore, was downright combative. I was a child when he left for Canada, and now I was an emboldened, protective, opinionated teenager, living in a state of perpetual fire and fury. Where Noel was concerned, I was a walking, talking arsehole. My respect for someone so callous and self-absorbed was zero, and it showed. Cursed with a resting bitch face on even my sunniest of days, Noel was never unsure about what I thought of him, but he had a foul temper too. He also used sarcasm as a weapon, and he taught me well. He would later learn to regret this however, when the passing of time allowed the student to become the master.

There is no way for you to fully understand Mum's decisions where Noel is concerned, because her life story is worthy of a biography of its own. I will however outline a few key passages from her life, as they directly affect my own psyche, and shaped the choices I have made.

Mum's early childhood was idyllic. Born in Northern Ireland to Patrick and Annie, Mum flourished in the security of a large and loving extended family. High achieving at school, Mum completely adored her Mum, Dad, older brother Graham, and younger sister Alison. Then one cold winter's morning, tragedy struck. Whilst ironing her niece's wedding dress, my Grandma Annie suddenly became unwell, collapsed and died of a cerebral aneurysm within the space of a few short heart beats. Graham was 22, Mum was 15, Alison was 8. The whole family were naturally shocked and devastated.

From there everything got a lot worse, the details of which I will spare you now, because that's Mum's story not mine. Suffice it to say my grandfather Patrick – or Pop, as he wished to be called – eventually remarried, Maggie. No, that's not your imagination, you really can hear the pantomime hissing and booing I've impregnated these pages with. Where Grandma Annie was a strong feminine power, but always warm, loving, attentive and nurturing, Maggie was emotionally cold, sharp and constantly disparaging. Maggie was a freezing shock to Mum's traumatised and grieving teenage system, to say the least. The very least. This was further exacerbated when Pop and Maggie had Eve within a year or two. Maggie made it abundantly clear to Mum that she was not welcome to bond or engage with the infant Eve. Unsurprisingly, the relationship between Mum and Maggie was fraught and rife with animosity and venom.

Events conspired, which led Mum first to Hampshire to live with her Auntie Irene, before relocating to Buckingham, where she eventually met Dad. There were many more hurts and emotional betrayals along Mum's path from Northern Ireland to Buckingham, but she ultimately fell in love and married Dad in April 1970. I was born in March 1971, closely followed by Paul in 1973, but our parents' marriage was not able to sustain, and they divorced. Mum married Noel in 1976, and we all moved into our brand-new council house together, where we were happy-ish. For a while.

Mum loved Noel deeply. To this day I will never fully understand why, but she did. Don't get me wrong, he was a good enough egg in the beginning, and Paul and I always had a summer holiday on the south coast, and generous Christmases and birthdays etc, but he was an emotionally cold and distant man; with Paul and I at least. Alongside Mum, he attended every school concert, sports day and parent's consultations with our teachers. He was engaged, and he did seem to care. We were always well fed, nicely dressed and provided for, but there was a warmth and a connection missing from him, like he was just going through the motions, ticking boxes. Perhaps it's because Paul and I weren't his? Perhaps it's because he had endured abrasive parents, and didn't know how else to be? Whatever the reason, this is who he was to us, and he shaped us.

Dad

Dad was tall, dark and handsome. He played football as a young man, until a knee injury curtailed the ambition he had. He was a carpenter by trade, and deeply in love with Mum. You can see the devotion and happiness in his eyes in many of the photographs they posed for, early on in their relationship, but the smiles quickly faded.

He told me in later life that he had always wanted children but admitted to struggling with the overwhelming responsibility when Paul and I came along, so soon after they were married. Their marriage was as tempestuous as it was short-lived, but they were able to remain friends enough for Dad to continue teasing Mum about her comically bad lemon meringue pies. Although he had one serious and long-term relationship post-divorce, Dad chose never to remarry, despite being aware of his partner's clear and present willingness. He just couldn't do it.

Dad struggled to cope when his mum, my beloved Nanna, died in 1979. *Ooof*, but Nanna was strong! I adored – still adore, even though she's long gone – my Nanna. I was eight when she died, following a devastating battle with a brain tumour. There is still a huge Nanna-sized hole in my heart to this day, because I have never come close to recovering from her loss. I should really have counselling for this, but I can't bear to let her go, so I choose to cling to her memory like a shipwreck survivor to driftwood.

Dad found his own way through the tremendous grief he felt, which again, is more his story than mine. This brought a temporary distance between us into play. I have never doubted his love for me, but our personalities diverged when I became furious and stronger for Mum, whilst he was weakened by the loss of Nanna. This was my first foray into being *too much*, but more of this later.

Dad went on to live a difficult life, punctuated with frequent bursts of serious, and sometimes life threatening, ill health. He died with me by his side in 2010, but not before giving numerous strangers the gift of life or respite, via the organ donation programme; of which I am now a proud registrant in his name.

Steve

The mythical "he" I was in love with once is Steve, and we have two magically magnificent children, Sofia and Alex. Yes, the retelling of this story will bring on more tears and snot bubbles because there are two innocent and precious children affected by what has happened. These tears and snot bubbles will also be fuelled by fury and disgust, and you'll understand why soon enough. Writing this is going to be as messy as it is cathartic, but it's always the process that counts. We are shaped by what we go through, to prepare us for what's next. We must grow into who we must eventually be, and this is my messy growth process you're invited to witness. I'm thinking eggs becoming scrambled eggs right now; as in you must first break to make, in the name of regeneration and creation.

Steve was born and raised by Bill and Mallie. As the man I loved, Steve was a pure soul. He had a huge heart and a tender temperament. Although tall and well built, he was a gentle bear of a gentleman, and had truly been the world's greatest daddy to our children. As our tale unfolds, it will appear that Steve has – in my opinion at least – lost his way, and shrunk down into a deep, dark, safe and secure space inside of himself... to heal, I hope. Despite his adultery, our subsequent divorce and his despicable treatment of our children more recently, he is not currently the man I knew or married. I accept this may well be Steve 2.0, and who he is for the remainder of his life, but he's not the man I was so deeply in love with, once.

This isn't just my opinion of him by the way. Even members of his own family have acknowledged he seems dead behind the eyes somehow. The once abundant warmth and softness in his kindly brown eyes is no longer there, now he's chosen to ruthlessly pursue some illusion of happiness he thinks he's found. It's like he's had to relinquish his humanity to pursue this affair, like a prisoner who must surrender his belt before incarceration. But then he couldn't do what he's done without changing into someone else, he was too tender hearted to have contemplated hurting me, or especially the children, in the way that he has.

Whilst Steve's eventual adulteress was able to inveigle away his mind and body, she has most certainly not taken "my Steve", who I believe – rightly or wrongly – is cowering, exhausted and broken behind an imposter's facade. Instead, she's saddled herself with a second-rate substitute, and she's welcome to him... and his emotional baggage. The children and I refer to this version of him as The Imposter, or Fake Daddy, because it feels like he's been invaded by The Body Snatchers to us.

His personality has done a complete 180°, and the few of us who knew him best, don't recognise him any longer. If I hadn't have witnessed it for myself, I would never have believed him capable of the cruelty that follows. With how heartless he appears to have become, the children and I feel blessed that we've been thrown clear of this metaphoric car crash, and hopefully karma will let us watch what happens next.

It is therefore my belief – rightly or wrongly – that Steve has [*temporarily, I hope*] manifested this Imposter persona, during some kind of midlife crisis spasm, essentially out of fear, exhaustion and panic. No, he didn't tear out and buy a Harley Davidson, because that's a tired and laboured screenwriter's metaphor, but his behaviour is otherwise textbook. If you should ever feel so inclined, do some of your own research into the concept of midlife crisis to see what I mean. I will discuss this issue in more detail as we get shoulder deep into Act II, but for now let's get back on track.

I specifically chose to marry Steve, to bear his children and spend the rest of my life with him, because I believed him to be the last man on earth who would ever do exactly what he's done. I thought I had found the Holy Grail of men, the ultimate, complete and Platinum Package. I felt beyond blessed, loved and thankful. He was loving, kind, gorgeous, thoughtful, sensitive, funny, honest, generous, hardworking, totally devoted, and he had *skills*. When other women in my orbit complained about their men, I would silently bask in the safety of *"Not my Steve"*.

He was the exception to every man-rule I was aware of, and he was damn near perfect. When it all came out in the wash that he was having an affair and leaving me, I was more devastated by how ordinary he was than by his desertion. It truly is such a tragic waste of a good man. I can only imagine what his late, honourable and highly esteemed father would have thought of his behaviour and choices.

As much as this request may surprise you, please don't cast Steve as the villain of this piece, because that would be too easy, and he isn't. Yes, he's made some disgusting choices, but so have I. He's made mistakes, and so have I. He's been a steaming heap of a man turd, and I've been an entitled, truculent bitch. So far, I've only outlined what he's done, when you still need to learn how I have contributed to it all. At the end of the day, this book isn't about who's to blame, it's about the process I have progressed through, and the hardships I have vanquished. It's about the lessons I've learnt along the way, which may be able to help you now.

Please know that I look upon everything Steve has thrown at me as a gift, because there was no other way, I could have learnt the lessons he gave me. There are some things you can only learn in a storm. I now like, love and respect myself, and I have Steve to thank for that. Sure, I lost everything in the tempest, but I now like, love and respect how I clawed back more than I lost. Don't believe me, just read.

I should be clear about this from the outset: there is a piece of me which still loves Steve, and I will never allow any harm to come to him. I believe I will always love Steve, but the nature of my love for him has changed shape. How can I tell? Well, when I have good news to report, he's no longer who I call. When I need help, he's no longer who I rely on. When I wake up, he's no longer a person I think of. When I'm singing [*badly!*] alone in the car, he's no longer who I'm singing at, err... I mean *to*. I do care about his well-being, safety and overall success, but whether he's having a bad day, or eating too many biscuits, is no longer any of my concern. I've let go to a large extent, but he needs to repair his relationship with the children, and pronto, before it's too late.

Another critically important point I want to make here, before we go much further is this: whatever his actions and behaviours, however much hurt and pain he's caused, I still choose to respect the fact that Steve is the father of my children. I may be respecting this fact more than he is, but that's something he's going to have to live with, if true. This man loves his babies, of that I have no doubt, and they continue to love him too. They just have no time or respect for this infected version of who he is right now. They have nothing to offer The Imposter.

I happen to believe – rightly or wrongly – that Steve is struggling with the shame and guilt of his selfish, knee-jerk reactions to his possible midlife crisis fear and exhaustion, and cannot look into the beautiful, innocent eyes of our children, so he chooses not to. If my theory is even a little correct, then allowing The Imposter to make his decisions, prevents Real Steve from having to face the hurt he's caused the children, or the hard choices he now needs to commit to, to atone for it all. For every day he hides behind The Imposter facade, the further away he's allowing his children to drift, because I can't hold them to the memory of who he once was [*and hopefully will be again*], forever. Whilst the sun has set on my marriage with him, Steve can still rescue the remnants of love and respect the children have for him, if he hurries the hell up!

I will obviously go into more detail soon, but I know from experience, that being furious and spitting bile gets us nowhere. As Dr Martin Luther King Jr teaches us: *Hate only breeds more hate. Only love can dispel hate. Only light can dispel the dark.* As a result, these principles have become the foundation stones of my decisions. I choose to lean into the light, and I choose love and compassion, however much that may infuriate my sideline spectators.

Regrettably, I am reasonably certain Steve harbours feelings of anger, dislike/hate and distrust towards me, and it is this apparent animosity towards me which now prevents him from choosing to see his children. It's all very cutting your nose off to spite your face, because there are no official documents or court orders preventing him from seeing them. This estrangement is his choice, which he renews every day.

It has been my strongly held belief since forever that children need both parents, wherever possible. Obviously if one parent is toxic or somehow detrimental, well then that's a different story. But assuming both parents are the best versions of themselves they can be, and both love their children unconditionally, then both parents have equal and essential contributions to make. I am not one of those mothers who use their children as a commodity, or pawns in vindictive little revenge games. My children are too sacred to degrade and objectify in this manner. They are teeming with love, compassion, intelligence [*and sarcasm*] and I respect them too much to merely move them around an imaginary chess board, to satisfy some warped agenda. They are people, and I honour their love for their father.

It is my suspicion, that on some level, Steve knows instinctively he's not currently the best version of himself and is choosing to withhold himself from the children; possibly to protect them from experiencing this (temporary) lesser Imposter. I could be seriously wrong about this, but I *just know* he loves the children deeply, and this is the most generous explanation I can think of. It is my sincerest wish for Steve to find himself, and true happiness, again. The world is a better place with him in it, and better still when he's happy and thriving. I hope he can find his way back to his children one day, and for he and I to regain at least a cordial means of interacting with each other. For now though, the children and I are here, and he is there. He is clearly happy enough, for now.

MY WAR COUNCIL

Q: What's a War Council?

Well, my War Council is comprised of those who coalesced around me at the point of impact and wouldn't let go. These are the nutters who listened to and counselled me for hours and hours for months on end. They patiently waited for me to work things out in my head, for my emotions to settle, for my vision to clear and for my logic to return. These are my platinum level angels, without whom I would probably have lost my mind.

But I have something important to add here. I was blessed to have been swamped with love and support from a humbling number of friends, who are not members of the War Council. This doesn't mean their contribution towards holding me upright was ever less-than in any way, it just means I saw or heard from them less regularly. Their time, advice, compassion and generosity of spirit were equally as valuable and valid, and for which I will be forever grateful. I would therefore like to take this opportunity to thank, with all my heart: Tracey W., Joan, Joe, Sarah, Phil, Cat S., Kellie, Melissa, Stephanie, Ms Ginns, Louise, Jane, Stevie, Sara, Wilkie, Tracey C., Susan, Elaine, The Berry, and Mandy. You all know who you are. Thank you for everything you did to support Sofia, Alex and I, I will never forget your love and support.

So, let's now get back to introducing you to my War Council.

Hayley

I'm going to introduce you to Hayley first, for the simple reason that it's because of Hayley this book exists. Hayley's responsible for a lot of things, which will provoke a hearty knowing laugh from her when she reads this. Hayley will not let me rest, not even when my world implodes. If I'm not living on the edge of myself, I'm taking up too much room!

Hayley and I have known each since 2010, when we met during a seminar. Hayley had previously read an article about my achievements and reached out to ask how I managed to get it all done as a working mum, and we haven't stopped talking since. It's dawned on Hayley more recently that if a friendship survives seven years, it's a locked in certainty. I'm sure I heard her gulp when she realised this, but it's too late, she's stuck with me now.

It's because Hayley and I set up our fortnightly Kick Up The Arse (KUTA) phone call sessions (she lives 150+ miles away), that my business was eventually born. We would motivate, inspire, empower and hold each other accountable for setting and achieving our goals. We would accept zero blather or BS about why a mission had not been completed, but we would also console and care for each other when the inevitable life shifts hit the fan.

Hayley is a strong, spiritual, artistically creative feminine power. She is intuitive, compassionate, perceptive, brutally honest, scathingly funny and wise. Hayley is also protective and not in the least bit concerned about getting in my face and telling me like it is – or pulling me up and telling me off if I'm being too hard on myself.

A true friend not only accepts who you are, but helps you become who should be.

Paul

My brother Paul was a peroxide blonde, blue-eyed angel of a boy when he was born, and definitely the apple of Mum's eye. There was an abundant cuteness overload where he was concerned, and he and I were close as children – despite me slashing his hand with a bread knife and breaking his toe with my bedroom door. War wounds he calls them, and I think I'd better clarify.

For reasons I cannot remember, or perhaps ever really knew, I once found an approximately 18-month-old Paul holding a bread knife in his closed fist, by the blade. My 3-year-old self, recognised the danger he was in, ran over and pulled the knife down and out of his hand. Yes, technically I slashed him, but I was trying to protect him. My intent was pure, but oh how the omens for the rest of my life are not lost on me now.

As for the broken toe, well that was entirely his own fault for being an annoying little brother. We were arguing about something, I stormed into my bedroom and he tried to follow, so I slammed the heavy wooden door to prevent entry, unintentionally fracturing his big toe. Which he still complains about to this day, like it was as painful as childbirth or something. Urgh, I didn't do it on purpose. These are just two of a million skirmishes we've had, but we have still managed to forge a deep and loving bond, nonetheless.

Now as adults we still occasionally annoy the bejesus out of each other, apparently. I can't imagine what he finds annoying about me, because I'm a delight! His annoying traits have lessened in their intensity over the years, certainly nothing warranting another broken toe or slashed hand, but seriously Paul, when we agree on 11 O'clock, do not arrive at 9 O'clock; people have been maimed for less!

[26]

As Mum and I had a complicated relationship, with the chemistry between us becoming more combustible the older we got, it became safer for us to accept our estrangement, for what eventually turned out to be the final six years of her life. This was never the plan. I for one never intended to never see her alive again. We'd had multiple histrionics in the past, but always found our way back to each other. It had been my belief and my sincerest wish to reconcile again, once the toxicity between us had dissipated over time. We did try to reconnect about a year before she died suddenly and unexpectedly, but alas it was not to be. We were both as stubborn and combustible as ever, neither one giving so much as an inch of ground. This I regret profoundly.

The reason I'm telling you this is because it affected my relationship with Paul, as I effectively lost him too, whilst estranged from Mum. I have always known and reluctantly accepted that Paul was enthroned in a place of Mum's heart that I could never even visit. There were so many instances where I was *too much* for Mum and Paul to handle: too arrogant, too strong in character, too opinionated, too forceful, too ambitious, too passionate and too driven. I can never operate at anything less than 100% full throttle, which can evidently make others feel like they're standing in a wind tunnel with a cocktail umbrella for protection. As alluded to earlier, this concept of *too much* is a recurring theme throughout my entire adult life, and few have been able to live with, accept, manage or even tolerate me. So, let's call me an acquired taste.

Events conspired in Paul's life to lead him back to living with Mum, so it's understandable how Paul became enveloped in Mum's perception of the estrangement, without ever getting personally involved. That being said, I missed him every day. Paul and I eventually reconnected when Mum died, and we have become closer than ever, as we bonded over simultaneous life changing events, which brought fear and turmoil to us both. Spoiler alert: we both vanquished our fears and conquered the tumultuous events, but goddammit they almost sent us both to the brink.

How the hell we did it needed much reflection from us both because it was all too much, and all at the same time, in both of our lives. We look back now and still can't string together adequate enough sentences to fully explain what we've been through, but damn are we stronger than strong as a result. Everything will be explained once we get into Act II.

I smile because you are my brother. I laugh because there's nothing you can do about it!

Lauren

Lauren is my oldest friend, although she's quicker on the draw than the Milky Bar Kid to point out she's five months younger than I am. We have known each other since we were ten, and in our middle school netball team together. Despite her comparative youthfulness, Lauren knows me, often better than I know myself. I once described Lauren as a pair of comfy slippers, before having to duck behind a quickly upturned table to avoid a hurtling coffee cup. Lauren didn't appear to like the analogy.

Once Lauren had been adequately sedated, I was able to explain what I meant: a comfy pair of slippers brings you a reassuring sense of relief at the end of an uncomfortable day, when you've endured being contained in circumstances you don't enjoy and appreciate nearly as much. Evidently, this explanation was enough to secure my continued survival. For now, at least.

Conversations with Lauren are effortless, because I must complete so few sentences, and I don't have to explain everything to the nth degree. She gets it, before it's even an it. More importantly, Lauren hears what I'm not saying and won't take my shit either. For all the people in my life who've somehow been intimidated by my *too much-ness*, Lauren laughs in my face. Lauren has never found me *too much* of anything, and has fought for me, and had my best interests at heart, even when I didn't thank her for doing so.

Oh, and we laugh. We laugh a lot. On the phone mostly, as we live far apart. If we were to ever have a crossed line, or our phone lines bugged, all they'd ever hear is our silent laughing. You know that kind of laughter where you're laughing so hard there is no sound, only tears streaming down your cheeks as you clench your pelvic floor, hope for the best and collapse sideways? That's us. One of us will say something funny, which the other one will respond to with interest, until we're eventually layering the ridiculous until we're unable to speak anymore. I love this, and I love us.

Loyalty is such a rare quality to be found these days, particularly in people you believe to be your friend. Alas, there are stone-cold drones in this world, who seek to penetrate their way into your life, exploiting any temporary vulnerabilities for their own nefarious ends. It will be the strong and high calibre friends like Lauren, who will flatly refuse to give up on seemingly worthless causes, and be there when it all shakes out, proving her right all along.

Lauren did just this for me. I knew someone once [*who you will be introduced to shortly*], who climbed up by their ragged fingernails to get into my world, and then attempted to destroy the friendship between Lauren and I, so my attention would become undivided. For almost three years, Lauren warned, coaxed and waited like a safety net for me to come to my senses. On the day

[29]

I phoned Lauren to ashamedly admit she had been right all along, and to apologise for my wilful ignorance, Lauren replied gently: "*I'd have given anything to have been wrong*". The graciousness and magnanimity Lauren offered me unconditionally in that moment, will forever define who she is to me, and to us as friends.

Lauren never gave up on us, even when it appeared to her that I had. For the avoidance of doubt, I had never given up on my friendship with Lauren, but from my choices, actions and behaviours, Lauren was well within her sense of foreboding to believe that I had. I am blessed to be loved and protected by someone as principled, steadfast and plain bloody fierce as Lauren.

A friend is someone who will calm you down.
A best friend will skip alongside you, swinging a baseball bat, singing:
"Somebody's gonna get it!"

Carrie

I've known Carrie since about 2004, but our friendship took a couple of years to really take root and blossom. This was mainly due to the fact Carrie cut our hair, so I was only able to spend any brief quality alone time with her every five weeks or so. It quickly became apparent that we both have the same warped and filthy sense of humour, but we didn't start socialising outside of the salon for a couple of years. Then things shifted up a gear.

Once I started to really get to know Carrie, and how her mind works, I was in awe. The polite, creative professionalism I was always greeted with at hair cut time, belied a kind of criminal genius mentality I could only bow down to in reverence. It became clear to me that Carrie was not to be messed with, and I deeply respected how she walked the walk with calculated laser focus, which always resulted in her desired outcome.

Carrie, like Lauren, Paul, Hayley and Dawn (who you'll be introduced to next), can see beneath a multitude of layers. Carrie does not accept what you choose to show her. If she senses there's more there than meets the eye, her mind is inquisitive and open to learning more, but then there are the consequences if you cross her, or those she cares about. All I will say is, if you're sufficiently mentally impaired enough to cross Carrie, the first thing you will know about it is when you've fallen into a hole of your own digging, wondering what the hell happened to you. I revere these qualities in such a like-minded soul.

Respect is earned. Honesty appreciated. Trust is gained. Loyalty returned.

Dawn

Dawn swooped in like Wonder Woman to save the day. There were no capes, lassos of truth, or bulletproof bracelets, but for the affect Dawn had on my life and mindset at the time of her arrival, there may as well have been.

I had been aware of Dawn for many years, as our eldest children went to school together and I often saw her around school, never really knowing who she was. Then in January 2014 a mutual friend, Tracey C, suggested I take Alex to local karate lessons. This was an ideal suggestion at the perfect point in Alex's now troubled young life. Karate would be a great way for Alex to channel his abundant physical energy, whilst temporarily distracting his 5-year-old distraught thoughts and emotions away from the turmoil of his daddy's wheel-spinning departure. Karate would serve as a weekly respite session for his grieving and bewildered soul. It was during these karate lessons that I met Dawn, as Tracey was happy to make the introductions.

Dawn is well connected locally for a variety of reasons and had been aware of the situation brewing around the children and I, at a time I was unaware of any such developments taking place. Dawn was also aware of me, and who I spent time with, but as she and I were essentially strangers at this point, Dawn kept her alarm and observations to herself and minded her own business.

The full essence of Dawn's character is going to be revealed later as my story unfolds, but I have never met anyone so crystal-clear cut in their thinking, logic and pragmaticism. When, for the previous three years I had been swept up in a whirlwind friendship full of hysteria, high drama, mental and emotional manipulation, Dawn was a welcome and refreshing change. If Lauren is my comfy pair of slippers, Dawn is my Nike "Just Do It" trainers. Both are equally essential in their own way.

Dawn showed up in my life just after it had crashed. I was feeling emotionally battered, exhausted and – when things got even worse – at a loss for how to turn things around to my advantage. I liken my mind at this time to a depleted phone battery, where I had spent many months at 100% usage, but with little or no recharging time. As a result, the quality of my thinking and logic suffered. Then came Dawn with her "Just Do It" attitude and energy, which charged me along the way.

I will state categorically, right here and right now, I would not be where I am today without Dawn's inherent kindness, compassion and generosity of spirit. People with Dawn's calibre of character are few and far between, and it is my honour and privilege to know her, and to be able to call her my friend. This is but a mere introduction to Dawn, so you know her name. The actual measure of this woman has yet to be revealed in context. Brace yourself.

Friendship is the comfort of knowing that even when you're alone, you aren't.

Eve

My Auntie Eve, Mum's half-sister, daughter of Pop and Maggie. Oh, how differently [*and much worse*] things could have turned out for me if not for her wise, wise counsel. Like the timing of Dawn's miraculous appearance in my life, a similar thing can be said for Eve's re-entry in my world.

I have pretty much hero-worshipped Eve all my life. Only five years older and living in Cheshire, Eve was a seriously cool auntie with a horse called Sovereign, a pony called Prince and I loved spending as much time with her as possible. She had a CB radio, was artistic, funny, with great taste in music. Eve is responsible for my love of AC/DC, and for a slightly obscene dance routine she and her friends devised for Status Quo's *Whatever You Want* back in the early 80's. Even though she's a mother and a grandmother now, Eve refuses point blank to be conventional, rides motorbikes and trikes, organises rock gigs and can still raise hell at a moment's notice.

Eve came to live with us in 1982 when her relationship with the combative Maggie reached boiling point, again. I was eleven and she was 16. We shared a bedroom and she taught me stuff no one else did, much to our guffawing amusement now. Eve eventually returned home to Maggie after a few months, fell in love and got married to the love of her life, Terry. They went on to have children and their lives got full and busy, right about the time my life got full and busy, so we lost touch there for a while.

Then, during September 2013, Mum died suddenly and unexpectedly. I will address Mum's passing in more detail and context as I get further along, but

I'm telling you now because this was how Eve was reintroduced into my life, after many years of quietness between us. We had never actually fallen out and had enjoyed sporadic bursts of telephone calls throughout the years, but we had drifted for sure. Now we were bonded back together again in mutual grief.

Living many counties apart, there were numerous phone calls between us during the days between Mum's passing and funeral, but I had yet to experience Steve's Bomb Drop, so these phone calls with Eve at this stage were largely funereal and logistical in nature, with long tears-and-laughter walks down memory lane. It was only about a month after Steve's Bomb Drop [which in itself was delivered a couple of days after Mum's funeral], that Eve became of critical importance to my journey forwards. Eve shaped my initial thoughts and tamed my wildest instincts, just in the nick of time.

What was incredible timing-wise about all of this is, once the funeral had taken place, I experienced the Bomb Drop, but had too much to deal with on every level to keep in touch with anyone. My immediate inner circle (Paul, Lauren, Hayley, Carrie and Julia) were informed straight away, but I didn't think to phone Eve. Besides, there's only so many times you can put yourself through phone calls like that, I was actually starting to run out of snot!

My immediate priority, of course, had been putting the broken pieces of my devastated children back together again. Oh, and to *not* throw up whenever I attempted to eat anything. That took a lot of time sitting beside the toilet, willing myself to keep food down. I'd seen this exact same solar-plexus reaction with Mum all those years ago, which seems to have developed into full-blown anorexia, so I was determined not to slide down the same slippery slope.

Then, halfway through October 2013, whilst hosting my very own Shit Show, Eve texted me from out of the blue to ask how I was, re: Mum and my grief etc. She was completely oblivious to everything that had happened in the past four weeks or so, concerning Steve's Bomb Drop. I sent back a very brief explanation of what had happened, not really wanting to go through it all over again, and the phone began to ring straight away. Eve and I then went on to speak for over two hours, and it's at this point she put me on the right track, which would ultimately serve me *very* well. Eve taught me things [*again!*] and completely changed how my mind was to operate going forwards.

It is this phone call that can be credited with changing the trajectory of Steve's chances of future success. My mindset was altered forever, and nothing would ever be the same again; the iron had been forged into steel. The nitty gritty of all of this is on its way, but when you read it, please remember how differently events could have unfolded, without the collective caring wisdom of my War Council.

The closer we get to being who we're meant to be, the brighter we shine.

These deeply beloved and cherished saints of my War Council are my heroes, plain and simple. They could have walked away. They could have dissolved into the background and become "too busy" like some who will remain nameless; for now, at least. Instead, they stood four-square behind me from start to… well, even now as it happens. Nutters they may be, but they're my nutters and I love them.

For the first couple of weeks post-Bomb Drop, Paul, Lauren and Hayley were talking to me every day, holding me upright. Often, they were talking to me multiple times a day, ensuring I was getting the right things done at the right time, to ensure the children's continuing needs and sense of security were being met. Every room was spinning constantly, and I couldn't think straight, so Hayley in particular did my thinking for me, and for once in my life, I just did as I was told. The continued love, support and criminal genius-level intellects of my War Counsel is the only reason I am where I am today.

If you've recently experienced a brutal separation, I strongly suggest you gather your own War Counsel as a matter of urgency. Your War Counsel should be made up of sincere, high minded, intelligent and wise souls who love and actively care for you. The empty vessels around you, who suddenly become "too busy" and vanish, should permanently make themselves scarce, because you need real concern and integrity at this point in your life.

You need kind people with love and compassion in their hearts, not the low energy, rubbernecking cling-ons who secretly delight in your temporary setbacks. Be careful who you share the details of your life with, because there are energy vampires who seek only to take away droplets of gossip to dine out on, whilst charging their empty selves on the outlet of your misery. Make room only for those who bring added value to you [*love, compassion, sound advice, a lasagne to warm up... wine!*], rather than those who have a habit of taking away more than they bring and depleting you further.

Avoid the Drama Llamas who will want to use what's happened to you as an excuse to behave appallingly in your name. Your name is better off steering clear of the mud it will be dragged through by such petty and counterproductive games. Remember the central wisdom I will repeat at least a thousand times in this book: **If you do your best in every situation, it puts you in the best possible position for the next situation**. Drama Llamas can't play the long game and have no regard for the consequences their pitiful drama addiction will inevitably produce. Like a junkie, their only concern is for the next hit of adrenaline and escapism, so they are blinded to the real-life consequences of their actions. *Your* consequences, for *their* actions.

I will make no apologies for how often I will repeat this wisdom, because it was the central game changer for me. This wisdom has shaped every decision, every action and every step of my journey since the Bomb Drop imploded our lives; and it has paid dividends. Petty, counterproductive games will only come back and bite you on the arse when you need it least. Always do your best. Never be less than you are. Maintain your dignity at all costs.

The function of your War Counsel is not – absolutely not – to conspire of revenge, or of any kind of hurtful retribution. This would be small, short sighted and detrimental to your strategy going forwards; watch my life play out to see what I mean. The function of your War Counsel is to oversee and safeguard your protection, self-preservation and best interests; nothing more, nothing less.

Your War Counsel must be able to stop you from succumbing to your wildest, most reflexive instincts, so choose these people carefully. Ask yourself:

- ❖ Who wouldn't hesitate to get into my face and fearlessly state how I was about to make an unforced error?
- ❖ Who has enough of my respect to be able to tell me I'm wrong?
- ❖ Who would be prepared to rugby tackle me to the ground, to prevent me from hurting myself (figuratively or literally)?
- ❖ Who would rather walk on their own lips than betray my confidence?

These people should make up your War Counsel. You may have two War Counsel members, you may have fifteen or forty-seven, the number is irrelevant, you need their high calibre minds, character, love, loyalty, integrity, energy and wisdom before all else.

Whilst my War Counsel members are relatively few, my god they are powerful energies to be around. Whilst they would never allow me to even consider exploring the darker side of my nature, they all have a handful of common traits amongst them. My War Counsel members are capable of critical thinking. Their ability to game out scenarios is second to none, and they are ruthless when it comes to planning, and the execution of those plans. They are ferociously protective, perceptive and patient. They are also hilarious, sarcastic bitches [*yes, Paul included*], who regularly leave me speechless with their savage wit. Humour has often been the vehicle by which my War Counsel has delivered their bluntest of truths, and I love them more for it.

Whilst we have always operated within the bounds of love and light, with a strict *harm to none* policy, we still revelled like medieval royalty when a plan came together. We didn't seek to hurt anyone, but we were damn well going to get what was owed... and then revel some more. *Hurrah!*

Last

There is one more individual I need to introduce you to, Helen, Steve's eventual adulteress. For good reason, Act I of my story will begin around the time I first met Helen. We met through a mutual friend during the school runs of October 2010. Our friendship began slowly and cautiously, but then quickly ignited into something that would eventually feel to me to be out of control, unhinged and suffocating. And that's before she slept with my husband after my Mum's funeral.

Don't be fooled into thinking this book is a hit job on either Steve or Helen, because I am more free and thankful to them, than I am angry and vengeful. Besides, I don't do vengeance and retribution, it's silly. It is without question Steve and Helen have behaved reprehensibly, and their actions brought untold heartbreak, pressure, plus financial and emotional hardship upon the children and I; but remember I have entitled this book *Too Relieved To Grieve*, for good reason.

Now the boiling pan of inflamed emotions, and the bewildered hangover of deception have subsided, I have crystal clear clarity. I can see clearly how and why it was all so necessary. Helen therefore is nothing more than a catalyst, a mere pawn in the larger game, sent as a kind of *Poundland protagonist* to propel me forwards, and out of my previously unacknowledged marital stupor.

Helen: Without you, I'd still be where you are now. Thanks babe.

ACT I

COMMENCEMENT

A Major Goal Accomplished

Let me take you back to August 2010. Steve and I (but mostly Steve) had been working our nuts off since April, designing and installing a product showroom with multiple displays. This had been a long-held ambition of Steve's, and now it was about to be realised.

You see, our business had taken a significant hit during the 2008 recession. We had had a couple of conversations discussing the merits of winding down the business versus fighting on. I remember so clearly sitting in the car outside the maternity ward of the General Hospital, when the decision was finally carved in stone. Alex had been born a couple of days earlier but had developed severe jaundice and needed to be cared for in the Special Care Baby Unit (SCBU) for a week. Tension was high when I asked Steve directly if we should just close the business and cut our losses. He thought for a nano second, and then stated how he wasn't prepared to give up on the business (yet), as we hadn't tried everything. He hadn't accomplished his goal of opening a showroom, and he would never have forgiven himself if we quit too soon, or too easily. As our lives unfolded in the years that followed, this courageous decision was eventually vindicated.

Almost as soon as we had agreed to fight for the business, and work towards building the showroom as quickly as we could, everything started to turn around for the better. There was a palpable energy shift. We were obviously busy for the first few months of Alex's life building him up and getting him on the road to recovery, as he developed gastric reflux too, which needed our devoted attention. In April 2009 however, the universe invited me to take a big new leap out of my comfort zone.

I had made playground friends with Linda whose son, Harley, went to school with Sofia. Both kids were invited to a birthday party at a local soft play centre, which Linda and I escorted them to. During our conversation, Linda referred to Harley's 10-year-old brother having created a website. This one casual remark felt like a whack in the face with a frying pan. I sat blinking and processing this information: if a 10-year-old boy can build a website, why can't I?

Unbelievably, Steve and I didn't have a website at the time, as we'd been blinded with science and discouraged by the huge costs, we'd been quoted to have one built for us. Whilst I would do everything differently now because I know better, at the time we had opted to channel our limited, recession-hit resources into staying afloat, during the quickly evolving financial challenge.

I got home from the party as quickly as I could and announced to Steve that I was going to build a website. He was intrigued and supportive, if not a little bemused by the idea. It amused him that I had left the house as a mum-of-two, off to play at a 5-year-old's birthday party with our young daughter, only to return as a self-appointed web designer, and entrepreneurial trouble-shooter, a couple of hours later. I wasn't kidding myself. With my non-existent knowledge and expertise in this area, there were no guarantees a Karan-designed website would work, or even help us at all, but it was worth a try.

By reading, researching and feeling my way around the project as I went, especially with regards to the ever-changing and mind-boggling search engine optimisation (SEO) algorithm dictates, I was able to keep costs to a bare minimum. I think the whole thing cost me less than £200 to put together and host. Obviously, I didn't charge the business for six weeks of my blood, sweat and tears, because this was another of my devoted investments into *us*.

Without a single clue about how to proceed, without a single second of training or experience under my belt, I embraced Arthur Ashe's *start where you are, use what you have, do what you can* philosophy. I spent the next six weeks working tirelessly on our website. I would work when Sofia was at school and whilst Alex napped. I would snatch the 20 minutes or so whilst the spuds were boiling [*dry*], or from any time opportunity I could leverage. I worked late into the early hours, before getting up again in the early hours before everyone else, to get what I could achieved. For *us*.

But here was another one of those occasions where I became *too much*. So focused and locked on to my target of publishing a website was I, that Steve began to complain about "... *only seeing the back of your head... you're always working!*" Frankly, I couldn't believe he was complaining about me working as hard as I could, on a project I hoped would help our business, because he felt neglected. The way I saw it, sitting watching TV in the evenings was not going to support our business, but this eventual website might. I ploughed on regardless and finally let Steve press the "Publish" button, once my opus was complete. We were live and online!

Even though I look back now at that clearly homemade website and wince until I blush, you would not believe the amazingly, spectacular effect it had on our turnover. The orders poured in like a dam had burst, resulting in Steve becoming perpetually booked up at least six months in advance. Within a year we had hit a financial target that had previously seemed too whimsical to even dream about. I bought Steve a personalised bottle of champagne to celebrate all the work my website had brought in, and that he had strived to complete. This was exciting. We were booming baby!

As Steve was [*and still is for all I know*] so highly sought after, he was insanely busy during the day, whilst also insanely busy during the evenings; either on client consultations, or in the office quoting for new business. Then at weekends, between April and August 2010, we would be working on our showroom development plans and construction. It must be said we were struggling to find exceptional, professional artisans to help him. We ran the gamut through a ridiculous range of Bodgit 'n' Scarper merchants, who had no right to trade at all, much less in our name. Steve was carrying a huge volume of work and becoming visibly fraught and exhausted for his noble efforts.

Then, on our eighteenth anniversary of trading, during the August Bank Holiday weekend, we opened our showroom to much acclaim and success. We had two Open Days, on the Saturday and Sunday, complete with the mayor declaring us open, the local press in attendance, a marquee with seating, stalls for our affiliated service providers to promote themselves, children's entertainment, wine, nibbles, music and general refreshments. We'd organised a free prize draw, with a variety of prizes ranging from £5 - £500. Both days were a triumph, even though the first day got off to an unceremonious start.

Steve worked right up until the doors opened on Open Day #1. He came down from helping with an electrical installation on the mezzanine floor, in work clothes he'd been wearing since the day before. He was clearly exhausted and unshaven, but the show had to go on as we had leafleted the entire town. And you know what? No one cared. Everyone acknowledged it was the measure of the man and applauded him. Existing clients who knew Steve well, just acknowledged how *typically Steve* this was; to be so hardworking and dedicated to his goals. It just goes to show you must never wait until you're perfectly ready, or until the stars are aligned. Start where you are, use what you have, do what you can. Just jump and watch the net appear.

I'm pleased to report we were able to get him showered, shaved and changed for Open Day #2, where the pair of us spent time talking to clients and prospective clients for the second day running. With Lauren in charge of operations to free us up, and to ensure everything ran smoothly, neither day could possibly have gone any better. It had to be Lauren to help us. There's no way I could have entrusted such an enormously important task or event to anyone else, and she did us proud.

At the end of each Open Day we would walk out of the showroom, blinking into the sunlight [*as I had remembered to order warm and shiny weather*], absolutely knackered and hoarse, but happy and proud. This was the culmination of a hard 18-year uphill slog. This was the eventual success after our relentless and determined efforts, focused belief and steadfast vision. We pretty much collapsed on the third day of the Bank Holiday, with huge smiles on our faces, and multiple orders on the books.

Then the hard work really began. Bearing in mind we were nationally only starting to see the green shoots of recovery following the 2008 recession, here we were in a truly enviable position of success. Steve however had been working flat out all day, every day, every night and every weekend for over a year at this point. He'd gone past exhausted and was now actively flirting with complete burnout. We stepped up our efforts to find qualified and conscientious help, but we were still unsuccessful.

Along with all of the work, I need to point out that our daughter, Sofia, was seven whilst our son, Alex, was two. If you think about how demanding a (successful) business is, and how much attention it needs to thrive and survive (a recession), and now add to that the time and attention two young children need, there was no time for us as a couple.

Nor did we have any willing childcare options available, to help us relax and connect on much longed-for date nights. The writing was well and truly on the wall for us a couple. Granted, Mallie had looked after the children almost every weekend between April and August 2010, when Steve and I were bringing the showroom to life, but that support quickly dried up once the showroom was operational, with no explanation as to why. Oh well, it's all water under the bridge now.

For now, I must scoot you along the timeline to when I first met my nemesis, Helen. Don't worry, it didn't take me long to bounce back, as I diligently began digging the ground out from beneath her feet to ensure what was mine. The only time she ever knew I was around or involved – post-Bomb Drop – it was already too late, and she was falling into the hole I'd dug. At the risk of mixing my metaphors, you may find it entertaining to start mentally playing the cello riff from Jaws, as you progress further through this book. After all, this book is all about your enlightenment and entertainment, to help you through similar circumstances.

So now I've laid some of the groundwork for your future reference, we can jump forward to late October 2010.

First Words

I was friends with Tracey, and we would meet up on the school runs for a natter. We had many well-intentioned plans to keep fit by route marching ourselves around the housing estate, within which the school was nestled, but we never did get around to it. Tracey's son had attended day nursery with Sofia, all the way back when they were two years-old, so we did the whole birthday party and starting school thing together. Coincidentally it was through Tracey that I met Linda, which led to the website being built, and eventually Dawn when the time was right, so Tracey has proven to be quite the unintentional catalyst in my life.

Tracey would often speak of a brilliant little cafe in town, which served the most authentic and exquisite Italian dishes. We said we'd visit there together one day, but that went the same way as our route marches, and never did happen. Then one day, sitting in what was referred to as the outdoor classroom (a timber framed rotunda built near the playground), Tracey started talking to Helen about how wonderful the cafe was. Seemingly Helen, and her then husband Lee, frequented the cafe regularly, and she duly raptured about the phenomenal food. Then Helen said something funny, which made me laugh, so I said something funny in response, which made Helen laugh. And that is how the ice was broken.

The following weeks allowed Helen and I to speak for a few moments twice a day during the school runs, and the subject of Helen's impending 40th birthday came up. I specifically remembered Helen's birthday on 31 December, as it falls on what has been my favourite night of the year since 1982; New Year's Eve. As Helen and I were not close enough at the time for me to have known her address to send a birthday card, I posted a birthday message on her Facebook profile. Helen later told me it had meant a great deal to her, that I had even remembered.

Robert

Our school run friendliness began to blossom into a tentative friendship, particularly on 12 February 2011. Helen had been outlining her beloved brother, Robert's, heroic battle against cancer for a few weeks. On Saturday 12 February 2011, Robert sadly passed away, devastating his entire extended family. I was never blessed enough to meet Robert before he passed, but I know with all certainty that he was a wonderful powerhouse of a man, with a mischievous energy, and was genuinely beloved by all.

The reason I remember the date of Robert's passing is because it was Dad's birthday too, and only my second without him. I woke up that morning with a heavy heart, only to find Helen had text me to inform me of Robert's passing. This text completely floored me, because here was Helen, so completely devoted to her brother, texting me to tell me he'd passed away. I was stunned she had even remembered who I was, much less that she'd thought to text me about this. This deepened our friendship significantly.

Warning #1

Events conspired over the coming weeks to push our friendship to deeper levels still. By now I was starting to plan my own 40th birthday festivities, which basically involved Helen, Lauren, Julia, me myself and I, and a whole lot of Pimms. Steve had always been a thoughtful and generous gift buyer and bountiful surprise pouncer, and he acquitted himself as well as ever with wonderful gifts (including the newly invented Apple iPad), and a luxury hotel stay and spa experience, complete with a reflexology session. Bliss!

Then came my girlie birthday drinkies night, *zoinks!* This was the first time Helen was to meet Lauren and Julia, having heard so much about them, and it was a disaster. Probably nervous about meeting my oldest friend (Lauren), and clearly revered friend (Julia), Helen overcompensated shamelessly from the beginning and just didn't look back.

Armed to the teeth with Pimms, pre-prepared Pimms accoutrements (a Tupperware box of chopped strawberry, orange, mint and cucumber), and homemade scones with whipped cream and jam, Helen barged into my home like a Hungry Hippo for the very first time, and completely took over. Now, I will be forever grateful to Helen for introducing me to Pimms, and the homemade scones were truly a delight, but damn did we pay a high price for it all.

Bearing in mind this was supposed to be my birthday celebration; I'd made it to 40 without the ulcer Mum had predicted, *woo hoo!* Helen however proceeded to contract, constrict and neutralise the happy with endless talk of her late brother Robert, and their seemingly endless caravanning trips to Scotland. There were more than a couple of "*Is she for real?*" glances between Lauren, Julia and I, as my birthday drinkies were actively being hijacked in front of our disbelieving eyes and ears.

Mindful and compassionate of Helen's recent loss, Lauren, Julia and I could only listen with bored courtesy, as Helen monopolised the conversation all night. We did try to recharge the energy in the room whenever we she went to the loo, but she kept coming back, so the evening was doomed and eventually consigned to the *well-it-seemed-like-a-good-idea-at-the-time* experience bin. Looking back now, it is clear to me how this should have been my first warning. The evening had been all about Helen, despite it being my birthday, which preceded a friendship that was all about Helen too. Everything, as I later found out to my cost, was all about Helen. If only I'd opened my eyes. If only I'd listened to Lauren.

Whilst Lauren and Julia have always been able to laugh and get along well together, Lauren's intuitive antenna practically burst into flames, where Helen was concerned. As hard as she tried to make allowances, Lauren could not quieten the blaring sirens going off in her head, warning her of some insidious and indistinct danger lurking ahead. To her credit, Lauren kept these opinions to herself for weeks after my birthday, until it became clear that my friendship with Helen was deepening.

Two Families Meet

It didn't take long for Helen and I to introduce each other to our husbands and children, and we started spending a lot more time together. As I'm an enthusiastic amateur photographer, with a rather lovely Nikon camera [*aka Whopper; another of Steve's generous gifts*], I offered to take candid photos of the birthday party Helen and Lee were throwing for their now 7-year-old son, Oliver, at a local petting zoo. This habit of photographically documenting our family's friendship continued right up until the end; I enjoyed it. I literally have thousands of photos of everything.

The photos I accumulated over each year would then be compiled into an A3 hardback photobook, complete with witty captions and references to our innumerable in-jokes, and given as a Christmas gift with love, for posterity. I gifted such a book to Helen and Lee for Christmas 2011 and 2012 and was halfway through compiling the 2013 edition, when Helen threw my love for her back in my face and embarked upon an affair with my husband. But I digress and have shot too far forward. We'll get to all of this in due course, but for now let's return to Spring 2011.

Warning #2

During Oliver's birthday party at the petting zoo, I was introduced to Mona. Mona was married to one of Lee's long-term friends and had herself been friends with Helen for a dozen years or so. Evidently the two families had been close forever, but oh how quickly Mona was dropped in favour of me in the weeks to come. This should have been my second warning, because as events transpire, you will notice how Helen appears to use and dispose of people – depending on their perceived value and usefulness at the time – before moving onto whoever is next. Let's look at the evidence.

Helen went from singing Mona's praises to disparaging every aspect of her life, and all within an unseemly blink of an eye. This *should* have rung alarm bells in my head. I *should* have acknowledged and paid more attention to what she was capable of, but I didn't and, as the divine Beverley Knight sang: "*Shoulda woulda coulda are the last words of a fool*".

What Helen was capable of was clearly being laid out for me to see, but I couldn't – or wouldn't – see it. Instead I chose to see only the favourable projected qualities of the funny, intelligent and charming version of herself that she wanted me to see; and I needed at the time. I needed her to be funny, intelligent and charming, so that's what I saw. I needed a life raft of some kind, to rescue and take me to someplace else. Lauren didn't fall for any of it though. By now, Lauren was starting to cautiously gauge my willingness to hear anything less than a trumpet fanfare where Helen was concerned, and was troubled with, what we're going to call, my *Helen-blindness*.

The first thing you need to know about me is that I'm loyal, to a fault. As I said earlier, I do everything with 100% welly and commitment (even at the risk of being considered *too much*), and that includes friendship. In this instance, if I adopt you as my friend, you are immediately upgraded to the Platinum Package, which offers you many enhanced features and benefits, not least me making time and space for you in my [*largely hectic*] world, my fierce protection of you and yours, every avenue of assistance I have at my disposal, and the best attention I can offer given my prevailing circumstances.

Looking back now, I wince at what I'm about to tell you, but I must sit here in my wrongness and be wrong, because it's the right thing to do. There's no growth without challenge, so here goes. During the innumerable instances where Lauren tried to alert me to her infallible gut feeling about Helen, I.... *wince*... wrote it off as envy on Lauren's part. I wrongly assumed Lauren was jealous of how Helen was enjoying the platinum benefits of my friendship, which she didn't want to share with this pushy, new and self-absorbed interloper. Nothing wrong with my ego there, aye?

Admittedly it didn't make much sense, because Lauren was able to play nicely with Julia and Carrie, but I clearly didn't want to believe her misgivings, due to my Helen-blindness. Choosing to insist Lauren was jealous was far easier, and more flattering for my ego, than believing she may have been right. So, I continued along Arrogant Street, before hurtling down the Hubris Bypass; still not taking my foot off the damn accelerator. Let me tell you this: 100% full throttle is not always the right option and is often *too much*. This is why we're given brakes, to negotiate life's bends and hazards safely. If we choose to use them of course.

Who the hell did I think I was? One can only assume the weather was lovely up there in my own arse, because that's where my head was stuck for more than three years. How Lauren didn't whack me in the face with a frying pan is anyone's guess, but then things got worse, from Lauren's point of view.

Love Bombing

I cannot begin to explain to you how much I loved Helen; I adored her. Separated from my brother as an unintentional consequence of my estrangement from Mum, it felt wonderful to feel a strong sibling link of love flowing towards me; or any kind of love for that matter. Steve was still slogging long hours, heroically providing for our family, but otherwise falling asleep everywhere when he wasn't working. Whilst he and I loved each other, we had slumped into becoming business and parenting partners only. The marriage bit was in trouble and I felt neglected, stifled, bored and frustrated. I have no doubt Steve was less than happy with our situation too, and I will get to that in a moment.

I hated myself for feeling bored and neglected, how dare I? Here was this gift of a man, whom I loved with all my heart, working relentlessly hard to pull our business through two recessions (1992 and 2008) to eventual success, and I had the nerve to feel neglected? Precious much, *moi*? The fact remains though, there was room in our marriage for Helen to give me the emotional fulfilment and attention I felt was lacking.

Now however – years later and with the benefit of 20/20 hindsight – I believe that I had become a victim of what's called Love Bombing. There has been a great deal written on this subject, which I urge you to research for yourself, but for now I will offer you this one short excerpt from an article written by Suzanne Degges-White, Ph.D.:

"Love bombing is the practice of overwhelming someone with signs of

adoration and attraction — think flattering comments, tokens of affection, or love notes on the mirror, kitchen table, or windshield, and you're beginning to get the picture. It's flowers delivered at work with hearts dotting the i's in your name. It's texts that increase in frequency as they increase in romantic fervour. Its surprise appearances designed to manipulate you into spending more time with the bomber — and, not coincidentally, less time with others, or on your own". [Source: Psychology Today, 13 April 2018]

Whilst my friendship with Helen remained wholly platonic, it's also worth noting what else Degges-White writes, in the same article:

"When someone tells you just how special you are, it can be intoxicating, at first. However, when a person uses such comments to keep your focus trained on him or her, or to keep bringing you back in if you've started to back off, it could be a case of manipulation. Not everyone who whispers sweet nothings in your ear is a narcissist or predator, of course, but if you're feeling that something just isn't right about the person or your relationship, these constant reminders of 'how good you are together' — when you suspect that you really aren't — can be an effort to keep you tethered. It's often the first line used by a potential abuser.

Why do narcissists love bomb? Narcissists in particular are known for their skills at manipulation, as much as their penchant for self-love. They may use flattery and attention as tools to build themselves up as the perfect partner, the better to gain your trust, affection — and, ultimately, adoration. Narcissists often learn through experience that once partners see through their facades, the relationship may self-destruct. Once they have convinced you of how good the two of you are together, a narcissist will try to shape your role in the relationship into a member of their 'supporting cast'. For this and other reasons, narcissists typically struggle to maintain equal, mutually satisfying relationships. Narcissists move quickly to avoid detection, so the more someone tries to flatter you into submission, the more diligently you need to explore their motives".

Interesting, huh? Now watch what happens in the following chapters, and perhaps place a page marker here for your future reference. For the time being though, let's get back to it, because I was oblivious to Love Bombing until years after Bomb Drop, but I'd like you to bear it in mind.

Neither Steve nor I were sleeping around, gambling the mortgage payments or beating each other up. We were both working hard with noble intent, but we were now seemingly taking it in turns to neglect each other. This inevitably takes its toll. After all, there are only so many coins from another person's goodwill you can spend before there's nothing left. Whilst it's true nothing lasts forever, it's also true that relationships never die of natural causes, they are always murdered by either ego, disrespect, selfishness or disloyalty. Neither Steve nor I were looking after us, as much as we were looking after people outside the marriage, which gifted Helen the perfect opportunity to make her entrance into our lives.

Helen gave me someone new to talk to and to laugh with on the endless lonely nights, when Steve was working, or snoring in front of the TV. Helen was interested in me, cared for, entertained and fascinated me. She was attentive, she stimulated me intellectually and encouraged me to grow personally and spiritually. There was nothing we couldn't talk about, and I grew to love her deeply as my chosen sister.

On Thursdays Helen completed her disabled mother's weekly food shop, and I knew she hated it. So, I would calculate the approximate time I thought she'd be standing bored at the checkout, to then send her funny and rude odes to make her snort with laughter. Helen loved these despite the temporary embarrassment, and it only occurred to me at the end of our marriage, that I used to write love odes and poems for Steve, all the way back in happier times. It's examples like this which quickly led Steve to feeling hurt and abandoned. He was correctly feeling replaced as my priority, but I still couldn't see the error of my ways, due to my insufferable Helen-blindness.

Helen loved me too, or so she had me believe, and here comes some of the Love Bombing I was blind to at the time. She told me: "*I actually have sisters, and I love you more than them*". She also stated: "*I didn't realise people like you even existed, much less that I could be friends with them*". Pretty effective ego-stroking, don't you think? We were so close, and went everywhere together, that other people began to suspect we were a couple. Even my kids called her their "other mummy", which really didn't help the lesbian rumours, but we cared not. When it all kicked off and Steve was leaving me for Helen, his sister Teresa told me she had felt sure it was going to be me leaving him for Helen.

After dropping off the kids at nursery and school, Helen and I would stand talking and laughing for far too long beside our cars, before eventually heading off to be late for work. Steve was becoming increasingly irritated with how late I was rocking up to the office, music blaring and defiantly unapologetic. This was the summer of 2011 and I finally felt alive again, having lain energetically dormant for too long. Helen had somehow awakened me, and it felt glorious.

My life force had been found decaying beneath layers of fraying greying *meh* and was now fully recharged every day. I felt vivid, effervescent and empowered, whilst Steve's energy levels were hitting the skids and unknowingly repelling me. He was feeling drained and discarded. Whilst I had no chance of winning Wife Of The Year, I simply had nothing left to give him; he'd absorbed everything I had to offer. If I could have thought of a new way to help or support him, I would have done so without hesitation. However, I was 20+ years into his dependency and was now bereft of ideas. Mentally, emotionally and energetically I was spent.

Soon enough I began to take Wednesdays off work, to spend time with Helen and enhance my personal development. We had a mutual interest in spiritualism, and I was starting to notice a strengthening in my lifelong abilities, so we set about learning more at a development and meditation circle. I had struggled to understand and manage these abilities throughout my life, and they had often freaked me out with their accuracy. I say this without an ounce of flippancy or disrespect, but I genuinely thought I could have been schizophrenic until I was 40, and that possibility frightened me.

In short, I heard voices who counselled me lovingly and guided me with care. I saw Spirit [*yes sceptics, "I see dead people" hardy, ha, ha*], and I *just knew* things I couldn't possibly know. I can also i.e.: smell someone's scent hours before they arrive by surprise, or if they're in need somehow, and I can feel, sense or accurately read the energy of other people, as effortlessly as blinking. Not all the time in every situation, just when there's something I need to know or share for my/their greatest and highest good.

Don't come at me wanting to know the winning lottery numbers and all that shit, because that's not how it works. I'm not privy to everything, I'm only given what's required on a need to know basis. For those stuck in the tired [*and frankly boring AF*] I-want-to-know-the-winning-lottery-numbers guff, let me say this to you. You may think money (or whatever it is you're wishing for) is what you need right now, but maybe just being handed a fortune by Lady Luck – without any real effort and endeavour on your part – isn't for your greatest and highest good. Whilst you may genuinely need the money, you perhaps need the lesson and personal growth in obtaining it for yourself, more.

It's also worth considering the possibility that not getting what you want can often be the greatest stroke of luck of all. Admittedly, this fact is often difficult to digest until enough time has passed to give you the necessary perspective to see it but take a look back on your life to see how it has already unfolded exactly as it should, in perfect time. It takes a big open mind to understand or learn these philosophies, and I don't expect everyone to respect what I'm saying here, but it may just spare me a handful of explanatory conversations in the future.

Anyhoo, back to me. All of my life I had been worried and confused about why no one else *just knew* these things or could see and hear what I was experiencing. I felt there was something intrinsically wrong with me. It didn't help matters when I routinely exasperated Steve in this area too, as I would meet people for the first time and *just know* I couldn't like or trust them.

Forever fair and just, Steve would defend them, urging me to give them a chance, so I would determinedly override these first impressions. Every time I would override my first impressions however, the person concerned would eventually validate my original sense, usually at my or our expense.

Unsurprisingly, I vowed to listen to my inner guiding voice from that moment on, to save time and to spare myself the self-directed fury for having known better. Obviously, I would override the guidance once more, but these were the choices I made. I often wonder if – on an unconscious or spiritual level – that I somehow *just knew* Helen was the catalyst to instigate the change my life needed, and that I shouldn't obstruct her. Who can say, but it's a thought that's going to fester?

Equally fascinated by spiritualism and my developing skill set, Helen and I would study the subject tirelessly. Because of our research and learning, I was relieved to learn I wasn't schizophrenic, I was merely clairaudient (clear hearing), clairvoyant (clear vision), clairsentient (clear feeling) and claircognizant (clear knowing); *phew!* Once this had been explained to me, the ordinariness of it all soothed me, and I began to lean into it.

Most of us have gut feelings and inner voices, so now that I knew I wasn't mentally unwell, I was able to relax; accepting myself whilst developing my full potential. The vast expansiveness of what I was studying and experiencing though, only compounded how small and suffocated I was feeling inside my life, outside of my spiritual exploration. Everything 3D was now slow, grey, mundane and draining, whilst what we were learning was 4D technicolour, dynamic, fascinating, and liberating.

Bless him, Steve did his best to understand what was going on, and why. He did try to encourage and support me to be my best self, but not-so-deep inside he was becoming seriously unhappy about my intensifying friendship with Helen, and the seemingly weird tangent we were heading off on. With sincere regret and shame now, I dismissively wrote off his feelings as jealousy too, because he had always been too busy to develop any significant friendships of his own. Yep, I was still clearly tanking it down the Hubris Bypass! Here was Steve making himself clear and communicating his innermost feelings, but I didn't care enough, because I believed he was only trying to lure me back into a [*metaphoric*] cage. Now I see his misgivings were perfectly reasonable for a once devoted husband, feeling as though his promised life partner was mindlessly drifting away from him.

In my mind at the time, Steve was Eeyore and Helen was Tigger from the Winnie the Pooh books. After 20+ years of hard work and uphill slog to build our business, Helen now represented fun, excitement, new, fresh, novel and stimulating. I felt my blood pumping when I was with her. We laughed so hard, all day, every day, either in person or via text messages. Helen has a great sense of humour, and I still remember some of our greatest hits fondly from time-to-time.

Compare this to my withering, exhausted relationship with Steve, where all we talked about was work, or the kids, before he fell asleep standing up from fatigue. Yes, Helen was shiny and new, and I wanted to enjoy some life, having worked so hard for so long. My marriage was either work-centric or crushingly low energy, and here I was being offered fun and enlightenment as *Karan;* not more of the same drudge as wife, mother and Steve's business appendage. Helen was a much-needed breath of fresh air, it's as simple as that. I had been starting to suffocate without realising it, until she breathed love, growth and laughter back into my life.

Don't get me wrong, Steve had been funny – no, he'd been downright hilarious – charming and wonderful. Steve has made me live, laugh and love like no one else ever has, but the business had systematically eroded the essence of who he was. I tried to implement boundaries on multiple occasions, where i.e.: we wouldn't discuss work after 9pm or at weekends to help him recharge, but that's impossible to enforce when one of you is still at work at 9pm, or still slogging away during the weekends! With nothing to grasp, I let go.

The worst mistakes I made are enormous and they started right about now. Dissatisfied in my marriage, and for all [*platonic*] intents and purposes, I was emotionally unfaithful with Helen. But I must make a critical distinction here. Mentally and emotionally, whatever Steve eventually did to me, I did to him first. I would never have left him, or deserted our marriage, because I loved him with every fibre of my being, but I did feel trapped in a small, colourless and expired life. Two things can be true at once. I believe we could have worked things out with some professional help, if we'd given ourselves the opportunity, and if Helen hadn't been allowed to pounce on the slowly dying heart of our relationship, denying us the time and space to defibrillate it.

I'm telling you this now, so you understand how I am by no means an innocent angel in any of this. I am certainly culpable for a lot of what has happened to *me*. What's going to be hard to forgive is, as deserving of the shit as I may have been, our children were most certainly not. Whilst I deserved a lot – but not all – of the lumps Steve has served to me over the years, for devolving into a less supportive and more absent wife towards the end, I didn't deserve a damn thing from Helen. I had epitomised the definition of friendship, at the risk of alienating my husband; only to be betrayed and usurped from my own life. Helen now sits in the chair I once occupied in my former office, and within the homes of my former in-laws. I imagine Helen to be the personification of a cuckoo in the nest. Should you ever meet her, please do proceed with caution, because she's likely to want what's yours. Those without talent or the wherewithal, or are otherwise incapable of achieving success for themselves, can only take from those who have what they covet.

I now see how I was tacitly, and explicitly, telling Steve that Helen was more important to me than he was, but from my perspective, it was only a matter of minutes before he was snoring beside me on the sofa. All I could see was how unhappy Steve was with my admittedly compulsive friendship, but also how he wasn't prepared to offer me a viable alternative, i.e.: working smarter rather than harder, or being available for family activities and marital pursuits. I had endured 20+ years of waiting for Steve to come home from work, to finish working whilst at home, or even to wake up. Granted, he was driven by a noble desire to grow the business and provide for his family, and I will forever commend him for that, but he had tacitly, and explicitly, been telling me the business, and our clients, were more important than I was to him since 1992.

Moreover, my gradual involvement in helping Helen to drive through her separation from Lee, in addition to my incremental distancing from our business in favour of my quest for personal and spiritual development, and Steve was starting to despair. Exhausted beyond measure and faced with a seemingly disengaged wife and business partner, Steve was now feeling the weight of having to manage the boiling hot business on his own; and it was simply too much to bear.

The problem from my side of this coin is that I had done everything in my considerable power to help, support and encourage Steve, but he was either unable or unwilling to help himself. I had now run out of ideas, patience and energy, and had all but given up on him. He either refused, or was unable, to implement the innumerable Work Smarter suggestions I had come up with and, by now, I had become exasperated. Steve had become too heavy for me to carry. I felt I had to save myself and rescue *me* for once, because how do you help someone when they're unable, or unwilling, to help you help them? You can supply them with a life raft all you want, but it's not unreasonable to expect them to climb aboard for themselves, is it?

Then I had one last idea, but you're going to need a little more history for context, so please bear with me as I lay this out for you.

Lee's Gone

During February 2013, following Lee's six-month affair with The Other Woman in 2009, and now having to deal with our intense friendship to boot, Helen and Lee's marriage hit a critical juncture. Relations had completely broken down. So close were Helen and I at this point, both Steve and Lee enquired separately from each of us if we were now lovers. We weren't, but Lee likened the situation to us having an affair in front of his eyes and expecting him to be happy about it. This looked and felt like Helen's revenge affair to him. Lee felt excluded and isolated from everything. He knew he was on the precipice of losing his heart's investment, and then he discovered further treachery on Helen's part.

By now, Helen was on the cusp of receiving her diploma certificates, having studied hypnotherapy during the past year. At a complete loss for anything else to do, but needing to do *something*, I suggested to Steve that Helen may be able to help him with some deep relaxation exercises; plus, maybe alleviating the depression he had been suffering, since his beloved father died in 2001. He clearly wasn't listening to me, so maybe he would listen to her? I had nothing to lose by suggesting it. Or so I thought.

Astoundingly, Steve agreed to try and was willing to be hypnotised by Helen. Looking back, I see now this was a tacit admission of desperation on Steve's part, because he hadn't previously rated Helen, or her training at all. If he was willing to try this, it was clearly as much his last resort as it was mine. I would only realise this a couple of years later, however.

By now, Helen had started a business and was renting a room in a local business complex. I accompanied Steve for both of the sessions he had with Helen (that I knew about) and sat in the waiting area whilst she hypnotised him. Whatever technique Helen used, Steve quickly reported feeling happier, lighter and as though colours and sounds were more vivid and vibrant than before. As an untrained lay person, Helen's mind influencing processes certainly appeared to have had a great and pronounced effect on Steve. He almost immediately set about losing weight and getting fitter; it was remarkable, and he was feeling better.

We had an old magnetic-resistance exercise bike which had been removed from the house and put into the back garden, theoretically on its way into Steve's work van before being dropped off at the recycling centre; but it never made it. An enthusiastic cyclist in his youth, when he didn't have time to hurtle around local lakes and landmarks, Steve would take to the exercise bike in the garden. It was all very Steptoe & Son, but how could I argue against his renewed lust for life and healthier exercise regime? Quite what my friend and neighbour thought to this, as she passed her overlooking window is anyone's guess, but it didn't matter because Steve was feeling happier within himself.

For what it's worth, and again in 20/20 hindsight, this was also the time Helen started losing a lot of weight, feasting on little else but Aldi rice cakes. Not that I'm endorsing such an ill-conceived weight loss programme; I'm merely remarking on how bloody obvious the signs were to anyone willing enough to see them. It all makes me smile ruefully now, but you really must see what's right in front of you – through an amateur photographer's lens if needs be – and not just what you want to see. You can only ever outrun the truth for so long. But these were my warnings to ignore and lessons to learn.

Now, are you ready for a supernatural twist?

As relations between Helen and Lee, and Lee and I were at an all-time low, the three of us agreed that Lee should never find out about Helen hypnotising Steve. With the imminent collapse of his marriage, and the inevitable separation from his children, Lee had been dealing with mild depression for a couple of months, and had no less than begged Helen, several times, to help him. Lee wanted Helen to help calm and focus his mind, using hypnotherapy if needs be, as he had been feeling swamped by negative emotions for far too long. Helen flatly refused all pleas for help, casting Lee further adrift and disconsolate; possibly by design.

Lee has been known to experience vivid dreams and had previously had his mum and other loved ones visit him whilst he slept. His dreams were so real to him, and he would verbally engage so comprehensively, that Helen had been able to comprehend all sides of the partially heard conversations. One night, following the second secret hypnotherapy session with Steve, Helen was woken up by Lee having one such dream conversation, apparently with Helen's late brother, Robert.

You should know that Robert and Lee were close. Closer than close in fact, as Lee has still not fully recovered from Robert's passing in February 2011. Every year Lee memorialises Robert on his birthday and other key anniversaries and remains close to Robert's devoted wife and children. Lee continues to attend weddings and other special occasions, despite his subsequent divorce from Helen, because he will forever be their beloved brother-in-law and Uncle Lee. Bewilderingly, Helen has opted not to attend such family events, if Lee has also been invited, and loses some of the ultimatums she lays out towards her loved ones. Evidently Lee's company is selected, whilst Helen chooses to fall further and further away from her own flesh and blood. No, I don't understand her decisions either, but then there's nowt as queer as folk.

So, Robert and Lee were close, and ended up having a chat together in Lee's dream. In the dream, Robert advised Lee to seek help from Helen as she'd been helping Steve for a similar condition. Lee expressed surprise out loud. Helen had been woken up a little earlier by Lee's dreamy preamble, was now listening to his half of the conversation, and was quickly able to put all the pieces together. Helen then braced herself for the inevitable aftershocks. Not only was Lee about to be justifiably hurt and angry by her apparent betrayal, but so were Steve and I for an unbelievable lapse in confidentiality.

I cannot overstate how careful we were in our measures to prevent Lee from finding out about Steve's secret hypnotherapy treatments. The business complex Helen was operating from was situated in a remote, rural setting, set well back on a single-track road. The sessions were scheduled on the fly, when we were certain Lee was suitably occupied elsewhere. There was no way Lee could have learnt about the sessions, so WTAF? If this had all been based on Helen's word alone, I would have assumed she'd left Steve's session notes laying around for Lee to see, but Lee remembers his chat with Robert also, so now what?

Let's agree the jury's still out on *how* Lee found out, because I can't possibly litigate this. All that I can tell you is, however Lee found out about Helen's treatment of Steve, the faeces well and truly collided with the air distribution unit. Lee erupted from hurt, Steve erupted from this bizarre and mysterious breach of confidentiality, and I erupted in my defence and protection of Steve, who had now slumped into a state of total disbelief and despondency. Helen initially appeared to be dumbfounded, but quickly started to revel in the possibility of this being the final, singular issue that could seal the end of her marriage, and Lee's departure from her life and the family home.

Helen saw an opportunity amongst the carnage, and she took it, telling Lee that either he could move out, or she and the children would move out. The natural, protective instincts within Lee wanted to ensure safety, security and stability for his children, and so he agreed to move out. He went to stay with his sister, approximately 45 miles away from the family home, but continued to travel to see his children every day. Until Helen put a stop to that too of course.

Fugly

Steve's first impressions of Helen were less than favourable. In fact, he uncharacteristically took her apart when appraising her privately to me after their first meeting. Specifically, he referred to her as Fugly [*which I don't have to spell out for you, surely?*], and was just as uncomplimentary about her trove of personal habits and character traits. For a humble and fastidious man, these were deal-breaking crosses in the negative column for Steve. He tolerated her in the early weeks and months, because he believed her to be a positive influence on me, as she made me happy. He even defended her to Lauren, saying *"She's good for Karan"*, which Lauren never was able to digest.

It is precisely because of his unfavourable first impression of Helen, that I decked myself out with an ironclad false sense of security and armour-plated complacency. This would eventually deliver my blindsiding. You see Steve and I were open about who we found attractive, celebrity or otherwise. I would roll my eyes playfully as Steve watched Lucy the weather girl endlessly on ITV, or Jennifer Aniston in Friends, and he would humour my appreciation of certain rugby players [*I didn't say Jonny Wilkinson, you said Jonny Wilkinson*]. We were secure enough within our relationship for Steve to admit he found my friend Julia attractive, whilst I found his friend David easy on the eyes. So, when he described Helen as unattractive and annoying (only in way more colourful terms), I had no reason to disbelieve him. Furthermore, with his opinion of Helen's appearance and eyebrow raising traits and habits, there was no way Steve was ever going to leave me for *Fugly*, right? Wrong.

By now Lauren was getting seriously upset, because every time she came to visit us, she would find me stressed, knackered and distracted by the war-torn events unfolding in Helen's world. According to Lauren I was a mere shell of my former self, eroded by the constant demand for my time, attention and energy. I can see clearly now how Lauren thought she was losing my friendship in the quicksand of Helen's apparent Love Bombing, but she really wasn't. I still loved and cared for Lauren as much as ever, but I was simply not allowed the time or space to express it in real terms, by spending time with her and being us. Regrettably, I didn't learn about the concept of Love Bombing until years after Helen had part-exchanged me for Steve, so my Helen-blindness really was just that: blindness.

As Hayley can also corroborate, Helen had an almost narcissistic need to absorb all of my attention and would unashamedly hijack any time I spent alone or with others; it's just so textbook now that I can see it. I once attended a seminar at Ascot racecourse, where I met up with Hayley. As we rarely get to meet each other in person (because we live so far apart), we thought we'd optimise our time together by going for dinner after the event. Helen knew I was spending the day with Hayley, that we planned to go for dinner, and that we hardly ever saw each other, but that didn't stop her bombarding me text messages, ostensibly because her young son, Oliver, had had a nosebleed at school. Whilst a nosebleed was a big deal for hemophobic Oliver, it certainly wasn't a medical emergency warranting Breaking News alerts at dinner. Needless to say, Hayley and I were more than a little annoyed and appalled by the unrelenting intrusive updates.

Helen also knew that I love and need to spend time alone. As an INFJ, if I don't get enough alone time to process and decompress, I begin to feel jangled and irritable, and ain't nobody got time for that. Steve could easily spend three or four nights a week either working late, or attending client consultations, leaving me alone to scratch this itch. Whilst I did begin to feel this was an excessive amount of solitude, I would utilise it well by reading, meditating or listening to music and drifting off into my head. Until I met Helen, who had other ideas.

I would try earnestly to lay out boundaries, by explaining that Steve would be working and how I intended to spend the time. Sweeping aside any possibility of giving me some personal space, Helen would invariably start a text conversation that'd go on for hours – despite my repeated attempts to end it – because she was bored at home, either with or without Lee there. Admittedly, I could have done any number of things to prevent Helen setting the terms for my precious alone time, but she had a nasty habit of going off at the deep end and throwing biblical hissy fits, if she didn't get her way. I'll give you an example from my contemporaneous journal notes.

Enough

On 26 June 2013 my 32-year-old neighbour, Evan, who reminded me intensely of my adored but estranged-at-the-time brother Paul, was blue lighted into hospital with a suspected stroke. This upset me disproportionately, which surprised me as I didn't particularly like Evan, although I was friends with his fiancée. I asked Steve if he would take the kids into school, so I could stay at home and go into my head – a process I go through to think deeply and analyse things I don't understand. I was happy to do the afternoon school run, but I just wanted some time alone to figure out why Evan's emergency had affected me so deeply. Steve understood this as much as either of us did, and duly agreed to take the kids.

I knew that if I did the morning school run, I'd collide with Helen, and any chance of alone time would evaporate, so I opted for all out avoidance. I then sent Helen a long and explanatory text, detailing what had happened to Evan and my unexpected feelings about it, so her suspected narcissistic streak wasn't unduly offended by some imaginary rejection. I also told her I wanted the day to myself, to mull things over, and that I would see her that afternoon at school. A rational person would have responded "*Yes of course, I'll see you later, take care x*", but no. Oh hell no. You'd have thought I'd just disembowelled her first-born as an offering to the Bunny Boiler Gods. Helen's hysterical text reply left Steve and I sitting open-mouthed, staring at my Blackberry [*yes, I know*] in disbelief. Steve commented in no uncertain terms: "*There's something fucking wrong with her!*"

Helen and I went on to have a long and heated exchange of texts over the course of the morning, which resulted in her coming around to our house by 12 noon. So much for the day by myself then, and by day, I mean the school 8.30am - 3.20pm day; so not an actual day in the literal sense. This one simple request I'd made for myself had now been blown so completely out of proportion, I couldn't believe it. When I wanted to know exactly what her problem was, Helen exclaimed: "*I don't know what's going on in your head!*", to which I replied: "*Neither do I, which is why I wanted the time to myself to find out!*" So now I wasn't allowed to have unexpressed thoughts or feelings either? This marks the beginning of the end of my Helen-blindness. Even though I was still clueless about the concept of Love Bombing at this time, I was certainly feeling its effects. The veil had dropped from in front of my eyes, and I could finally see her for who she truly is, and it ain't pretty; it's Fugly. It was exactly who and what Steve and Lauren had been seeing all along.

By the school summer holidays of 2013, I was full-on suffocating and wanted out of this so-called friendship, but I didn't know how to extract myself from the clutches of Helen's increasingly unhinged displays of emotional neediness. I was exhausted and couldn't think straight, as I was so comprehensively jangled from having little to zero introvert time in over two years. My strength of character and force of will, which had once been all *too much*, was now wilting in the heat without respite. I was shattered and frantically searching for a way out of this trap. Lauren was right [*again!*], I was now a shell of my former self. This is exactly how manipulators operate, they wear you down by relentless and imperceptible degrees, so you don't notice until it's too late that you're too weak and foggy of thought to escape.

Throughout the summer of 2013 I was also plagued with frequent bouts of agonising gastritis, a stomach condition where the stomach lining becomes inflamed, irritated and eroded by the harmful effects of stress [*in my case, but there are other causes*]. And if this wasn't a clear enough sign from my mind and body that I needed to escape the toxicity of Helen, my migraines increased from every few months to weekly clusters, and my back went out more than I did. All of this was stress induced, I was in a right state.

It's plain to me now what was happening, but that still didn't show me the way out of the massive hole I'd dug for myself. I swam around mentally in a simmering, jangled pea soup for weeks, trying to think of ways to extricate myself, without bringing another shit show down around my ears. I needn't have worried though, because Steve and Helen were about to deliver me from this toxic swamp, and ultimately save the children and I from any further carnage… by first throwing us under the bus.

Prised Open

Having endured the summer surrounded by Helen, her boisterous, ubiquitous, attention-seeking daughter, Emily, and her perpetually Minecraft playing son, Oliver, I wanted out.

It hadn't always been bad, we'd had moments of supreme fun, but they were now the exception, not the rule. Helen had spent over two years trying to prise me open, to relax, lighten up, work less and play more, and her efforts were rewarded by, i.e.: me relaxing enough to start a food fight. I do have a childish streak, which I rarely let see the light of day, but Helen had accepted this part of me without prejudice, and it was delightful to let go and have some fun.

It's true that I had become too tightly wound, after years of i.e.: being criticised by Mum for simply reading a newspaper: *"You're like your father, reading the ink off the page"*, or by Steve who felt ignored and neglected if I read a book, or designed and built a website for our business. All of these things I seemingly did *too much*, and it evidently offended people, so I stopped. If I couldn't read a newspaper without being *too much*, then how could I do anything else without causing harm? This hammered my confidence and self-esteem, as I was clearly capable of unintentionally offending people without even trying, so I started to live smaller and dimmed my own light.

I once started a water fight with my young nieces and nephews in Mallie's back garden, which was enormous fun for all involved, but it was met with

Mallie's *"I've just sucked a lemon"* face, so we never did it again. In fairness, I don't suppose many people would be happy to have their garden churned into a quagmire, but this is the same woman who promoted noise and fun whenever it annoyed others (i.e.: Bill, Steve's Auntie Doris, me). The times I'd urged my children to tidy up after themselves before we left for home, only to be overridden with *"You're at Nanny's now, so mummy shouldn't worry so much"*. Infuriating! There I was trying to teach my children personal responsibility, only to be shot down, repeatedly. I didn't matter whether I was promoting fun or responsible tidiness, I was wrong.

Anyway, Helen had genuinely been able to prise me open, but now I was starting to withdraw into myself again, and I think she noticed. On top of this, Steve was starting to talk to me about his developing feelings for Helen, which I *still* didn't recognise the significance of. Here is an example of just how Fugly Complacent I was, taken from my contemporaneous journal notes again.

On Saturday 10 August 2013, we were at Helen's for dinner, but my gastritis flared up from out of nowhere. I tried to ward it off and put up with it, but my tablets were at home and it was becoming unbearable. Even though the night was still young, I had to call it quits and went home in a taxi, leaving Steve and the kids at Helen's having fun. The following day, Steve told me that he and Helen had been sitting close enough together for Helen to put her legs up onto Steve's lap. He wanted to be honest with me, and to ask me if that was okay, and I said it was; so cocooned in my complacency was I. I want to slap myself now, but that's what happened. He went on to tell me how they had bounced on the trampoline together, and then lay on it, looking up at the stars. I know, I know, you want to slap me now too, don't you?

With every step Steve took during the summer of 2013, he stopped and either told me about it, or asked if it was okay. He told me about his deepening feelings towards Helen, he told me he was experiencing an urge to kiss her [*which was definitely not okay*], and what was going on between them (legs up on lap etc). Steve didn't lie to me. In fact, it's as though Steve was begging me to notice, to care, to give the tiniest of shits about him getting close to my chosen sister, but I didn't. And I still don't know why, although I have my suspicions.

Fool If You Think It's Over

You may need to strap your lower jaw to the rest of your skull for this bit, because you're not going to believe some of what I'm about to tell you.

First, let me time hop you back for a moment, because it's important. Steve and I used to be visited by a Romany gypsy in the showroom from time-to-time, who told me my estrangement with Mum was not necessarily permanent. Whilst Mum was unwell, I would be given a choice before she eventually passed away. No specifics were given about what constituted unwell, or when Mum would pass away, but there was certainty I would have a choice before anything happened. Okay. I all but forgot this, but I need you to remember it.

Years later, on Monday 12 August 2013 I woke from a vivid dream with the song lyrics *"Come on, get happy"* ringing in my ears. Initially I was heartened by the seemingly happy and positive message, but I couldn't place the song or the singer from those lyrics alone. In the dream I was standing in a place I

[77]

just knew to be the Ulster Festival Hall, in the 1940's era. I was standing on the first-floor level, looking at a proscenium arch to my right, which was framed by two broad parallel burgundy bands painted around its edge. To my left was another undecorated arch, which led to a short corridor with a metal spiral staircase down to the ground floor. At the top of the stairs a trio of musicians were accompanied by a short and fragile looking black lady singing *"Come on, get happy"*. This lady's stature put me in mind of Edith Piaf, as she was so delicate and tiny. I felt compelled to Google the song lyrics, which you'll have to do too now – if you want to – otherwise I'll be in violation of copyright laws. Don't worry, I'll wait whilst you go and do that, and we can resume when you get back.

All done? Okay, good.

So now I was alarmed, as I perceived – rightly or wrongly – this song to be about death. The fact I was in the Ulster Festival Hall, listening to live music in the 1940's, put me in mind of Pop and Grandma Annie. I have several photographs of Grandma Annie waiting for Pop to finish playing drums, guitar or piano on New Year's Eve, before they could celebrate and Auld Lang Syne together. These photographs were all taken in the 1940's.

Now, I have only been to Northern Ireland a handful of times in my life, and I most certainly have never been to the Ulster Festival Hall. In fact, I text my (Northern Ireland resident) Auntie Alison to ask if such a place even exists, or has existed, because I seriously didn't know what I was dreaming about here. Auntie Alison told me there was an Ulster Hall, but there wasn't – or hasn't been – an Ulster *Festival* Hall, to the best of her knowledge.

Perplexed, I recounted all of this information, as well as my perceptions about what was happening, to Helen via text. The song lyrics also gave Helen pause. Likewise, the link back to 1940's Ulster where my family are from. Helen offered the possibility that perhaps a spiritual message was being sent to me, via my late Pop or Grandma Annie, preparing me for a possible death in the family, but who could they mean?

We shortlisted either Mum (because of the direct and obvious link to both Pop and Grandma Annie), or Maggie (because of the historic link to Pop, and to her continuing residence in Northern Ireland). Helen suggested I phone Maggie to check she was okay, which I did, and she was. Then Helen asked me: *"Do you think you can phone your Mum?"*, to which I replied: *"No"*. I had initiated contact with Mum the year before, and it had ended badly. My last tearful, heartbroken words to her were: *"Okay, goodbye Mum"*.

Besides, how on earth was I supposed to explain my reasoning for calling her this time? The truth was obviously out of the question: *"Hi Mum, how are you? Is everything okay health wise?"* I didn't want to raise that kind of fear or suspicion, which would only have inflamed our relationship further. I lived in the eternal hope we could both grow up one day, and love each other wholeheartedly again, so I didn't want to spike that.

I was sitting up in bed, facing our bedroom window, during this text exchange with Helen, and brief telephone conversation with Maggie. Then, just as Helen was asking me if I felt I could phone and check on Mum, a large black crow landed on my windowsill. I kid you not. My blood ran cold. This had never happened before in the 20+ years we'd lived in the house, and it never happened again. Crows are said to be the harbingers of death, as they purportedly escort the soul into the afterlife; but I still couldn't bring myself to phone Mum. Our relationship really had become *that* toxic.

So now we skip forwards a fortnight or so to Saturday 31 August 2013, which saw us all at Helen's house for dinner, again. We stayed late, but we were still texting each other into the wee small hours. Picture this: Steve and I sitting next to each other in bed, both texting Helen until about 4am. There was much hilarity between Helen and I, so I wasn't paying much attention to Steve's text conversations with her.

Then suddenly Steve burst into tears, which prompted him to tell Helen he could no longer be friends with her, because his feelings towards her were deepening and he couldn't handle it because it felt wrong. I suggested we call it a night and sleep on it because we were clearly tired, and that we could discuss it in the morning. Helen on the other hand had other ideas. Helen was imploring Steve not to make any hasty decisions, and that the three of us were "...*stronger together than apart*" [*refer back to your page marker, because this a textbook Love Bombing technique for when targets pull away*]. Steve eventually settled down enough for us all to stop texting and sleep.

Steve couldn't sleep though. Steve hadn't been able to sleep for months, so troubled had he been about his deepening feelings towards Helen; despite the miles he was pounding on the exercise bike each night. For what it's worth, he told me everything, he was as clear and as honest as he knew how to be. He tried valiantly and repeatedly to warn me, to get me to notice and to care about what was happening, but I could not be roused.

Despite trying to settle for sleep after 4am, Steve found himself sitting on the edge of the bed at 7am, when a text from Paul came in, it read: "*Hi Steve, please get Karan to phone me urgently, thanks, Paul*". Steve reached over and gently woke me up, advising me of Paul's text message. Having not heard from him in over six years, I sat bolt upright, immediately frightened and alert. Paul had left a similar message on my phone too.

On Sunday 1 September 2013, I phoned my brother and was told that Mum had passed away suddenly and unexpectedly a couple of hours ago. I asked him what had happened and was told the following: on Tuesday 27 August, Mum had been feeling increasingly unwell, which resulted in her asking Paul to call an ambulance and being taken to hospital. After an initial battery of tests, the doctors confirmed she'd not only had a mild heart attack that night but had had a minor heart attack two weeks previously – on or around Monday 12 August, when I'd had my "*Come on, get happy*" dream.

Mum was admitted to hospital and underwent several further exploratory tests. These tests confirmed that Mum had advanced liver cancer, amongst other things, as well as the cardiac issue which needed immediate attention. On Friday 30 August, Mum and Paul discussed the additional tests and likely treatment plan she was going to have to undergo with her doctors.

Whilst Mum was gravely ill, there was no sense of immediate mortality, which is why I wasn't called; they wanted the full facts before contacting me. This I don't doubt, because I would have unloaded 10,001 questions and expected clear and concise answers. I have little patience for vagueness or sugar coating when the chips are down, I want facts and evidence. Paul assures me now that had he known the end was so near, he would have called me, and I believe him.

On Saturday 31 August, Paul visited Mum in hospital and stayed for a few hours but began feeling unwell himself and so went home. He left promising to return the following day. Later that evening though, Paul got a call from the nursing staff advising him to come in, which he did. When he arrived at her bedside, Mum was unconscious and no longer connected to any medical equipment. He was told Mum's condition was now end stage and just a matter of time. He stayed all night, eventually falling asleep on the floor beside her bed, because a back injury prevented him from sleeping in a chair. At approximately 5am Mum passed away quietly, without ever regaining consciousness, and with her darling Paul asleep on the floor beside her; she was not alone. The nursing staff woke Paul into his new reality.

The grief hit me like a truck and took me clean off my feet. The seven stages tried to arrive in order, although I'm pretty sure I leapfrogged the second stage of denial, to land right in the middle of anger. I raged at the universe: "I THOUGHT I WAS GOING TO HAVE A CHOICE?!" Helen would gently remind me later of her question following my *Get Happy* dream: "*Do you think you can phone your Mum?*" So, I had been presented with a choice, and I had chosen to decline it. This placed me squarely in front of the self-recrimination firing squad. The *what ifs* ran rampant through my mind, pointing self-accusatory fingers and setting fire to my peace of mind with the flames of regret.

Steve woke the kids and got them ready to be dropped off at Helen's, so he could take me to the hospital to see Mum. I was numb initially, in shock, but then I started to question what right I had to grieve for her. How was I entitled to grieve for my Mum, who I hadn't seen in more than six years? How big a hypocrite was I, to be sorry for losing her now? How dare I go and see her now, when I wouldn't see her whilst she was alive? Thoughts like these didn't stop swimming around in my mind for weeks, I was powerless to stop them or answer them.

We arrived at the hospital at the pre-arranged time, but still had to wait. I honestly thought I was going to throw up on the floor right there in the corridor, but I'd not eaten anything to throw up. Eventually we were escorted into the ward where Mum had been treated whilst alive, which surprised me as she'd been gone for more than five hours at this point. The curtain had been pulled around her bed, and the accompanying nurse left us to take all the time we needed.

I took a deep breath and tried to mentally prepare myself as best I could, but nothing really prepares you for seeing your Mum lifeless and empty. I slowly pulled the curtain back, focused my eyes on Mum and immediately my knees went out from under me. Steve caught me as a rolling thunder of emotion erupted from inside of me, as the grief and regret of my entire life, was released as a kind of howl into his chest. The sense of aloneness was strange and overwhelming. The realisation I was now parentless ached and feared. Even though I was quite grown up at 42, and a mother myself, I felt small, orphaned and bereft; untethered and floating.

My shock was as much to do with Mum's appearance, as it was with her having left me. Mum had been a larger lady in June 2007 when I had seen her last, but now here she was a tiny, sparrow like version of who she once was. She put me in mind of Edith Piaf. No, the symbology was not lost on me, as the pain of dream recollection struck me unforgivingly. What if I had have phoned her? What if I had dared to tell her about my dream, could I have persuaded her to see a doctor? Could I have prevented the heart attack(s)? If only I had said something! Could she have beaten the liver cancer, had her heart not given out? We will never know.

Just in that moment I felt like a little girl, alone and desperate for her mummy to wake up, terrified that the unquestionable reality might actually be true. I began bargaining with God to press the Undo button, because this wasn't what I wanted. How could she be gone; she was *my Mum*? I had taken her for granted and now she had been taken. I chose not to see her for years and now, after today, I would never get that choice or chance again. The abyss was deep, dark and wretched.

Ideally, Paul should have prepared me for the significant change in her appearance, but then he'd been swallowed by grief too and was naturally focused on his overwhelming loss. Mum had allowed her hair to grey naturally, rather than continually fighting the good hair dye fight. This I never thought I'd see, and she had also had it cut shorter than she had worn it in a very long time. Then there was her jaundiced skin hue, savagely shaded by cancer's remorseless attack on her liver, with her suffering clearly etched on her face. There appeared to be no serenity in the instant of her passing.

I do question the wisdom of seeing her that day, but at the time I felt I had to push myself, as I believed it would help with closure. I have often wondered over the years if my inability to move on from the loss of Nanna was in some way related to not attending her funeral. I was eight, completely distraught and grief stricken, and Mum thought the whole process would have overwhelmed me. I can't argue with her logic, but I do wonder if attending the funeral would have given me closure.

Too Many Variables

Whenever I think of Mum, it is her warm brown doe eyes, that I recall first. For all their beauty, Mum's eyes were also a window to the vast well of emotional hurt, which simmered within her. Mum loved and trusted deeply, and only ever asked for that love and trust to be returned equally, but her bleeding emotional scars could wall her off inside herself, disallowing any display of vulnerability. This made reaching her difficult sometimes.

I know Mum loved me, but it's only by writing these pages it's occurred to me how my *too muchness* possibly gave her unconscious mind post-traumatic Maggie flashbacks. Oh God, how I wish I had realised this earlier: Grandma Annie was a strong character, albeit kind and nurturing, and she left Mum. Nanna was a strong character, albeit kind and nurturing, and she left Mum. Noel had a strong character, and he left Mum. Maggie had a strong character and rejected before exiling Mum to Hampshire. So, my less than fluffy *too muchness* was never going to be well received and accommodated, was it? Perhaps, unconsciously, Mum pushed me away before I inevitably left her, like everyone else of my ilk had done before? And left her I had. I'll let a qualified therapist help me to answer that one day.

Mum had a wonderfully dry and witty sense of humour, and I delighted and marvelled in her clever use of words. As the daughter of a wordsmith herself, this should have come as no surprise. Pop had worked with all things communications-based during World War II. He later went on to work for the government, whilst publishing sports articles in his spare time. He was a vastly intelligent, erudite and witty man, and I remember him laughing more than anything else. This man loved Monty Python, and when others complained it didn't make sense, he responded: *"Exactly!"*

Maggie really was the personification of a cheese grater, where Pop was more of a toaster, leaving you warm and popping up. How – *just HOW?!* – those two ever got together after Grandma Annie passed away is anyone's guess, but Pop could only tolerate the cold serration of Maggie for so long, before falling into the soft and nurturing arms of his third wife, Patricia.

Mum shared Pop's sensitivity and vulnerability, in addition to his wordsmithery. Soft-hearted by nature, Mum always rooted for the underdog, and believed in second chances, but once her limit was reached you could kiss your arse goodbye. When Mum finally turned, you were faced with impenetrable steel and the game was over, as she'd endured too much hurt in her life already, to tolerate more. She had paid her dues and it was time for you to fuck off now, and that included me.

When Mum and I got on we really got on, with much hilarity and sentimentality, but where there was friction, we could burn your house down. There seemed to be no middle ground, where we could just muddle along without The Hague having to invoke articles from the Geneva Convention. Both of us were born naturally gentle, sensitive and caring souls, only to be forged into the fire breathing She Devils we both had the potential to be.

Like everyone else on the planet, life shaped us both. Life hardened us both, which is a shame, because our natural selves had so much more to offer the world, had it just passed on some of the chances to give us a kicking. I don't know, maybe we were too alike without ever acknowledging that fact? Whilst our spirits may have been kindred, how we perceived and interacted with reality was diametrically opposed. This is where the friction lay in waiting, and with the friction came the decimating sparks of dysfunction.

One thing is certain though, whatever the prevailing condition of our relationship at any given moment, I was devoted to Mum. I loved her so adoringly and completely, and only wanted her to be her true self around me, rather than who she thought I wanted her to be. Mum always seemed to be looking for my approval, which made me uncomfortable and squirmy, because I thought her divine perfection as she was; as her true self. It was only when she tried to be someone she wasn't, that it agitated and infuriated me. Why couldn't she see herself as I saw her? I cannot abide falsity on any level, it makes my skin crawl, and I didn't understand why I was feeling like this. My "gut instincts" were so strong and accurate, how? Why? What the hell?

Now I understand why; way too late of course. Now I understand I saw, recognised and felt Mum's true self, on a spiritual and energetic level, and was offended by the false personas she tried to put forth. Her true self was beautiful and felt like home to me, so I needed nothing more from her, but she couldn't appreciate this. Having endured and survived so much trauma and rejection in her life, I think she may have felt something was intrinsically wrong with, or faulty or deficient in her; not good enough, not worthy of devotion. You can't live through what Mum had lived through without it rewiring your mind into a default, defensive position. But of course, I've only realised this since she's been gone, and can't do a damned thing about it now. How my heart grieves and repents.

I Left The Planet

Back to Sunday 1 September 2013. As I'd had less than a couple of hours of sleep, by the time we got back from the hospital I was fit to drop. I was more than happy to accept Steve's offer of letting me sleep at home, whilst he went to collect the children from Helen's. In fact, to ensure I got as much sleep as possible, he pitched the idea that he should stay at Helen's, so the kids didn't wake me. This sounded utopian to me. All I wanted to do was collapse, weep and sleep, without having to pull myself together for appearances sake. I needed to unravel desperately, but I needed to be alone for that to happen. Once alone, I duly came apart, before falling deeply asleep for many, many hours.

Steve did indeed stay at Helen's with the kids into the early evening, when they returned home so we could get them bathed and ready for school in the morning. I honestly have zero recollection about what happened, or what was said during this time, it's all one big grey, fuzzy blur.

To be honest, the entire three weeks between Mum passing and her funeral on Thursday 19 September, was one big, grey, fuzzy blur; I remember so little. I know I spoke with Maggie, Auntie Alison, and Mum's cousin Pam, but I can't remember the content of those conversations. I do remember the conversations I had with Eve, that she was unable to attend the funeral, but otherwise joined me on a tearful journey down memory lane. What I remember most during these three weeks was the baffling quest Helen roped me in on, to try and find out where Lee's new girlfriend lived. Yep, you heard me. *Urgh!*

Mentally and emotionally I had left the planet. Physically I was limp and heavy. I felt so consumed by the magnitude of the grief I was feeling, but so undeserving of feeling it. This was a massive internal conflict I was struggling to wrangle and reconcile, so I did what I always do in such circumstances, I went into my head to try and make sense of it. The inside of my head at this time can be best described as a deafeningly loud, pulsating kaleidoscope of thoughts, visions, memories and recriminations thrown into a blizzard. My thoughts were fragmented here, and my emotions were fragmented there. By going into my head, I was striving to perform a kind of mental defrag; to pull it all together, so I could grasp my new reality.

A defrag, in the usual sense of the word, is a routine clean-up operation you initiate on your computer, to collect pieces of data that have been strewn across the hard drive, to then put back together again to aid operational efficiency. This is precisely what I felt I was doing when I went into my head; and yes, it was as complicated, painful and time consuming as it sounds.

With the daily needs of Steve, the children and our business to juggle, in addition to Helen's relentless demands on my time and attention, my defragmentation took infinitely longer than it might otherwise have done. In accordance with Mum's wishes, Paul was making all the funeral arrangements and had politely rebuffed my offers to help, so I wasn't needed there. I was however able to talk with Auntie Alison and Pam to discuss their flights from Northern Ireland, and travel to and from the airport on the day of the funeral.

Wandering around in a daze, perfunctorily fulfilling my daily duties as best I could, Steve stepped up and took on many of the school runs. I seemingly shut down when spending time in my head, and I think it's to limit my exposure to unnecessary stimuli, for which I know I will have insufficient RAM to process well. By Steve completing the school runs, I could limit my exposure to Helen, but also forgo those superficial playground chats I just didn't have the social skills or inclination to navigate. How could they be planning a holiday, or little Jimmy's birthday party when my Mum had just died? Don't they realise the world had stopped on its axis?

[89]

Whilst Steve was taking on more responsibility, you know... with all that surplus energy he had [*not!*], I was trying to come to terms with the loss of Mum, and my newly rebooted relationship with Paul. It was a lot to process. Meanwhile, Helen still wanted to hunt down Lee's new girlfriend, who reportedly lived a couple of streets away from me. I have no idea – or memory – of how she came to know where his girlfriend supposedly lived, but I do remember Helen driving us around looking for Lee's car parked outside a house.

Quite what we were going to do had we found it was never explained, but around and around she drove, diving into all the smaller side streets, searching hungrily for sight of Lee. It was quite beyond my care or comprehension. It was madness for sure, but these are the things I'd been whittled down into doing for a quiet life. If I complied, she might leave me alone, because I wouldn't hear the end of my selfishness otherwise.

Why did finding Lee's new girlfriend's house matter? I do remember thinking it strange how she had worked so diligently at removing him from her life, that she should be so questionably jealous about him having found someone to be happy with. As with most things at the time, this too is largely a blur, but I wonder if Helen was irritated that Lee had found a new love, whilst she was still very much alone? Did she somehow feel the loser in their fractious battle, and couldn't bear him prevailing? We will never know.

Unbeknownst to me until months later, Dawn had been observing some new developments during the school runs Steve was attending. Habitually, Dawn would park up in the same place each afternoon and read whilst waiting to collect her kids. As a result, Dawn was aware of Helen and I, without really knowing either of us to speak to. She would repeatedly see Helen and I walking from our favoured parking spot, talking and laughing ourselves into the school gates. So now Helen was being accompanied by a tall man she knew wasn't Helen's husband, Dawn's antenna twitched with suspicion.

Dawn had accompanied her kids to Oliver's 7th birthday party at the petting zoo a couple of years earlier and had orbited Helen and Lee in the process. Whilst she would have undoubtedly seen Steve and I there too, it is reasonable to assume Dawn would not have been able to place Steve specifically as my husband. Once Steve had collected Sofia (whom Dawn knew to be my daughter) from school however, the pieces fell into place for Dawn, and her sense of alarm grew.

Steve doing the school run and meeting up with his wife's friend in the process was not newsworthy and wasn't what caused Dawn's antenna to twitch. What troubled Dawn was the sustained improvements in Helen's appearance and demeanour, on the days Steve went to school. As a couple of ordinary slummy mummies, Helen and I were generally dressed in jeans, T-shirts and trainers or walking boots. I tend not to wear makeup unless pinned to the ground and Polyfilla'd first, whilst Helen always wore a modest amount.

Why would we dress up to simply fling the kids into school? We certainly weren't interested, or able, to compete with the perfectly coiffed and high fashion mums, who had some place else to be. Dammit, our kids were bloody lucky we ever got changed out of our pyjamas at all on some days; and this was Dawn's usual vision of us.

Now, whilst I was off the planet grieving for Mum, planning to collect Auntie Alison and Pam for the upcoming funeral, taking tentative baby steps with

Paul, and running the business, Dawn was noticing a little more effort in Helen's wardrobe choices. And high heeled footwear. And bright red lipstick, which was now applied heavily rather than modestly. Something was rotten in the state of Denmark, because this only occurred when Steve collected Sofia from school. On the few occasions I did the school run in this time frame, Helen was back to her slummy mummy self. *Hmmm.*

Dawn repeatedly watched agog to see which of us was collecting Sofia on any given afternoon, and whether Helen rocked up in high heels and bright red lipstick for me. Which she didn't, because that was evidently just for Steve. Dawn's antenna crackled an intuitive warning but because she didn't know me to speak to, she didn't feel she could, or should, interfere in our affairs. Perhaps there was a perfectly innocent and logical explanation? Hmm. Only if you tilt your head and squint.

Just for the record though, Steve would always be wearing his tradesman's work clothes, but don't forget he'd been working out like a man possessed for months by this time, so was looking fit, fabulous and handsome. And I was consciously oblivious to it all. For those of you wanting to slap some sense into me, please form an orderly queue behind my friends and family. In the meantime however, stay tuned to find out how this all unfolds. It ain't pretty.

Did Helen Try To Spike The Funeral?

So, the three weeks between Mum's death and the funeral seemed to drag on forever. I felt like I was climbing uphill through treacle to complete even the simplest of tasks, like washing my face and brushing my teeth. My interest in Lee was now extinct. I no longer gave a flying wah-hoo about what he got up, even if that meant deserting Helen and leaving her to fight her own battles, for once.

Still very much in my head, trying to complete my defrag. Still swimming in shark infested self-recrimination waters, I now had another perceived problem to sort out. In my mind I was concerned about the reception I was going to get from Auntie Alison and Pam. Whilst I had previously had a loving and respectful relationship with them both, I was now defensive and concerned about their opinion of me, and how well we would get on, on the day of the funeral. The last thing I wanted was to cause, or to be the cause of, any additional drama on the day, as they were grieving as much as I was.

What I didn't know was what Mum had told them, how accurate any of that may – or may not – have been, and what their opinions of our situation were likely to be. If Mum had pitched it to Auntie Alison and Pam that I had simply just walked out, never looked back and denied Mum a relationship with her grandchildren, who could blame them for being cool and aloof towards me? But our relationship was so much more complex than that, and we had both tried so hard to make it work, repeatedly.

As Paul and I were still trying to find our new footing together after so long estranged, I didn't feel I could ask him such potentially inflammatory and self-serving questions. His life had just imploded around his ears, he was trying to live his life without Mum, and had a heart-breaking funeral to plan. The last thing Paul needed was me bleating on about whether Auntie Alison and Pam were going to be mean to me or not. I had to Woman Up and get on with it.

Whilst I was fretting about the potentially disastrous consequences of meeting up with Auntie Alison and Pam, Helen was trying to influence my thinking. She made it clear that she didn't want me driving the 60 miles or so to the airport and back, twice on the same day, with two people who may have taken exception to my relationship dynamic with Mum. Helen was persistently insistent on this issue, but I have never allowed myself to be held hostage by a challenging situation like this, and Helen knew that better than anyone. This was to be no exception. If Auntie Alison and Pam were operating under a misunderstanding or misrepresentation, then I would clear it up, if and when it came to a head.

Running away from perceived disputes or challenges like this solves absolutely nothing, the problem just sits there waiting; growing in magnitude. Better to nip it in the bud, as there's less work and hurt involved. Helen disagreed, and I was surprised and puzzled by the ferocity in which she was holding her ground. Why did it matter so much to her? I ran it past various members of my War Council, in case I was missing a valuable point, but as they were as unaware of the potential Love Bombing deployment as I was at the time, none of us could answer the question. Still wading through life with pea-soup fuzzy brain grief, and certainly not anticipating malfeasance on Helen's part, I couldn't grasp any sense in her argument, so I largely ignored it. I didn't have that kind of time or inclination to be perfectly honest. I was frayed and exhausted.

Looking back now, and trying to piece the puzzle together with hindsight, I question whether Helen felt uncomfortable with all this "new" family showing up in my life again. Remember, I was "hers" [*her words, not mine*], she'd had me increasingly to herself as Steve had been systematically side-lined for almost three years, and she didn't want to share me, or so she said. She verbalised and text these sentiments to me often. Now here was my beloved brother Paul, and revered Northern Irish tribe, re-entering my time and consciousness, and this was perhaps unacceptable to her. Obviously, I can't read minds, so this is simply my best guess whilst trying to make sense

[94]

of it all. Only Helen can speak to what she was actually thinking and feeling at the time. All I have is what she text.

Helen had also fought long and hard to try and oust Lauren from my life, with little success, but now she had new family to deal with too... *come on!* Helen was aware of my deep love and admiration for Paul, Auntie Alison and Pam, and they represented the potential dilution of my time and attention in the weeks, months and years to come. Who can say for sure? As I said a moment ago, this is largely conjecture on my part, having painfully acquainted myself with the outwardly projected workings of Helen's mind for so long. But to me, this felt like Helen was trying to isolate me further from my loved ones. What I couldn't understand at the time was why she would want to do that. This isn't how you love someone. This isn't how you positively enhance their life. I just couldn't fathom it, so I continued to pull away from her because our values started to feel very different.

Alex's Fifth

In amongst all of the funeral preparations and discussions sprang Alex's fifth birthday and birthday party, which needed to be thought of, bought, wrapped, organised and facilitated by yours truly. Birthdays are a big deal in our family, and we duly swamped our beloved baby boy with lots of love, kisses, cuddles, attention and presents; going so far as having a fully erected set of junior goalposts in our front room, waiting for his explosion of happiness.

Yes, the goalposts had to be dismantled again to fit through the door and set up in the back garden, but that was beside the point. We wanted to see the delight and excitement in his big blue eyes, and he needed to be able to play with, not just look at his new gift from a window in his pyjamas. He shared his joy in abundance. Our hearts were throbbing with love for our most glorious boy. Whatever has happened, Alex has always been, and will always be (even when he's 6ft 8" and built like a tank), *Mummy's Big Handsome*. From his first precarious week in SCBU, here he was now five years-old, healthy and perfect in every way. I felt so blessed and happy.

The following Saturday saw us all converge on his favourite soft play activity centre. This was going to be the first time I would meet Mallie and Steve's family since Mum had passed away, and I was in no mood for Mallie's snark. She walked towards me in the activity centre, starting to convey her condolences, but my skin crawled, so I just held up my hand to cut her off and said: "*Thanks*". They largely kept their distance for the remainder of the party, and I took lots of photographs which helped to maintain the divide.

Having roamed the party with Whopper [*my camera*] taking photographs, my energy eventually crashed, so I sat down to watch the fun and festivities. Alex was a hot and sweaty mess, having huge amounts of fun with his friends. The hotter and sweatier he is, the more fun you can safely assume he's having, so all was well. Whilst observing the noisy, frenetic action, I happened to look up to the top of the play structure, only to see my tall, well-built husband, with Helen, leaning against the netting and throwing plastic ball-pit balls at each other. They too were having the time of their lives, and *still* I didn't twig. Or perhaps on some level I did twig, and just didn't care? Having rested sufficiently, I continued taking photographs and video for posterity.

From the activity centre it was all back to Mallie's house, where we flung the kids around a nearby park to burn off the excess cake and ice cream energy. Helen and Emily tried to start a grass cutting fight with me, which I resisted initially, before throwing myself in with gusto and launching an overwhelming counterattack. There was much laughter and lots of childish behaviour, and it felt good to relax and let go a little. This is a prime example of how Helen was able to prise me open and encourage me out from inside my head, particularly if she thought I'd been in there too long. On this occasion I was genuinely thankful for her intervention, as things had gotten entirely too heavy in my head, and she was right to pull me out.

Alex was being supervised hurtling down an infant-friendly zip wire by an attentive Steve and Uncle Len and revelling in his moments as a Super Ninja Hero Commando. This was thankfully drying out his sweaty shirt in the process. [*Note to Self: Pack more spare clothes for your sweaty little monkey boy*].

It wasn't long before Steve came over to join in our grass fight, when I noticed something. [*Finally!*] Bearing in mind I was witness to his sobbing willingness to cease being friends with Helen, due to his burgeoning feelings the week before, which Helen had initially talked him out of, and Mum's subsequent death had distracted us from. Now here he was trying to stuff grass cuttings up and down Helen's top, WTF?! This I noticed. This I told him was unacceptable. This dampened the overall mood of our park play, and we returned to Mallie's shortly after that. Len for one seemed to register something was amiss but said nothing.

Mum's Funeral #1

The day of Mum's funeral finally arrived. I woke up, realised the date and the enormity of the dreaded day ahead of me, and felt sick to my stomach. I was up and out of the house before the kids got up, as Auntie Alison and Pam's plane got in at 8am, and if I wasn't there ten minutes early, I was late. It had been a while since I'd last had to navigate the airport complex, so by the time I found the right car park, an actual parking space, walked over to the terminal

[97]

and gone to the loo, there were Auntie Alison and Pam walking towards me on the concourse. I was met with sincere, bone crushing hugs and a lot of love and sympathy. All these weeks, I'd been worried about nothing. Bloody good job I hadn't listened to Helen then, isn't it?

If I had given Helen the entirety of all that she had insisted upon, not only would I have petulantly refused to collect these two dear and wonderful women from the airport, but I wouldn't have attended the funeral either. By not attending the funeral, I would most certainly have invited suspicion and disapproval upon myself, whilst fuelling a feud that hadn't previously existed. By shaking free of Helen's influence, I had regained my objectivity, thought long and hard for myself, and opted for courage under (imaginary) fire. My Helen-blindness was rapidly receding in the rear-view mirror and she knew it.

Helen had said she was worried I was walking into an ambush, that I was being tricked into collecting Auntie Alison and Pam, to then be trapped in their disapproval to and from the airport, and throughout the day. Helen had never met either woman, and if she had, she would have realised this is not how they operate, and it is not who they are. Perhaps Helen was projecting her own character or family dynamics onto my family, who knows? The important fact is that I ignored her and went to meet my family, to share in our collective sorrow.

I drove from the airport to what was once Mum's house (now Paul's), with what felt like bats and pigeons turning somersaults in my stomach. Auntie Alison was a godsend insomuch as she came armed with 101 questions for me to think about answering, rather than focusing on what awaited us at Mum's house. We all tried to stay upbeat and positive whilst catching up on each other's news, but our destination was upon us relatively quickly and easily. Thankfully the motorways were kind to us that day.

We pulled up outside Mum's house, and Paul came to the door, eventually. His appearance took my breath away, he looked skeletal. This was the first time I had seen him since Dad's funeral in February 2010 and he had lost a lot of weight. This is a big deal, so hear me when I tell you that Paul has always been tall and thin, but this was beyond tall and thin. In the past, he had been able to eat anything, and the calories seemingly found their way to my hips! I really don't remember signing up to this bargain. Perhaps I got the brains and beauty instead? Okay, you laughed a little too hard and long with that one, what about my feelings? My broader point is this, Paul never had any weight to lose, and now he looked like death... literal death!

Unimaginably frail for his mere 40 years, he slowly shuffled his way towards the car and hugged Auntie Alison and Pam first. I steeled myself, because I was frightened about how many of his ribs I might now break unintentionally as we hugged. He felt as bad in our embrace as I'd feared. Although he was wearing an overcoat to keep himself warm on this mild autumnal morning, his coat looked like it was hanging on a coat hanger. He looked grey of hair, sallow of skin and thoroughly drained and exhausted. I would find out exactly why in the days and weeks to come.

For now, I thought his frailty was the result of having been crushed between some industrial racking and a forklift truck, several years earlier. He shuffled slowly, hunched over almost 45°, with every step pouring searing agony up and down his damaged spine. His employers at the time of the accident had hired some powerful lawyers and essentially scared his claim away, so he received nothing in the way of compensation, even though it was all caught on CCTV. They exploited the fact he couldn't afford high powered legal representation for himself and crushed him again under the weight of their corporate, callous, greed and malfeasance. But there was even more to it than that.

After our hugs, Paul invited us inside for a coffee. This was it. This was one of the moments I had been truly dreading for weeks; going back to Mum's house for the first time in six years. As Paul and I hadn't quite found our footing just yet, and as Helen's demands on my time had been as demanding as ever, I hadn't had the opportunity to visit him beforehand; to desensitise myself for this day. In truth, it's equally valid to assume I was probably trying to delay the inevitable heartache for as long as possible too.

Mum's house had a unique and specific smell, and I was worried about the emotional impact that would have on me when I smelled it. It's a medical fact that the sense of smell is most closely linked with memory because the olfactory bulb is part of the brain's limbic system, which is commonly referred to as the "emotional brain". This means the limbic system can call up memories and powerful responses almost immediately, but what if the smell was no longer there? What if three weeks without her, the house now smelled more of Paul than Mum? I didn't know which option was preferable. Do you see what I mean about my thoughts being like a kaleidoscope thrown into a blizzard? Clearly my defrag was still a work in progress.

I stepped through the front door and the collection of Mum smells hit me like another truck! The polish she'd always bought, which had recently dusted the furniture, the fabric conditioner on Paul's clothes and the cushion covers, the million candles *[I counted!]* and endless pot pourri [*"I don't think much to these snacks Mum!"*], I was warped back in time. My emotions burst the dam and poured forth inside of me. This rendered me unable to speak or to unclench my jaws, as I fought to keep the welling contained within. Paul was clearly on the edge of his stoicism too, and if I started, he'd have started, and we would all have started, with a very long day ahead of us. One of Mum's most enduring lessons to me "*Maintain your dignity Karan...*" played loud and on a loop in my head "*... because we don't fade, we don't buckle, and we don't cry out loud*".

Auntie Alison and Pam had bought old family photographs with them to help us reminisce, and I have no idea how I held myself together. Everywhere I looked there were our family photographs, the souvenirs from holidays past, the ornaments I'd grown up with all my life. The presents I'd given her and the studio portraits of Sofia and Alex, whom she so clearly adored. This was Mum's time capsule, and it felt so desperately empty without her.

Auntie Alison and Pam were working hard to keep things light, by recounting tales from their shared childhood with Mum in Northern Ireland. We were given a stronger sense of who Grandma Annie and Pop were as people, which made me love them more. I would love to have spent time with Grandma Annie whilst she was here, as she sounds like my kind of woman, but alas it was not to be. I know with all certainty she's here with me now though... correcting my grammar mostly.

Whilst Mum and I were estranged, it was clear I still resided in her heart and mind, as much as she had in mine. The problem with us seemed to be that one was a stick of dynamite, whilst the other was a permanently lit match, and only one thing was ever going to happen when you put the two together; BOOM! Over the years we had finally learned this about ourselves and stayed apart to spare the carnage and ensure the safety of bystanders.

As the funeral was to be held at 2pm, and with the return airport run to negotiate, Steve and I decided to pull the children out of school for the day. There was no way we could be back from the funeral to collect them at 3.10pm, without negatively impacting upon the service and wake. Alex had only just started his Reception year a handful of days earlier, and I had appraised his teacher of our family bereavement and planned absence, so we were all set.

Crazy Gamma

Alex was clearly too young to experience a funeral and had never met Mum. Amazingly, Mallie agreed to look after him during the service, where Steve would then collect him to be part of the wake. Conversely, Sofia had known and adored her *Crazy Gamma*, so she was going to attend the funeral, once Steve had dropped Alex off at his mother's.

Why was she called Crazy Gamma? Well, Mum and I had had another period of estrangement between 1998 and 2003, where we shut ourselves down from communicating with each other. Then, in February 2003, I finally fell pregnant after one miscarriage and months of trying. I operate from the basic principle that my children should have as many people in their world, who love and adore them, as possible.

This mindset was mostly fuelled by my own idealism but was bolstered by Mum's stories of what her early childhood had been like, living in the organically warm embrace of a close-knit, extended family. She told me tales about how she and her cousins could wonder freely into any aunt's home, to then be fed, watered, cuddled and cared for without distinction. They were all one big happy family and it sounded heavenly to me. I wanted this for my children.

The closeness was never more apparent than when Grandma Annie passed away suddenly, and the whole family convulsed together around a shared open wound of grief, shock and unconditional love. For the good times and the bad times my children will inevitably face in their lives, *this* was the kind of love and emotional security I wanted them to grow up in, surrounded by and cosseted within. So, I rang Mum.

In May 2003, shortly after my 12-week scan, I rang Mum to tell her the news. She promptly burst into tears. We then cautiously tried to iron out our differences in the name of our one shared goal; family unity for the love of Spud. Spud was the nickname of my baby bump because, although we didn't know the baby's gender yet, my bump was all out front – which meant a boy, right? Lauren predicted a boy too, so it was obviously going to be a boy...*eye roll*. For what it's worth, Mum predicted a girl based upon the scan images, which I scoffed at. Mum said that from the curve of the cheek on the baby's face, she was certain of a granddaughter. So adamant was she that we were having a girl, Mum bet me 50p that she was right, payable after our 20-week scan. You know what's coming, don't you?

The more our pregnancy news sank into Mum's consciousness, the bigger my baby bump grew, the crazier she got; in the over-excited sense of the word. She was knitting blankets and cardigans, buying clothes, toys and nappies. She had us pinging to and from baby stores to buy bedroom furniture, travel cots and buggies. When Steve and I baulked at all of her huge expense, Mum shut us down with one seriously well-rehearsed line of reasoning: "*I helped Paul and Rhea buy their house, so I can do this for you. Now be quiet and let's go to Mamas and Papas!*" But it wasn't just about spending money either.

[103]

Mum would write Sofia long, loving letters for the future, introducing herself, detailing what I had been like as a baby, child and young person, in addition to my [*good!*] qualities now and what a perfect daddy Steve was going to be. Mum wrote poetically about how we were all so completely ready to love and welcome Sofia into our world. Yep, Mum fell crazy in love with our little Spud and never came up for air.

I Have Never Faked A Sarcasm In My Life!

On the day of our 20-week scan we made it clear we wanted to know the gender, but the baby had other ideas. Bearing in mind the entire capacity of my bladder is slightly less than a miniature thimble on the best of days, when you go for a scan, they want a full bladder to help bounce sound waves off the baby. I was already uncomfortable and irritable. So, there I was bursting to pee, but really wanting to know the gender of a baby who was now playing hide and seek!

Evidently Sofia – because we all know I had a girl first – thought it would be fun to turn her back to the scanner. As the ultrasound operator chased the baby around my womb, Sofia was clearly winning this battle of wits. I was advised to go for a walk around the pocket park, lugging my sloshing bladder over my shoulder if needs be, to see if the baby would be kind enough to shift position. After about ten minutes I returned to the scan room, and we were told our beautiful Sofia was on her way. We cried. Mum cried, then told me to pay up, triumphantly.

Now, those who know me personally will attest to my penchant for sarcasm. I honestly think it's the highest form of wit because you have to be suitably attuned to understand it. Nothing irritates me more than wasting perfectly good sarcasm on people who smile wanly, clearly not appreciating its beauty.

Mum loved sarcasm too, so I was in good company and on safe ground with what I did next.

To pay off my 50p gambling debt, I found the newest, brightest, shiniest 50p coin available. Then I buffed it and polished it some more with a silver dip, before having it professionally framed and mounted, with a plaque on the back, commemorating Mum's winning wager; indelibly admitting my wrong, wrongly wrongness. There would be no simple handover of a 50p picked randomly from my purse, *oh no!* This was in response to an oft-repeated accusation of never being wrong being levelled at me. Here I was now making a huge production out of being exactly that. Mum threw her head back and laughed, cherishing the rare admission of fallibility. It was the only one she had or would ever get!

Just one little sidebar point. On the day we found out Sofia was on her way, and she really did have the cutest little cheeks we'd ever seen, Steve was so smitten with her that he took a pink onesie from her layette and slept with it under his pillow until she was born. *This* is who he truly is. *This* is who The Imposter has walled off. *This* is who I hope is healing.

The Gamma craziness continued. When Sofia was born, oh my god the world caught fire for Mum. Sofia wasn't due until Wednesday, but I was woken up at 5.50am on Monday, needing to pee. So far so unremarkable. However, just as I was about to assume the position on the loo, my waters broke. Then came the tsunami of pain, which washed over me suddenly, violently and so completely overwhelmingly. The unrelenting, escalating pressure building to a crescendo of excruciating agony was like nothing else on earth. You know, like when a man stubs his toe on the corner of a coffee table?

[105]

I phoned the maternity ward to tell them of my tsunami leakage, and they told me to call back when I was in labour. Wait, what?! This was my first baby; how would I know when that was if *this* wasn't it?! Barely able to breathe to articulate a suitably polite response, and swear words being so much shorter and on the tip of my tongue, I snarled that I was in labour, and of that I had no doubt – or some expletive riddled variation thereof. The maternity ward duly agreed I should come in as soon as possible, because it sure sounded like I was ready to have this baby.

The pain was ceaseless. Where the hell were the pauses between contractions, I'd heard so much about in our *How-Not-To-Kill-Your-Baby-By-Accident* classes? Steve suggested we try out my brand-new TENS machine to help with the pain. Great idea. So, we broke open the virgin box without stopping to read the instructions. Who needs instructions? We didn't have time for instructions. How hard could it be? What could possibly go wrong?

By now I'm on my hands and knees trying very hard not to have this baby on the sodding floor, as Steve approached me gingerly with electrical equipment. He placed the electrodes to my lower back, switched on the TENS machine, whose dial was set at 10 (the maximum), when you're supposed to start at 1 and work up. The air turned blue, my hair turned curly, and I'm sure I smelled burning. How I didn't *vag-ject* that baby out of the open window I will never know. Steve apologised profusely, citing panic as a mitigating factor for not checking the settings. I was beyond words, just grunting, snarling and looking for something heavy to throw at him. Luckily anything worth throwing was too high for me now.

The TENS machine was put away before I could smash it and then, inexplicably, I decided to shower, because of the tsunami leakage moments ago. Steve didn't dare question the wisdom of this, as my lower back was still smouldering, so I had the shower. Ridiculous! If you're expecting a baby, please take it from me that you absolutely do not need to have a shower before giving birth, because the worst is yet to come. It's like rearranging the deckchairs on the Titanic. It's a totally pointless exercise, and a complete waste of time and water. In a few short hours I was sitting waist deep in the residue of my baby's birth, waiting to be stitched up like an Austrian blind.

Predictably, once I'd showered, I couldn't get out of the bloody bath. As I had SPD [*Symphysis Pubis Dysfunction; look it up so I don't gross out the disinterested*] and was in the throes of labour, lifting my leg to step out was near on impossible. Moreover, now I was the size and density of a fully-grown Silverback [*only less charming and charismatic*], Steve wasn't going to be able to lift me out either. Somehow though I made it out of the bath and Steve helped me get dressed and into the car.

Every route to the hospital had 47,529 speed bumps [*I counted!*], so there was no smooth way to get there. I was trying to levitate in my car seat, but gravity was having none of it, so when Steve phoned Lauren to say: "*Hi, we're on the way to the hospital, because Karan thinks she's in labour*", whilst driving over every speed bump and pothole possible, I growled: "*I AM IN FUCKING LABOUR!*". Steve correctly announced the onset of labour during all subsequent phone calls. This man was not having a good day.

We arrived at the maternity ward, where there was a 7½ mile hike to the delivery ward – obviously – and not a wheelchair to be found. I waddled, pain-riddled and irritated to the maternity reception desk, thoroughly indignant in my capacity as the first woman to ever give birth, and they'd offered no trumpet fanfare. Rude! Steve and a nurse, or six, heaved me onto the world's highest hospital bed, so that I could be examined – and I was 8 centimetres dilated! You must be ten centimetres dilated to have a baby. Karan *thinks* she's in labour, my arse!

The nurse asked me to "*hop down off of this bed*", so I could "*hop onto that bed over there*". *Sure! Maybe I'll throw in a little ankle sock triple axel en route, if you like.* There was no way I was budging off of bed #1, possession is nine tenths of the law. As I had been suffering with SPD since about Week 25, the only way I was moving now was if I was craned, winched or carried. The nurse blanched at that suggestion, and duly wheeled me into a delivery room. I'm going to spare you any further details of this birth story, except to complain bitterly about my lead midwife looking like Jennifer *Fookin'* Aniston; are you kidding me?! Women who've had babies naturally will understand and nod in solidarity. There is a god, and she thinks she's funny, but Steve knew better than to acknowledge how ridiculously attractive my midwife was.

Sofia was born by about 12.50pm. When Steve phoned Lauren, she thought she was getting an update, but was surprised and jealous of my sub-seven-hour labour. Lauren had three long labours, so it took a while for her aghast to wear off [*until Alex was born even more quickly, *chuckle**]. Steve then phoned Mum who was coiled beside the phone, positively fizzing with excitement. Once the call had come in it was all systems go. Paul and Rhea drove round to collect her, only to drive "too slowly" all the way to the hospital, about 25 miles away. If they weren't hurtling at warp speed or arriving looking ten years younger and sporting centre partings, it was too slow for Mum. Thankfully Paul's excitement was contained, his common sense prevailed, and he continued to drive to arrive, despite Mum's alternating pleas for speed laced with threats of bodily harm.

Mum's energy burst into my ward about twenty feet ahead of her body, where there I sat – sore and exhausted – holding our beautiful Sofia. Mum's face was a picture, and it was in that moment all was well between us again. For a while at least. To my eternal regret we would combust again in June 2007, only this time forever, despite my last-ditch attempt in December 2011 and Helen's *"Can you phone your Mum?"* suggestion in August 2013.

Mum's Funeral #2

With all that water under the bridge, I was back again, in the house where the 50p trophy still sat pride of place in Mum's bedroom. Steve had dropped Alex off at Mallie's and then brought Sofia (now aged nine) to the crematorium to meet up with the rest of us. We stood at the door of the crematorium, waiting to accompany Mum's casket into the chapel. Paul and I stood together, holding hands, trying to hold it together, just as we had done for Dad's funeral three and a half years earlier. Sofia looked a little bewildered, but Steve was hugging her, explaining and comforting her throughout, so I could focus on saying goodbye to my Mum. Well, sort of.

The pallbearers removed Mum's casket from the hearse and began the solemn march towards the chapel. Overcome with a wave of grief, Auntie Alison grabbed Paul and I and hugged us both tightly, releasing our barely contained tears in the process. As clichéd as this sounds, none of it felt real. It felt ethereal and like it was happening to someone else. How could this be my Mum, wasn't she invincible, immortal, too special for death? How could she not live forever, we needed her to look after us? We hadn't sorted ourselves out yet or made up again! The pea soupiness of thoughts in my mind were stirred around and around, going nowhere and resolving nothing.

Following the service, we returned to Mum's house to pause, breathe and reflect gently. After a while, Paul began looking like he wanted his home back to himself, and to unravel in his own personal solitude. He'd been holding himself together for weeks to endure this godforsaken day, and now he needed to let it all out, privately. He politely thanked Mum's friends for coming and gave us his blessing to go ahead to the wake without him.

Steve left with Sofia to collect Alex from Mallie's, to meet up with us again in a short while. Auntie Alison, Pam and I stayed with Paul for a little while longer, wanting to make sure he was going to be okay by himself. We were concerned the house was going to be too big without Mum in it. Despite being only 5ft and a nth of an inch tall, Mum's energy was huge, and so now was the void in Paul's life. He wanted more than anything to be left alone, and so we left.

I drove Auntie Alison and Pam to a local restaurant, where we met up with Steve, Sofia and Alex. Already enamoured with Sofia's beautiful face, character and demeanour, now they were enchanted by Alex's shock of blonde hair, big blue eyes and his *I'm-cheeky-and-I-know-it* charm. The kids were a dream all day, well behaved and a complete delight. My babies did me proud and I could not have loved them more.

Our meal celebrated Mum in a style she would have approved of. There was much laughter, many memories and deep, genuine family love around the table. As small and as scattered as our family is throughout the British Isles, Pop and Grandma Annie's values run through us all; proudly defining us as people of strength and integrity. I am proud to belong to this family, and I love being loved by these two awesome, wonderful women who shared in my grief.

[110]

We stayed at the restaurant until it was time for us to make our way to the airport again. Following more hugs, kisses and meaningful eye contact between us all, Steve eventually took the kids home, as Auntie Alison, Pam and I departed, so they could catch their flight home. It was a punishingly long day for us all.

I drove home from the airport in complete silence, replaying the day's events in my mind and allowing the tears to flow freely in the privacy of my car. I finally arrived home to an empty house. Steve had taken the kids to Helen's, where they were having dinner. Having not had a minute to myself since collecting Auntie Alison and Pam from the airport, almost 12 hours earlier, I desperately needed this alone time to settle myself and decompress. I assumed Steve had predicted this, which is why he'd taken the kids to Helen's, although it would have been nice to have been hugged and looked after when I got home. Oh well, never mind. I poured myself a Famous Grouse, sat alone in the candlelit quiet of my living room and cried some more.

Steve brought the kids home eventually, so we could get them ready for bed and school the next day. I must have crashed to sleep early that night, because I don't remember much of anything else. I do remember Helen texting me before I slept to tell me I was going to spend the day with her tomorrow, "*...because you need looking after*". According to Helen I'd had a horrible September, starting with Mum passing away on the 1st and ending with her funeral today, and she was going to try an lighten my load a little. This sounded really quite lovely; some much-needed TLC that I felt was lacking from Steve.

I have to admit there's a huge argument to be made here that Steve couldn't have gotten it right for getting it wrong at this point. He was damned if he did and damned if he didn't. After knowing me better than anyone else for 24 years, he was right to predict I wanted alone time after a long day of grief, and 200+ miles of airport runs. But I had wanted hugs and looking after too, so he was damned for giving me space. I couldn't have both, I understand this, but I'm telling you this to demonstrate the pea soupiness of my thinking. There's no way this man could have won this day.

Friday 20 September 2013

So, Steve couldn't win, but in swooped Helen to pick up what he'd left on the table. I initially viewed Helen's plan for this day as a loving and caring gesture. I thought it was lovely that she cared so much about me that she'd bought ciabatta, brie and bacon for our lunch. I thought it a good idea when she engaged me in a calm and soothing task of binding lavender smudge sticks, only to start a lavender fight to lift my spirits. She genuinely seemed to care, and I was – uncharacteristically – letting her.

Privately, I don't like being the centre of attention or being made a fuss of, it makes me uncomfortable; and don't even think about pitying me! Whilst I've conducted seminars, training sessions and team building events in front of hundreds of people at a time, that's all fine because I'm Karan + Job Title; I suit up for occasions like that. Steve noticed this during my motorsport career. He noticed that once I was dressed in the team uniform, I became a whole new extraverted version of myself, able to talk to anyone about anything.

Privately however, I'm really quite shy and I'd rather not have a fuss made (outside the embrace of my nearest and dearest). I always marvelled at Lauren's effortless ability to talk to checkout operators at Tesco, where I could only muster the politest of socially awkward nods and smiles. I'm better now than I used to be but allowing Helen to look after me was a big deal for me back then. Whilst I was struggling to get out of the relationship overall, I had seemingly suspended my escape attempt since Mum had died, focusing on the more important matters in hand. For now, on this day, I needed the care Helen was willing to give me, and I was genuinely thankful for it.

Little did I realise what Dawn had been observing on the school runs during the preceding weeks of my Horrible September. I wouldn't learn this for another seven months, when I'd eventually be introduced to Dawn for the first time at Alex's karate lessons. I had no idea that September was about to get a whole lot worse.

I often wonder if Helen was softening me up for the killer hammer blows, she planned to rain down on me, my children and our world? I was already operating at half power due to grief, exhaustion from many months of fighting Lee and being jangled. But if she knew what she was about to do to me and my family, then maybe she'd want as many Brownie points in the bank as possible – who can say? I know I sure as hell can't speak to Helen's intent and motives. Only Helen knows the reason why she ever did anything, and only Helen must live with the karma and consequences of her choices. I wouldn't trade places with her for quids.

The day together turned into another evening together. By now, Steve was lean, strong, tanned and feeling better about himself, having lost weight and gained tone whilst cycling; he looked gorgeous. During the evening, I think it was Emily who suggested they polish the long, laminated hallway floor, so they could slide up and down it in their socks, and then eventually on a skateboard. Now, I'm all up for a bit of childish fun and can food or water fight with the best of 'em, but there was no way I was taking part in this.

Following a car accident in 2004, resulting in a degenerative back injury, my back has little tolerance for such trivial adventures. Sliding up and down a polished hallway floor wasn't my idea of fun anyway, and only offered more long-term pain if I risked it for a biscuit. I gave it a hard pass, whilst everyone else took part. I cared not, although I did get very bored very quickly.

The night finally ended with Helen insisting we come back the following day for a BBQ and a bit of a party to cheer me up. Emily jumped at the suggestion and invited her school friend Megan to attend. It was a date apparently.

F.Y.I.

All that I'm about to tell you from this point forward, is supported by the contemporaneous notes I made in my journal. Oh, I had been journaling like a normal person up until this point – handwriting in bound ledgers – but from here on my entries became significantly more detailed; where even the minutia was recorded. Some of these journal entries are more than 5000 words long; I really purged. Hayley had encouraged me, immediately following the Bomb Drop, to get all of my thoughts and feelings out and written down to help my healing journey, and duly recommended an app for my iPad. This advice I followed, which I encourage you to follow too, because it really helps.

As I said in a previous chapter, the thought of ever recounting the collapse of my life in a book was repellent to me. I was too private a person, and too hurt to bare my soul in public; it was never going to happen. Because I was specifically journaling to heal, it was essential for me to record every minute detail, and refuse to deny any thought, feeling or occurrence the light of day.

This is how I can recall so many accurate details from so long ago, and the writing of this book continues to heal through the acceptance of that pain. We must feel our feelings, otherwise they become stagnant and then toxic within us.

No two ways about it, I had to face my fears to write this book. As so much time has ticked by, and so much water has passed under the bridge, the children and I have very much moved on with our lives. Having endured so many years of heartbreak, poverty and psychological trauma, we are now in a better place mentally, emotionally and financially. Finally, the past hurts are starting to fade, and here I am having to dredge them all up again to write this book; *urgh!*

The whole time I have been writing the previous chapters, I have been feeling a burgeoning sense of foreboding. A dark cloud has been looming and growling at me overhead, and I have had to call myself out for wilfully procrastinating on the task in hand. I knew there was going to come a time where I'd have to charge up my old iPad and read my old journal entries. This exercise I recoiled from undertaking though, until the very last minute.

I procrastinated right up to the point where the book couldn't progress any further until I got over myself. I knew I was going to have to go back into that deep, dark, hurt place and relive it all, because how else were you ever going to understand how our lives collapsed, and unfolded from there? This was the prising open of the slowly merging flesh of a machete wound I had predicted it to be, but the following chapters could not be written without reacquainting myself with the facts and feelings. So please now follow me into my nightmare.

—— ❀ ——

Saturday 21 September 2013: On Your Marks

We arrived at Helen's early afternoon, and the hallway skidding recommenced, much to my annoyance. Within an hour or so, Sofia had worn a hole in her leggings, so Helen and I shot off down to Asda to buy her a new pair, amongst other bits and pieces for the BBQ later. When we returned, a water fight had broken out, which eventually resulted in Helen's long-sleeved top being soaked. The first alarm bell rang loudly in my head when Helen removed the long-sleeved top and proceeded to run around in a vest top for the remainder of the day. This level of immodesty was new for her, and I noticed. Whilst I missed a lot in the fog of grief, I still remember thinking *Why is she doing that?* – but I said nothing.

The rest of the day followed in much the same vein, and I was not enjoying myself. I even started to shrink down inside myself, getting quieter and more insular, as the day turned into evening. Something was wrong, and I didn't know precisely what. Surely it couldn't just be the vest top that was bugging me. I didn't know, and with the loud music and general cacophony of voices and good-natured chaos around me, I couldn't tune into my guiding inner voice to find out either; I was severely jangled. They say the quieter you become, the more you can hear, but this was a rumpus and I didn't stand a chance.

The original plan was for the children to stay overnight at Helen's, supposedly to give Steve and I an evening together, which I was very much looking forward to. However, the night just went on and on, the hallway skidding felt interminable, and Steve was having fun taking part. It didn't look like we were going home to spend time with each other anytime soon. By now Steve had finished at least one bottle of wine and started to become over familiar with Helen.

One example I witnessed involved Helen bending over slightly to put something in the microwave. For reasons never explained, Steve thought this was a prime opportunity to walk up behind her, bend and hug her from behind, all in front of me and as brazen as you like. For her part, Helen didn't flinch, complain or even look shocked and uncomfortable. This was too much for me to accept though.

Once everyone had scattered into alternative rooms, I followed Steve back out into the kitchen and told him I thought he was being over familiar with Helen, and that it was not okay. I explained that I loved him, and his behaviour was rousing a possessive streak in me. He looked uncomfortable. I asked him if he wanted me to be possessive, and he pulled a face as if to say *well this is awkward*. He wasn't apologising for the over familiarity either, WTF? Hot, hurt anger blasted my heart apart, but I chose to leave the room rather than create a scene in front of everyone else, especially our young children.

I sat seething alone in the dining room for a few moments, before finding Steve – crying on the steps in the garden – to tell him his food was ready. Without lifting his head from his folded arms, he told me to go away and, without caring sufficiently for the anguish he was clearly feeling, I left him on the steps and decided it was time to go home; it was very late.

I called for a taxi and was given a 15-minute ETA. Steve was still sitting alone on the garden steps, still with his head on his folded arms, still crying and I still didn't care. I informed him factually that the taxi was due in 15 minutes and immediately walked away; I was in no mood for his shit. I didn't recognise a single element of who he was at this time. He already felt like a stranger to me.

I started hugging and kissing the children, telling them to behave themselves on their sleepover, and to not play up. I put on my coat and shoes and waited in the doorway of the home office, so I could see when the taxi arrived through the window. Steve walked up behind me, put his arms around me and said that I had tricked him with alcohol. I had no idea what that even meant, because I certainly hadn't forced the wine down his throat. In fact, I hadn't even poured him a glass all evening.

He then proceeded to tell me he needed to talk to Helen, and I still didn't know what he was talking about. It was like he was halfway through a conversation I hadn't been invited to, so I firmly suggested he sleep on it and deal with it in the morning, sober. Of course, I was working on the mistaken assumption that he was wanting to apologise for his over familiarity. Seems I was wrong.

The taxi arrived, so I kissed and hugged the children goodnight again, but Steve wasn't gathering his things. It didn't look like he was coming home with me. With my mind scrambling to compute the reasons for what was happening, I hugged Helen and walked out towards the taxi. I steadfastly refused to look back, for fear of looking weak and hesitant in the hurt and indignant position I'd assumed. Heartbreakingly, if I had have looked back, I would have seen Sofia breaking down in tears and partially following me out to the taxi, confused and upset about that was happening, and why. The taxi drove away, and I still didn't look back.

No, I'm not proud of my actions, I hate that I caused Sofia pain. I would have returned to comfort her if I had looked back. I wouldn't have been able to stop myself from holding her close and kissing her cheek reassuringly, probably taking both children home with me. Every time I'm responsible for hurting my children, my soul is indelibly branded with searing regret, but my heart was breaking too, and my mind was racing. What the hell was happening? Why did Steve need to talk to Helen? Why wasn't my husband coming home with me? Why was he choosing to stay overnight with my friend? I felt embarrassed and uncomfortable for Helen, having to put him in his place once she'd listened to his drunken and wildly inappropriate ramblings. When did he turn into this person I didn't recognise anymore? Why was this happening? Didn't he realise the irreparable harm he was inflicting on our marriage?

Once I had left in the taxi, Steve went back into the house, through the kitchen and into the garden. He sat with his head in his hands initially but came inside to sit on the floor by the back door, with Sofia sitting on his lap, cuddling. Sofia asked him what had happened, and he told her not to worry, because everything was going to be okay. By now, Helen had walked into the adjoining kitchen and was leaning against the oven, listening to their conversation. Sofia went over to Helen and they hugged before Helen asked: "*Do you want to speak to Mummy?*", Sofia nodded. Helen took Sofia up to the master bedroom and sat with her whilst we chatted on the phone. I made a conscious decision to tell Sofia I was cross with Steve (which was obvious, so there was no point denying it), that he was an idiot, and that it was all going to blow over in the morning.

This seemed to settle Sofia sufficiently to stem her tears and fears, whilst allowing her to sleep. Whilst I had never been more alarmed and afraid for the condition of our marriage, I did think we could work through whatever the hell it was we were going through and was finally prepared to sever the friendship with Helen to safeguard us. In that moment however, I had no earthly idea what it was we were going through, and how any severance was way too little and way too late.

After the call, Sofia went downstairs and looked for Steve by the back door where she'd left him, but he wasn't there. She found him comforting Emily, who was sitting next to her friend Megan at the dining table with her head resting on her folded arms, obviously upset. *Why isn't Daddy comforting me?* Sofia saw this, turned and went to sit with an oblivious Alex in the living room. Steve came in shortly afterwards and told them both to start getting ready for bed.

Once the children were settled in bed and asleep, who the hell knows what happened next? All I knew in the immediate backwash was what Helen told me via text, which was that Steve needed time and space, and would be going to his mother's. This is where I thought the game was paused. No. Nope. Not even close.

Sunday 22 September 2013: Get Set

I woke up alone in the house for the first time since Mum had died, three weeks earlier. It felt like an aftermath. I text Helen as I'd promised to do upon waking, who informed me Steve had slept in Oliver's bed. She asked me if I wanted her to look after the kids for the day, so Steve and I could talk, but I was still furious and confused and needed to calm down before I engaged with him. Steve has always accused me of being "clever with words", which isn't good for him when combined with the fury-fuelled sarcasm which spits effortlessly from me, when ignited. Intuiting this was something far greater and more significant than anything we had worked our way through before, I acknowledged it was important to take the heat out of me before we spoke. I declined Helen's offer and kept Steve safe from a verbal evisceration.

What's interesting to point out here is, when Sofia woke up in the living room following their sleepover, she went upstairs to be greeted by Steve and Helen coming out of the master bedroom. They were both fully dressed. Steve was still in the clothes from the day before, and neither offered an explanation to Sofia for why they had been together behind a closed bedroom door. I wouldn't learn this fact until years later, when it eventually wriggled itself free from Sofia's unconscious mind during counselling.

I mention it now, because I think it could put Helen's morning after offer of having the kids "so Steve and I could talk" into an entirely different perspective, i.e.: *"Do you want me to have the kids, so Steve can tell you he's leaving you for me, because we've just slept together?"* Only the two of them truly know what happened that night, but I don't think it's unreasonable for me to consider this possibility, given the duplicity of the pair, do you?

Without realising at the time that Sofia had witnessed them leaving Helen's bedroom together, I was so confused with what I *was* aware of. My Fugly complacency was upending in slow motion. He couldn't be leaving me for Helen, surely? After all he'd said about her, really? Whilst Steve may have been considering slumming it, it occurred to me that I had no idea if Helen's position had shifted opportunistically, on the back of Steve's newly revealed interest in her. So, I text her. I text her five times in 26 minutes, to ask her directly if she wanted Steve. On each occasion she typed a lot of words, but not one of them was "*No*".

In fact, after the fifth and final time of asking, I had to wait more than an hour and half for an answer. I had blown Helen's mind apparently, poor lamb. According to her conversation with Steve in the moment, which he later disclosed to me, Helen had not allowed herself to explore her feelings towards him up until this point. Now she had, and she had discovered she loved him and wanted him. Just like that.

Hands up all of those who believe her. Hands up those who remember the upgraded wardrobe choices, high heels and bright red lipstick on the school runs Steve attended, in the three weeks prior to this proclamation of innocence. Not that I was aware of these facts in real time, but they happened, nonetheless. Hardly commensurate with "*I haven't allowed myself to explore my feelings for Steve*", is it? She was still playing me for the fool I'd been throughout our entire friendship; talk about a long con! As much as I loathe the word, because it really is beneath me to use it, it was at this point Helen was forever defined in my mind as an opportunistic _____. I simply couldn't think of a more suitable adjective or noun. I still can't. And I'm supposedly "clever with words" remember.

If you're outraged and offended by my use of a profanity [*which I haven't actually written, so it's whatever you think it is*] to define Helen, please offer me a suitable alternative. Please define a woman who claims to love her friend eternally and unconditionally, spends more than two years prising them open and establishing their trust, to then be presented with the opportunity to take a big, strong, handsome, successful man [*who's teetering on the brink of a crisis*] for herself in an instant, to spare a life of inevitable loneliness and singledom. I'll wait.

An actual friend, an actual sentient human being with a soul and a conscience, would have made herself unavailable to Steve's wild, panicking, crisis-driven meltdown and supported me through my troubled marriage. An actual friend, an actual sentient human being with morals and even a sliver of self-respect, would have recognised and cared about the haste in which these life changing decisions were being made, and the metaphorical grenade she'd be lobbing at my children. Children she purported to love. Children who referred to her as their other mummy. Children who trusted, adored and respected her. But instead, Helen appears to have sold her soul and sacrificed my baby's hearts on her altar of self-interest. This is the definition of an opportunistic _____. I rest my case.

Without a single thought or care for our children, who she claimed to have loved as her own, without a second backward glance at the unconditional love I'd offered her, Helen told Steve to jump because she'd catch him. I don't believe Steve had the man-stones to jump without a soft place to land. Even his mother agreed with me on that one. Mallie told him that if he wanted to leave me, that was one thing, but that he had to go through with it, in its own right. Mallie counselled Steve not to jump straight into Helen and Lee's former marital bed, without spending some time alone, reflecting.

Of course, Steve dismissed this advice because Helen was offering him something shiny, new and fun – exactly as she had done for me two years earlier. Well, almost. If he landed on Helen, there wouldn't be the stress of looking after two very young children, because Emily was 14 and self-sufficient and Oliver was perpetually gaming... easy! There'd be no parental responsibility, because these children weren't his. Yeah, he'd keep them safe, feed them and drive them to school, but the emotional investment wouldn't be nearly so exhausting or time consuming; he'd have more time to think about himself. The business wouldn't suffer either [*or so he thought*] because Helen is AAT qualified (Association of Accounting Technicians) and could do his books. It was a win-win whichever way he looked at it, through his rose-tinted Hall of Mirrors spectacles.

After decades of responsible mortgage payments, dedicated marital fidelity, developing a successful business and raising the two beautiful children he had been desperate to have, Steve had now buckled under the pressure. His burnout cycle was complete. A midlife crisis episode appeared to have taken hold and he bolted from all his responsibilities. Like a lost and frightened little boy, he ran away, rather than straighten out his life like an grown up. Steve was now on the cusp of becoming a deadbeat dad, something I never believed he could be. Damn, my levels of wrong, wrongly, wrongness were orbiting the epic!

Steve told me weeks later, that as I was texting Helen on the morning after (asking her five times in 26 minutes if she wanted Steve), he was telling her that he loved her and wanted to be with her, whilst asking her if she wanted to be with him. This is what had blown Helen's mind apparently. They had initially been discussing Steve's plan to maybe leave me in Spring 2014, because it was too soon and heartless to leave me now my Mum had just died. Once again, Helen walked him back from decency.

Apparently, she couldn't risk waiting six months for him to leave me, hell no. By then I would have moved on through my grief, been restored to full power, and Steve and I could perhaps have sorted ourselves out. It's unlikely Helen could hazard the bet. Who knows when she would find another man in her own right? Even Lee had been dating someone else when she met him 25 years earlier. High value men are sparse, and discerning. Too risky. So, her inner opportunistic _____ grabbed at the low hanging fruit that was an unstable Steve throwing himself at her, and she was saved. Hey, better someone than no one, and I was pulling away from her anyway, so it really wasn't that much of a choice; and Steve really was the complete package. How great was life for Helen right now?

As a world of opportunity had now opened up in front of Helen and, rather than be a single mother of two children herself, she took Steve whilst she had the chance. She told him that if he waited until Spring to leave me, she would find it impossible to choose between us, to know which of us she wanted most, so it was now or never. Ultimatum delivered to a weak and wavering man, looking for any light and relief in an oppressive world of work, depression, burnout and fatigue. A strong move. Helen 1 v Karan 0.

Helen's *Not-Exactly-Sophie's-Choice* dilemma was further validated by my friend Wilkie, who met up with Helen on the school run a day or so after Bomb Drop. Helen was complaining to Wilkie that I wouldn't speak to her or let her explain what had happened. Wilkie snapped succinctly: "*You're fucking her husband, she gets it!*" But still she continued to try and woo Wilkie over to Team Helen by wistfully stating: "...*if I could have them both, I would*". Whatever that means. Disgusted by Helen's betrayal of a once deep, loyal and adoring friendship, Wilkie shunned Helen and remains resolutely Team Karan to this day.

Back to Sunday 22 September 2013, and the morning after. With all the kids waking up from their sleepover, Helen made breakfast for her newly enlarged family [*possibly recreating the one she grew up in, as the youngest of five*

children?]. Sofia asked Steve if they could go out somewhere that day. Steve suggested they all go for a walk in the woods about 20 miles away, and the place our two families used to take our caravans for long weekends away. Sofia liked this idea, so that's what they did. Still wearing the clothes from the day before, Steve bundled the children and Helen's dogs into his van and Helen's car, and off they went for a tramp in the woods. I'm going to sidestep the obvious joke there, because I can do better.

Whilst at the woods, the oblivious and carefree children and dogs ran freely, having fun, getting fresh air and exercise. Meanwhile Steve and Helen continued to talk about themselves and what they wanted, before kissing each other, in front of Sofia. This I didn't learn until years later, when again, the memory was released from Sofia's unconscious mind during counselling. After their walk in the woods they all went back to Helen's for dinner.

It was only at 7pm, when I text Steve to ask him to bring the kids home, that we had communicated directly with each other since the night before. They were home within 20 minutes. Once I'd bathed the kids and got them into bed, I showered and went to bed myself, clearly still seething. Steve showered and then said he needed to put the child seats into my car, and that he was going for a drive after that. I didn't care. Going for a drive is something Steve had always done when angry, or at times when he's needed to think and decompress. I sure as hell didn't want him anywhere near me, so going out for a drive was fine by me. When he eventually came home, he slept on the sofa, and I cared not.

Monday 23 September 2013: Boom!

Steve was up, washed and dressed for work early, so as not to alarm the children with his sofa sleeping that night. I got up and pretended like everything was normal as well. Whatever the hell "normal" was.

Helen text me early, like nothing had happened and referring to me as "*my lovely*", stating that Oliver was unwell and wouldn't be going into school. She added that I was welcome to go around to hers after school for a coffee if I wanted to. I replied quickly, saying I was sorry to hear that Oliver was unwell and wished him a speedy recovery. I deliberately didn't refer to the coffee invitation. She thanked me for Oliver's well wishes and invited me again for a coffee and a chat – all the time having kissed Steve in the woods the day before, and again the night before (as I would learn later from the man himself). Unaware at the time of all the kissing but pissed off with the piss poor answers to my five questions in 26 minutes, I replied: "*Nothing to say*", to which she replied: "*That's a shame but it's your call. I love you. Always will* ❤ " We had no further contact until evening; she actually left me alone.

Inexplicably, our house was always the place where washing machines and kettles went to die. It didn't matter if we bought bottom, middle or top of the range, they all died unreasonably quickly, but always outside of their warranty period; typically. Having sounded like we were washing breezeblocks with six-inch nails and screaming baby lambs for a couple of weeks, this was the day our washer-dryer finally ceased to be. I phoned Steve and told him we needed a new machine today at all costs, no excuses. He said he'd sort it out and, at around 5.30pm he arrived home with his friend David, to remove the old and install the new. How prophetic.

This was most unlike Steve, as nothing ever got done or finished in our house; my antenna twitched. Then I was alarmed by David's complete inability to make eye contact with me, which had not been an issue in the past. My antenna twitched again; something was wrong. It was clear to me that Steve and I would need a huge clearing-the-air conversation – or a fight if we had to – to get this sorted out. No. Nope. Not even close.

We had dinner and got the kids to bed, then Steve started his shower. So far so unremarkable. But then he started shaving in the shower [*waterproof electric shaver*], WTF? Why was he shaving at 8pm? Now I was alarmed. I ran upstairs to look for his phone. I was intent on becoming one of those suspicious wives and I didn't care, I wanted answers. I had every intention of reading his text messages to and from Helen, but I couldn't find his phone. Most unusual. So, I rang it (via the bedside landline), and from beneath a pile of clothes in his wardrobe I heard it ring. This was sneaky, defensive and reeking of deceit, not qualities I'd previously known in Steve. I entered the pin code he'd used for years, and it didn't work. Now my guts went off and I was starting to boil. I stormed into the bathroom and demanded the pin code, and he asked me why I wanted it. I stated clearly that I wanted to read his text messages and he said: "*You can't, they've all been deleted*". So, there was no problem with me checking that for myself then, was there? He still wouldn't tell me the pin code. Who *was* he?

Now he was out of the shower, so we moved our pre-war dance to the bedroom. Standing beside our respective sides of the marital bed, like two opposing chess pieces, I just went for it in the name of clarity and asked: "*Are you leaving me for Helen?*" With my rapidly fading Fugly complacency, I thought I was going to get a big, shocked, and disgusted "*Oh my god NO!*"

response, but instead he stated coldly and factually: "*It's highly likely, yes*". Bomb drop.

Trying to contain my hurt and emotion long enough to establish the facts before responding, I asked if they had slept together, which he said they hadn't. I then asked if they had kissed, and he admitted they had the night before – when he was supposedly out for a drive – leaving out the kiss in the woods beforehand. So now he's a liar and an adulterer. Kissing counted as adultery in our book, and if you don't agree then get over it, because this was us. Without saying another word, I charged downstairs to my Blackberry and text Helen: "*We're done*". They were the last words I exchanged with Helen (at the time of writing), and she didn't respond.

Steve and I didn't speak again that evening, because he got dressed, left and spent the evening – until the wee small hours – with Helen, before coming home and sleeping on the sofa again.

Our marriage was over.

ACT II

Tuesday 24 September 2013: Cry Later

Steve and I repeated the pattern of getting up and dressed before the children woke up and having nothing to say to each other. I couldn't even look at him, he disgusted me. I can't speak for him obviously, but there were no visible signs of sorrow, regret, pain or shame. For me though, it felt like I was carrying a flailing washer-dryer around in my stomach. I felt a lurching sense of heaviness and nausea, but I had to focus on normality and getting the kids to school, like nothing had happened. Steve went to work. Or at least that's where I think he went.

I first text Lauren the news, who asked me if I wanted to talk, which I didn't. I still had to process and evaluate. I had to spend innumerable hours inside my head, before I could coax enough composure, just to be able to articulate recognisable words out loud. I knew I had well-meaning words of comfort and platitudes coming my way, from everyone who cared for us, but they were only going to make me cry. I knew I was going to face vociferous venom directed at Steve, but he was still the father of my children, who adored him, and I didn't want to hear it. I knew I was going to have to listen to hate-filled invective directed at Helen, but I really didn't need the encouragement. It was all I could do to quell the worst instincts of my dark side, because once that cage door was opened there'd be no going back. So, I focused on love and light, my children.

I decided there and then that I would have to be strong now crushed, calm now livid and light now heavy with seemingly insurmountable grief. I had lost my Mum, my husband and my friend within the first 23 days of Horrible September. The void was incomparable to anything I'd ever experienced before, and I couldn't think straight. I was clinging to debris whilst spinning in space.

Telling Lauren what had happened, that she'd been right all along to dislike and distrust Helen as vehemently as she had, was hell. To have to admit to *myself* that I had been so wrong, and so blind – Helen-blind – to everything that had been so crystal clear to Lauren was agony. I felt humiliated and beyond stupid for falling for the Love Bombing, whilst wholly believing in her false persona. The past three years flashed before my eyes, now the veil had dropped, and I winced and grimaced with all the bad, bad choices I'd made, all the lies I'd swallowed, all so unquestioningly. How could I have been that stupid? What the fuck had I been thinking? Who the fuck had I been?

Lauren tended to me gently, without so much as a hint of self-congratulatory smugness. In fact, I sensed empathetic pain from Lauren as she said to me softly: *"I'd give anything to have been wrong"*. For sure Lauren wanted Helen gone, but not like this. Having known Steve for many years, Lauren was infuriated by Steve and Helen's betrayal, not just for the hurt they had caused me – two days after Mum's funeral – but for the inevitable grenade that was about to explode in my children's faces. Lauren is the antithesis of Helen. There isn't a narcissistic bone in Lauren's body that screams *Me! What about me? Me first!* Furthermore, Lauren is all about the children first, which you'll appreciate further on in this book, when even some members of Steve's family behave almost as abysmally as he has.

Lauren has held both of my babies just hours after they were born, and has watched them grow, in her capacity as Auntie Lauren, ever since. There have been cuddles, babysitting and presents throughout, always ready to gang up on me with the kids when they're teasing me; usually about my catastrophic cooking atrocities. In this sorry state of Steve's affair, Lauren was enraged by the world of hurt Steve was about to rain down upon the babies, she knew he had been desperate for. Lauren had lived through it all with us; getting married, the miscarriages, the pregnancies, the business growth, everything. Lauren was there for it all, and she was there for me now, and she understood better than anyone that I needed time and space to process, to go into my head.

Hayley on the other hand gave me no choice. Having endured more than her fair share of trauma over the years, Hayley knew I wouldn't be able to think. Hayley knew from her own experiences that every room would be spinning, and I'd be unable to grasp anything tangible. Hayley knew I had to take control of my life and, unable to think a thought for myself, she started to do my thinking for me. This is where you need trustworthy and wise members of your own War Council to step in and take charge, with only your best interests at heart. It would have been too easy for me not to trust anyone ever again, because Steve and Helen had betrayed me so completely, but there is no way you could ever put Lauren and Hayley in the same bracket as Helen.

Hayley and I shared many phone calls that day, whether I was composed or an emotional wreck, whatever. Hayley wanted me to focus on my future, to march forth from now on, without Steve. It was clearly just a matter of time before I would have to leave the business, either willingly or forcibly. If I left voluntarily though I would have been unable to claim any benefits, which I would now have to rely upon to feed the children, so I waited. Not long as it happens, as I had to issue my own P45, effective Friday 20 September 2013. You know, the day after Mum's funeral.

[134]

Great. Now I didn't have a job or an income, after 20+ years of devotedly growing the business, and making sacrifices to ensure its eventual, hard slogged-for success. Now the business was thriving, I was surplus to requirements and severed from the fruits of my labours. I was rendered penniless and powerless. A thunderous sense of panic swirled within me; how was I going to feed two children without an income?

How long was it going to take me to find a job? How would I pay the bills in the meantime? Was Steve going to financially support us, or pocket everything for himself and his new family? As the sole name on the title deed for the house, was he going to force us out to force a sale? I had no answers. I couldn't bear to think of the answers, because I suspected if Steve had been reduced enough to leave us in the first place, there were now no depths he wasn't prepared to plumb.

Hayley told me to phone the Tax Credits office to open a claim and, once I'd done that, I was to phone her back with an update on my progress. She told me I didn't have a second to lose and I could cry later, it was essential I got this done right now, no excuses. I phoned the Tax Credits office and spent over an hour sobbing down the phone, trying to articulate recognisable words to explain what had happened – and breathe, all at the same time. Thankfully, I got a beautifully sweet, patient and sympathetic DWP agent, who let me work through the agonising process in my own time.

Steve had ended the marriage and the best thing I could do was to accept that and move on. I had to focus on myself and the children exclusively from now on. Thankfully I was able to claim Tax Credits and Income Support and, although it wasn't much, with some severe budgeting and major lifestyle cutbacks, we shouldn't go cold or hungry. Boy how your focus and priorities can change in the blink of an eye. Never take anything for granted, because it can all be taken away from you in an instant. I was now a 42-year-old skint, single mother of two. I had become exactly what I had been protecting Helen from becoming, when Steve begged me to reduce the intensity of my friendship with her, a mere six months earlier. I could never have thrown her under the bus and left her to fend for herself with two kids alone, but here I was now under that very same bus.

The rest of my day followed in much the same vein, with Hayley giving me tasks to do, me completing them and then reporting back to her. I can't tell you how grateful I am to her for helping me in this way. There was no bullshit and blather from Hayley, she just launched straight into a *you're going to have to protect and provide for yourself mode*, and never looked back. I doubt I would have taken such decisive action, had it not been for Hayley. But oh, how that decisive action pissed off Steve later that day.

We had still not told the children we were separating at this point on Tuesday 24 September 2013. Steve was still coming home late, sleeping on the sofa and getting up before the kids. As far as the children were concerned, all was well. A bit weird, because we weren't seeing as much of Helen as usual, but that was fine with them, because they were getting me all to themselves for a change.

That evening, Steve arrived after work, had dinner with us and discreetly referred to sleeping at his mother's, in a private moment. Following dinner and baths, Steve put the children to bed and started his own shower preparations, after which I told him there were some changes he needed to know. I advised him of my Tax Credits claim and future Income Support benefits, along with all the other changes I'd made in light of his adultery. He was visibly shocked with how proactive I had been, less than 24 hours after being told of his *likely* plans to leave me.

By taking such decisive action to separate myself from him, for one apparent kiss (as much as I knew at that time), I was now dictating the end of our marriage on my terms; I had grabbed that power back or myself. If Steve was ever doubtful about moving in with Helen and ending things with me, tough, because now it wasn't his decision to make. I'd taken him at his word, it was all over bar the shouting.

I had spent 24 years telling him, the only way he would ever be truly rid of me, was to be unfaithful. There was no way I was going to make the same kind of decisions Mum had made with Noel. Perhaps Steve forgot this? Perhaps Steve hadn't taken me at my word? Why else was he surprised by my proactivity? We had met, right? He knew the inner workings of my mind better than anyone, so why the shock? My guess is, by taking such decisive action, I was effectively removing his safety net. He now *had* to make things work with Helen, because there was no return ticket available to bring him home. I knew this would apply maximum pressure to him, to her, to them, but it was their pressure to deal with. After all, I had two soon-to-be heartbroken children to repair and soothe, so I still got the fuzzy end of the lollipop.

In all honesty though, whatever Steve was feeling at this time, I certainly wasn't picking up on any kind of doubt or jitters about the future he saw for himself. Outwardly, he seemed cool and calm, despite his surprise with my chosen response to it all. Maybe he was expecting more shouting and screaming? Well, that's just tacky [*"Maintain your dignity Karan, because we don't fade, we don't buckle, and we don't cry out loud!" – Mum*]. Maybe he was expecting sobbing and begging? Hah, dream on Sunshine. Only Steve can know for sure. Lauren did ask me months after the split: *"Did you ever ask him to stay?"* – and in that moment I realised I hadn't. How remiss of me.

Remember, I had witnessed Mum's repeated disintegration at the hands of Noel, and there was no way on earth I was following suit. There was no way on earth my children were going to witness such a thing. My disgust with Steve was all pervading and I could barely look at him, much less consider reconciliation. For all intents and purposes, Steve was now diseased to me, forever and always. He had been where Lee had been. He had slept where Lee had slept. He was able to contemplate a life without feeling the arms of his babies around his neck, or their rosebud kisses upon his cheek, every single day. I couldn't fathom how he'd survive without them. This revolted me. There was something deeply wrong with him. His energy repelled me.

During our discussions, Steve expressed his interest in telling the children about our separation as soon as possible, because he couldn't sleep on the sofa forever, and he obviously wanted to sleep with Helen. He initially wanted to tell them the following day, Wednesday, but I insisted he wait until Friday. I argued that he couldn't throw a virtual grenade at the children's lives, and then expect them to concentrate at school the following day. At least by telling them on a Friday, I would have two days to adjust their perspectives and expectations, before maintaining the continuity of going to school on Monday. Reluctantly, Steve agreed.

Just before Steve left to spend another evening at Helen's, he told me Oliver would be returning to school the following day, now that Helen no longer felt she had to avoid me. I told Steve, in no uncertain terms, that Helen *should* avoid me, because it would be unwise to poke this Mama Bear. He acknowledged my warning and left.

Wednesday 25 September 2013: Not Giving In

Mentally I was starting to wobble. Mentally I was starting to question whether I could get through a life, with two broken children and a perilous financial situation, alone. Every time I looked into the pure, innocent eyes of my babies, I knew those eyes were soon to be filled with pain, distrust, confusion and anger. I knew their world was about to explode because of something their darling daddy wanted to do for himself, and to hell with the consequences for them. And I also knew there wasn't a damned thing I could do to stop it.

All I wanted to do, when I looked at their cherubic faces and listened to their carefree, playful giggling was to scream, rage-filled and venomous into the self-absorbed face of Steve, revealing my black contempt for him from the windows of my soul. I wanted to burn his idiocy with the fire of my fury, for hurting these two precious little ones he had once cherished before anyone else. Who the fuck was this? When had he become this thoughtless, selfish pig?

This barely contained rage against Steve, combined with my all-consuming love and protection of the children, plus conflicted grief for Mum, almost sent me over the edge. There were simply too many competing emotions, all at once. I briefly questioned my sanity. I briefly questioned my ability to hold it all together. I briefly questioned my inner strength, because I had too much to handle all at the same time, alone. Then I made a critical decision. Whilst staring out of the window, under the dark cloud of overwhelm so quiet and still, I decided – *decided* – there and then this was not going to break me. I *decided* there and then that I was going to be stronger than Steve, stronger than Helen, stronger than the two of them and stronger than anything – and everything – they would throw at me. It was an intense, growling, laser-focused and unyielding decision; polished with the oft repeated affirmation: **IT AIN'T OVER. UNTIL. I. WIN***!*

Don't get me wrong, "winning" didn't mean winning Steve back, he was diseased to me now. Winning didn't mean seeking revenge against Helen, because I believe karma will do a far greater job on her than I could ever do [*I just hope I'm allowed to watch*]. No, winning meant the children and I prevailing against the worst of times and coming out on top; better than, stronger than, more successful than and happier than those who had sought to cause us misery, poverty and heartbreak. I adopted "Not Giving In" by Rudimental as my anthem from that moment on, until the words and sentiment were forged into the neural pathways of my brain forever.

Steve had forewarned me that Oliver was back to school on this day, which opened the possibility of running into Helen. This made me fearful, because I was barely holding onto my temper. I couldn't guarantee her safety if she was stupid enough to approach me, or either of the children. She no longer had the right to even look at me, much less speak to me; she was worth less than dog shit to me now. My protective instincts had been fully activated and no inch would be given, which is why I told Steve she should keep a respectful distance.

By all accounts, as I mentioned earlier, Helen was champing at the bit and eager to justify her choices to me in person. But she had already taken enough of my time, energy, attention and spouses, and she wasn't getting any more. Playground friends, like Wilkie, coalesced around me once the news broke into wider circulation, resulting in Helen dropping Oliver off in another nearby school's car park, for him to walk in by himself. Yes, really.

I felt so sorry for Oliver as I watched this poor nine-year-old boy, clearly aware of what his mother was doing, having to walk past me twice a day at school, whilst sharing a classroom with Sofia. Of course, I made no issue of his presence near me, as he would walk the 200-yards or so with his head down, shoulders slumped and broken shoes slapping against their uppers as he passed by my friends and I. We truly felt for the poor lad; he'd experienced so much loss in his young life. Happily, his shoes were scarred with glue before winter, despite Lee contributing to his wellbeing and for essentials such as these. This was now Oliver's reality.

F.Y.I.: I found out via Wilkie, following Sports Day in July 2015, that Helen was telling people I had been having an extramarital affair, which is how she and Steve had got together. Honestly, the brass balls on this woman! Helen repeated this falsehood to a friend of Wilkie's, who told Wilkie, who then duly shot it down as an outright lie right there and then.

When exactly would I have had the time to have an affair with A.N. Other; when Helen demanded all the free – and not so free – time that I had, in addition to two young children, a husband and a thriving business to look after? Not that the wider population of our town would have known these details of my hectic life, but I have every reason to believe Helen (and Steve) have peddled this guff to his family; possibly to make themselves the victims not the villains. Oh well. If Steve's family are inclined to believe it, having known my character and devotion to Steve for 24 years, then their opinion of me really is none of my business. They can have at it, be happy and go in peace, but I no longer have to make room for them in my life. The truth will out one day, and they can live with the consequences. *Toodles!*

Back to September 2013, where Helen was refusing to have Oliver moved into another class, despite his discomfort and anxiety. The pressure on Oliver must have been immense but Helen had a point to prove. Surrounded by Sofia and all of her supportive friends, something eventually snapped in Oliver and he started to bully Sofia. Whilst I could easily separate Oliver from the actions of his mother, I would never allow my child to be bullied by anyone, and duly received the school's full support. Following a number of meetings and emails, the situation was resolved efficiently.

I understood Oliver was still suffering with the separation anxiety from his own father, whilst being expected to accept Steve as a new "Farshier" (the title he was given by Emily after watching Austin Powers: Goldmember). I understood he had experienced unimaginable turmoil in the past year. I understood he was frequently losing people from his life (i.e.: his Uncle Robert, his daddy, the kids and I), and I was genuinely sympathetic to his circumstances, but lashing out at Sofia was not an acceptable release mechanism. Thankfully the issue was quickly neutralised.

Sofia had initially asked Steve to intervene on her behalf with Oliver, but all he ever said was: *"It'll sort itself out"*. He was between a cock and a warm place, so he put his balls into storage and opted to do nothing. How could Steve take Oliver to task without alienating Helen, and destabilising their fledgling relationship? He couldn't, so he didn't. First test as absentee father:

FAILED. Perhaps it's because he knew he didn't have to jeopardise his relationship with Helen by tackling Oliver over the mistreatment of his baby girl? The baby girl whose pink onesie he had slept with under his pillow. Perhaps he knew I would do the dirty work for him, when he failed to step up as a father and protect his child? He was right, I did, and my contempt for him solidified further.

For what it's worth, as the months went by, Sofia and Oliver were eventually able to keep the tiniest embers of friendship warm-ish, for which I am proud of them both. For example, another boy in their class kicked a chair out from under Sofia, as she was about to sit down. This resulted in her hitting her head on a radiator, with enough pain and shock to make her cry. Oliver rushed over and asked her, sincerely, if she was okay, which Sofia appreciated. I guess Lee had enough time to instil some chivalry into Oliver, before his enforced departure from the lad's life.

Another example involved Oliver's blood phobia, which Sofia was well aware of, but their new class teacher was not. A class discussion went off on a tangent and started to include the subject of blood, which made Sofia look over to Oliver reflexively. She saw the precursor signs that Oliver was about to have a negative reaction and alerted the teacher. Because of Sofia's quick and caring intervention, Oliver was able to avoid a significant head injury and personal embarrassment.

Whilst I didn't see either Helen or Oliver on the school run during the morning of Wednesday 25 September, the afternoon was a different story. Clearly Helen was feeling feisty and brave. You'd think having been told to stay away from me, would have included parking somewhere else on the school run, wouldn't you? Helen decided to test me.

[143]

For the years running up to all of this, Helen and I would park alongside or near each other in a side road, within a two-minute walk to school. As Alex had only just started his Reception year at Infants, and was only going in during the morning sessions, I had him with me on the afternoon pick up for Sofia at Juniors. I reversed into my usual parking spot and then watched in total disbelief as Helen swooped in, to park on the service road right in front of me, just to our left. This meant Helen and her car were clearly visible to Alex, as we waited a while before walking up to collect Sofia.

Less than a week earlier, Alex would have gone bounding out of our car and over to Helen for a hug and a hair tousle. On this day though he was confused, as I wasn't moving or getting out of the car. He told me: *"Mummy, Helen's right there!"* thinking that perhaps I hadn't seen her. As this wasn't the time or the place to get into it, I simply told Alex I was cross with Helen and we wouldn't be going over to see her today. His five-year-old logic seemed to accept this.

Things took an unexpected twist once we'd collected Sofia though. Clearly avoiding the playground mums and their savage judgement of her, Helen waited in the car and had Oliver walk down to her by himself, for the first time in his life. Apparently, Helen's right to be happy didn't extend into her children's right to be happy. Helen's name and reputation were now largely in tatters, especially with the parents who remembered what she'd put Lee's Other Woman through in 2010. Oliver now carried the weight of this on his young shoulders. He was infinitely more courageous than she was.

Sofia had wanted me to allow her to walk down to the car in the afternoons, prior to the Bomb Drop, and I had said I would think about it. Originally, if she and Oliver walked together for the two minutes or so it would take to reach us, I was leaning towards letting her do it. Now however, walking with Oliver was not an option, but he hadn't been in school for the past couple of days, so it wasn't something I'd had to address. On this day however, Sofia saw Oliver start to make his way down the hill to our preferred parking spot and wanted to know why she couldn't walk alone too.

Mindful again this wasn't the time or the place, and that Steve and I had agreed to tell the children of our separation in another two days, I tried to fob Sofia off by changing the subject. This tactic failed, and Sofia had her first ever public hissy fit, right there and then. She'd only ever had two hissy fits in private before now, so this startled me. This was not how she had been raised or had ever chosen to behave in the past; I was flummoxed. Why in god's name was she playing me up now, on this day, over this issue?

She wasn't letting up and demanded to know why Oliver could walk down to Helen, but I was still collecting her from school like a baby. When we got down to the car, and didn't go over to see Helen, her tantrum worsened. I decided to try and make a run for home. In the ten minutes it would take me to get there, I could come up with something suitable to say, which would hopefully placate her. I started driving towards home, but Sofia persisted.

In the end, to be brutally honest, I just snapped and thought *fuck it*, in respect of my pledge to Steve to tell the children together on Friday after school. Yes, it had been my idea, which seemed like a good one at the time and I genuinely meant it, but he wasn't here having to deal with this Devil's Spawn hissy fit. Fuck him! Wasn't he about to throw away his paternal privileges anyway? He only wanted to be part of telling them so he could put his own warped spin on his own perverse choices. *Fuck him!* These were my children, who I'd have to comfort to sleep and console for evermore, and he wanted the

[145]

privilege of putting himself in as good a light as possible? *Fuck him!* FUCK. HIM.

It wasn't ideal, and I wasn't able to make it the four miles home before I had to start explaining why we weren't talking to Helen anymore. I explained that although their daddy still loved them very much, he no longer loved me, and wanted to live with Helen instead. Obviously at age nine and five, this was beyond their comprehension. It was beyond my sodding comprehension, so they didn't stand a chance. Once home I had us all sit on the floor in the living room, with my arms around them both, and told them it was all going to be fine, that very little was going to change. I assured them, in good faith, that they would still see as much of their daddy as ever, but he would just sleep somewhere else; he wasn't dead. I was trying to limit the spray of shrapnel, i.e.: Yes, it's bad, but it could be worse.

Alex was worried that Steve wasn't going to be his daddy anymore, so I took some extra time to explain simply that he was made up of half me and half Steve, and where Steve chose to sleep wouldn't – couldn't – change that fact. There were lots of tears and snot bubbles, as you can imagine. There was a lot of fear, confusion and uncertainty, but I remembered this one key point from when they were both starting to toddle, which may help you if you ever have to deal with a similar situation.

When babies start to toddle, they fall over a lot, we know this. At the beginning of their toddling career, babies often have two grownups waiting to catch them in an otherwise soft and safe environment. The chance of pain or damage is negligible to begin with. Once the child is a little more experienced, confident and toddling outside, the probability of bumps, scrapes and grazes increases exponentially, it's how they learn... fall down, get up, fall down again, get up again. That's life.

However, when toddlers fall, particularly when they fall down hard and hurt themselves, the first thing they do is look at Mum, or the grown up in charge. They're looking for a cue from you, about how serious this fall was. If you cluck around, laying an egg and fret like the sky is falling in, the child will become unnecessarily frightened and cry more. If, however, you can at least feign nonchalance, the child will grow up to be more resilient than coddled. Obviously if there is serious pain or injury, then that needs to be tended to appropriately, but you still need to remain as calm and comforting as possible, whatever happens.

This was the model I was mindful of when trying to explain to my children how their realities were about to change forever. I was mindful throughout that they'd be looking to me for cues about how serious this all was. That doesn't mean I didn't cry or release more snot into the wild. Quite the opposite. Whilst I knew I was going to have to be stronger than strong for these two bewildered wee ones, they had to know I was human, and that feelings of sadness, anger and grief were natural, normal and absolutely necessary. If I had become some ridiculous caricature of stoicism, they'd take their cues from that and bury their feelings too. No, their feelings had to be acknowledged, felt, expressed and respected, and so we sat on the floor, in each other's arms, crying and grieving for our past lives lost.

Unexpressed emotions are like torpedoes, which hurtle unseen beneath the surface, only to explode causing maximum damage at a later point in time. This was not going to happen to my babies. I let them ask me every question they could think of and, if it made me cry, I cried. I explained why I was hurt and upset, so they could understand my feelings more fully, should they ever see me crying at another point in time; which they obviously did.

I had to take the fear out of tears for them, and duly taught them how tears accompanied healthily expressed emotion out of our hearts, which is a good thing. Whilst having a bad thing happen, which warranted tears was horrible, not letting the emotion out of our hearts made it a hundred times worse. I gave them an analogy of unexpressed emotion being like a chunk of cheese, which would slowly go mouldy and then rot into slop altogether if it's not dealt with appropriately. I really didn't want to have to explain torpedoes and weapons of mass destruction to them.

I did my best to demystify everything, to give them as much information and clarity as I thought they could handle. Taking the time to explain everything in terms they'd understand was the secret to success here. Children are more perceptive and understanding than many parents give them credit for, and they appreciate being respected with the truth. They know when something is wrong, so shape the messaging to allow them to understand, without being unnecessarily hurt by finding out by mistake, or stealth. Palace intrigue frightens children, because their imaginations will often conjure up far worse than anything you have to offer, so gentle age appropriate honesty is best. You're in control of what they know, when and how they know it, so massage the truth for the palatability of your young audience. Hiding and running away is not an option.

I urged Sofia and Alex not to think of Steve as a bad man, but as a man who suffered with a sad mind (depression). We agreed that if his leg was broken, they couldn't expect him to run with it, so if his mind was sad then we couldn't expect him to think well with it. They were aware of how hard he had been working, how tired he was and how much he still loved and missed his own father. So, when I told them this had all given him a sad mind, they could see the logic in that, and they empathised with, as well as sympathised for him.

I specifically wanted to encourage their innate compassion to lead them, rather than anger and bitterness blind them. Anger and bitterness would have made my babies cold, hard, cynical and smaller people. I didn't want this for them, so I showed them how to lean towards the light, with love, hope and inclusiveness. I taught them that life is sometimes horribly unfair and hard to figure out, but that doesn't mean we quit. It means we rise to meet the challenge. It means we work harder to become better people, from learning the lessons these horrible experiences are teaching us. It means we conquer the bad things by being as good, and as great as we can be. We don't sink lower by pointing to horrible events as an excuse to fail or not even try. No, not ever, we're better than that. We maintain our dignity, we don't fade, we don't buckle, and we do not cry out loud. Right there on the carpet, in each other's arms with tear streaked cheeks, we chose to rise. Then we decided we would eventually soar.

I knew I also had to reassure them that they weren't going to lose me, so I played them my new anthem – Not Giving In, by Rudimental – and I played it loud. I then put one hand down on the carpet, until all of our hands were layered alternately on top of each other. We were now bound not only as family, but we had just created Team Mentals (Alex's suggestion), and this was our anthem. We were not giving in, we were going to work harder, we were going to be stronger, we were not giving in. If my babies were looking for my cue, this was it. Yes, we were in pain, but we were not giving in.

Sofia and Alex began to dance to the song on a loop, and I was deliberately letting them exorcise their energy and emotions, I didn't want anything bottled up. They were still dancing when Steve arrived after work. As we had pledged to tell them at the end of the week, he assumed they were just in a good mood following a great day at school. I remember standing in the kitchen, looking into the living room where Steve was sat watching them, smiling and laughing on the sofa, at their seemingly joyous exploits.

With the music still blaring and their feet still dancing, the kids were oblivious to me bursting Steve's bubble by mouthing "*They know, I've told them*". This took a second to compute in Steve's mind, but when it landed, he was confused initially and then flat out furious. He was riled because I had "*done a number on him*", but I really hadn't. He was angry because I had reneged on my pledge to tell them on Friday, when it was admittedly my suggestion to do so. I understood how he thought I'd set him up, and tried earnestly to explain why I hadn't, and how events had conspired on the school run. He wasn't having any of it. He decided there and then that I was out to destroy him in the children's eyes and didn't believe my protestations to the contrary. I tried repeatedly to explain exactly what I had told the children, and why, but his mind was made up, I was the Devil.

Steve stayed for dinner and until the children were in bed. He wasn't *that* offended then? In fact, he stayed until gone 9pm, which irritated me no end. The kids had long gone to bed, but here he still was with the wife he no longer wanted, WTF? In the end I couldn't help myself and asked if he intended to stay this late every night when he stayed for dinner, because he was eating into my private time. There were things I needed, or wanted to do, which he no longer wanted to be a part of, so his departure would very much be appreciated. Yes, I know this sounds a bit cold and harsh, and was possibly the time I could have begged him to stay (had I the mind to), but his physical presence made my skin crawl. He *had* to make it work with Helen or move in with his mum and, as the record shows, he chose the lesser of two evils.

Steve was visibly hurt by my attitude towards him, but what did he really expect? He had told me 48 hours previously that "*it was highly likely*" he was leaving me. In that time, I had taken him at his word, opened a single person's Tax Credit and Income Support claim, and told the children of his intentions. I was respecting his wishes. If he wasn't sure or serious about leaving me for Helen, he should have thought about his words and actions before acting on them. Perhaps he was hurt, again, because I still would not fight for him, and didn't seem to care he was wandering off? Who knows? If he wasn't expressing these things out loud, how was I supposed to know them?

I later discovered that by leaping into immediate action the day before and claiming Tax Credits (i.e.: whilst declaring the end of our marriage and moving Steve in with Helen to the Department of Work and Pensions), Helen's own Tax Credit benefits plummeted, now she had the advantage of Steve's income. Steve told me how my "rash actions" had caused them considerable financial hardship, possibly veering Helen towards the criminally fraudulent or a penalty of some kind, because she had not reported a significant change in her circumstances. How was this my fault exactly? Steve's argument was that I should have let things stand as they were for a while, rather than rushing in; but why if this was our new reality? I got a sense he wasn't as certain about his course as he would have had me believe, but that wasn't my problem. Feeding and providing for my children was my priority, especially when it felt as though Steve attempted disproportionate vengeance in the months and years to come.

Thursday 26 September 2013: Only One Safety Net

Sofia asked me to invite Steve to have dinner with us, which I did, and he accepted. I cooked lasagne, Sofia's favourite at the time. The stress from the loss of my Mum and husband within the first three weeks of Horrible September however had caused my cortisol levels to surge. This resulted in a drastically reduced appetite and now noticeable weight loss. I served myself a small portion of lasagne, not certain I could even keep that down, so nauseous was I, and Steve noticed. He asked if I wanted some more from his plate which, although well intentioned, caused another caustic belch in my stomach. I feigned nonchalance and lied about having had a large lunch; which I don't think he bought.

Once the kids were in bed, I asked Steve if he could move all his stuff out of the house in one go, rather than by piecemeal as he had been doing since Monday night. He didn't like this and commented again on how proactive I'd been re: the Tax Credits and telling the children. Exasperated, I asked him what his problem was. He had ended the marriage to be with Helen, I was simply responding to his wishes and giving him what he said he wanted. His reactions to my actions however were telling me something was off, but I wasn't going to wait, wringing my hands, hoping for him to change his mind. If he wanted out, he was free to leave, but my focus was on resettling the children into their new reality, and I didn't want him exacerbating their pain by moving out slowly or doubtfully. The children were still looking to me for cues, confidence and guidance, so Steve and I had to both behave decisively for their benefit, if not our own.

I was still sensing doubt and hesitation from Steve, like he wanted me to wait with a safety net in case he changed his mind about being with Helen. That was non-negotiable however, as the deed had been done and he was diseased to me now. The only safety net I had in my possession was fully deployed ensuring the kids' safe landing. I sure as hell didn't have the time, energy or inclination to create a second safety net for him. He was Helen's project now; I'd served my time.

On an entirely different subject, Steve and I had been talking about replacing the boiler for over a year by the time we split, but as ever, we had never got around to it. We had been experiencing intermittent pressure problems and the timer had completely died. Winter was promising brass monkey 4am wake calls, so I could put the heating on for the kids to get ready for school. Now the kids and I were about to start living off £77 per week, I certainly couldn't afford to heat the house all night, so the kids' beds were layered with blankets and I'd do the "brass monkey leg it".

On this day however, two days after opening my Tax Credit claim with DWP, there was a knock at the door. Long story short, as I was now in receipt of Income Support, we would be entitled to a government grant, which would afford us a free replacement boiler. This would subsequently result in reduced fuel bills too, due to greater heating efficiency: bonus! My luck was already starting to change for the better.

As it turned out, the company who knocked the door were not able to install a replacement boiler, I forget why. This experience however piqued my curiosity, and so I started to investigate whether alternative options were available, hopefully before winter arrived. This took several months to resolve, with the boiler issue further illuminating Steve's imposter traits. This part of the story will continue to unfold later in the book, so please bear with me, and we will return to this issue shortly.

Saturday 28 September 2013: Transference A-Go-Go

Whilst wading through a biblical pile of ironing *[aren't all piles of ironing biblical, or is that just me?]*, a voice in my right ear said: "Transference". This stopped me dead in my tracks. I put down the iron and stood motionless for a moment, processing the possibilities and ramifications. Abandoning the ironing, I quickly Googled the definitions of transference and countertransference for my own personal enlightenment, to try and understand how this may, or may not, apply to Helen's hypnotherapy treatment of Steve earlier in the year. I was thoroughly interested to read this one of many alternative articles available:

"In a therapy context, transference refers to redirection of a client's feelings from a significant person to a therapist. Transference is often manifested as an erotic attraction towards a therapist but can be seen in many other forms such as rage, hatred, mistrust, parentification, extreme dependence, or even placing the therapist in a god-like or guru status. When Freud initially encountered transference in his therapy with clients, he felt it was an obstacle to treatment success. But what he learned was that the analysis of the transference was actually the work that needed to be done. The focus in psychodynamic psychotherapy is, in large part, the therapist and client recognizing the transference relationship and exploring what the meaning of the relationship is. Because the transference between patient and therapist happens on an unconscious level, psychodynamic therapists who are largely concerned with a patient's unconscious material use the transference to reveal unresolved conflicts patients have with figures from their childhoods.

Countertransference is defined as redirection of a therapist's feelings toward a client, or more generally as a therapist's emotional entanglement with a client. A therapist's attunement to his/her own countertransference is nearly as critical as his/her understanding of the transference. Not only does this help the therapist regulate his/her own emotions in the therapeutic relationship, but it also gives the therapist valuable insight into what the client is attempting to elicit in him/her. For example, if a male therapist feels a very strong sexual attraction to a female patient, he must understand this as countertransference and look at how the client is attempting to elicit this reaction in him. Once it has been identified, the therapist can ask the client what her feelings are toward the therapist and examine the feelings the client has and how they relate to unconscious motivations, desires, or fears". [Source: ClinPsy, 3 February 2008]

Huh. I called the General Hypnotherapy Register, with whom Helen was reportedly registered, to discuss this matter in more detail, and to try and learn a bit more. They listened intently and took down some details, before advising me that as a breach of professional ethics and standards hadn't involved me personally, i.e.: I wasn't the hypnotherapy client whose therapist had started sleeping with them, I could not escalate this matter further. Okay then. I went back to the ironing, having learnt what I thought of the General Hypnotherapy Register.

Sunday 29 September 2013: Absent Dad

Steve's first Sunday as a weekend dad saw him collecting the kids at 10am, before collecting their bikes from his workshop and taking them to a country park for a cycle; when they'd actually asked to go swimming. Once again, Steve's needs and interests came before all others. You'd have thought he'd have taken the opportunity to undo the imagined damage I had supposedly done days before, when I *did a number on him*. Here was his opportunity to talk to them, to explain himself to them, to make amends and put right any wrongdoing he'd judged me guilty of earlier. But no. He squandered the opportunity to delight the kids by making them do something he enjoyed [*expletive, expletive, something about rectal re-engineering, expletive, expletive*].

After the park, Steve took the kids to see Mallie, where they went out for lunch together, before shopping in a local garden centre. Really scintillating stuff for young children, huh? When Steve dropped the kids off at home, Sofia became seriously upset about him leaving, and took a long time to be settled and soothed. Steve was visibly uncomfortable, perhaps even feeling guilty, about the level of Sofia's distress, but not enough to phone or text and check on her later. Out of sight out of mind.

In other news and following some quiet thinking alone time whilst Steve had the kids, I reviewed my recent past and forgave Lee on this day. Not that Lee was made aware of it, but I did let go of all the animosity I had stored and directed towards him. The veil had now completely dropped from in front of my eyes, and my Helen-blindness had been finally cured. Everything started to slot into place, and I could see what had happened with this new clarity and perspective I was enjoying.

Lee had never been my fight. Lee had never actually wronged me, or mine. I had willingly been recruited to help Helen fight her battles – against the falsely reported tyranny of Lee – because she had portrayed herself as too weak to fight them, against a much stronger opponent, and I hate injustice. Whatever she may – or may not – have lacked in battle prowess however, she made up for in manipulative guile. I had been played for the fool that I was, and I now had to accept personal responsibility for this massive error in judgement. My first act had to be releasing the negative thoughts towards Lee, because he was no longer my problem or enemy. I felt instantly lighter and freer. The manufactured acrimony was dead, long live peace and harmony!

I made this pact with myself: I would not contact Lee directly, or indirectly invite him to contact me, but should he ever choose to reach out to me of his own accord, I would respond favourably. Then, on 30 April 2014, Lee did exactly that. He knocked on my front door, walked to the end of my long drive, held his hands up in an act of peace and conciliation, and asked if we could talk. I said: *"Yes, of course, please come in"* and, before he'd even crossed the threshold, I stated: *"Lee, I'm sorry, I was wrong. Very wrong!"* He walked into my house, we hugged as we had as friends in the very beginning and got straight into setting the record straight between each other. Within moments it was clear how we had been played off against each other and never allowed to be friends. We had been fed a diet of pure bullshit about the other – to stoke the animosity and further scorch the earth between us presumably – but we vowed to start again with clean slates.

It wasn't long before I met Lee's new younger and more beautiful girlfriend (who Helen had hunted so remorselessly just six months beforehand), who truly understands, appreciates and loves him. They make a lovely couple, gallivanting hither and thither, enjoying Lee's passion for football, country pursuits, and enviable holidays. Lee has well and truly landed on his feet, and I couldn't be happier for him; it's been a long time coming.

So that's us allowed to be mates finally, and the air cleared between us, let's get back to the end of September 2013, about a week after Bomb Drop...

Horrible September was all wrapped up. In 30 short days, my life, and the lives of my children, had been blasted into shards. My Mum had died, Paul and I were on the road to recovery, Alex turned five years-old, Eve, Auntie Alison and Pam had been wonderful, Mum's funeral had been agonising, and then my husband left me for my "friend" and destroyed our family.

In the years to come I have vowed to reclaim September as a happy, joyous month.

Don't believe me, just watch!

Kintsukuroi

Somewhat hilariously – now I look back – I declared October my rest and recovery month. Month?! *A fookin' MONTH?!* Just the one batch of 31 days to recover from an intense and devoted 24-year relationship, with the man of my dreams then? You have got to admire my blind optimism if nothing else. Needless to say, 31 days is not a realistic time frame to get over the person you considered the love of your life, and who warranted being the father of your children. I'm not sure I will ever get over him, how can I?

To be perfectly honest, I'm not even sure I want to get over him. Steve's presence in my life lifted and enhanced it so completely. To love someone as intensely as I did is a gift, so why would I discard it now it is broken? The Japanese believe in something called Kintsukuroi. This means when they mend broken objects, they aggrandise the damage by filling the cracks with gold. They believe that when something's suffered damage, and has a history, it becomes more beautiful and valuable, not less. I love and have adopted this philosophy.

Until September 2013, Steve was the most pure and beautiful soul I'd ever known, and he has gifted me so many wonderful memories, and so much valuable life experience, not to mention the two most precious children I could ever hope to have been blessed with. How and why would I ever choose to get over that? I don't want to dump the memories of our happy times together; I want to fill them with gold and cherish them forever. Loving Steve was not wrong, or a mistake, it just ended horribly. Our pot (our life together) is broken, but we can still make it something beautiful if we try. It will look different to how it looked before, but it can still be something valuable to us, if we refuse to sink into negative thoughts, and choose instead to rise. I was not a bad person during my Helen-blindness, I was just temporarily lost. Steve is not a bad man during his Helen-blindness, he is just (temporarily) lost. There is still a place of love for him to dwell in, in the children's hearts. It can still be beautiful, if he chooses them at any time.

October 2013 didn't start so well. At 9.20am on Wednesday 2 October, Steve visited his GP and was prescribed another course of antidepressants. This was a positive step in the right direction for him, as he had foolishly taken himself off of the last course when he had started to feel better. It's worth noting this decision was against strong and established medical advice. There is a methodology to follow when ending a course of antidepressants, so *just stopping* can often harm your desired outcome of improved mental health. A careful protocol supervised by a medical professional must always be followed. By going back to his GP, Steve was at least recognising he needed some help. Now I just hoped he'd listen and heed the advice accordingly.

He visited me at home after the appointment and, over a civilised and emotional cup of tea, we talked about what was happening to us. The client he was working for at the time interrupted our discussion by phoning to ask where he was. They had been advised of his early morning doctor's appointment, but this was now so much later; where was he and when was he coming back? Visibly stressed and under pressure, he told me how he planned to take a couple of days off work, despite being only halfway through a job. Once again to my horror, this wasn't *my Steve*. The man I had loved, married and worked alongside for 24 years, would never have inconvenienced a client so grievously. Part of the reason why he was so burnt out and exhausted now, was because he had always put his client before himself, and his family, for *their* greatest good.

Only a little more than six months previously, Steve had taken his birthday (a Wednesday) off work, but because of an affiliated contractor's poor workmanship, a client's bathroom water pipe had leaked, causing significant water damage in the room below. Steve called the contractor to ask them, in no uncertain terms, to visit the property immediately and repair the fault and water damage, but the contractor "was busy" with a social engagement himself. Long story short and without missing a beat, Steve cancelled his birthday plans to repair the fault and the damage during the same day. The contractor never worked with us again.

So now here was the man I recognised physically as my ex-partner, shirking responsibility and gambling with his impeccable professional reputation. I was horrified, again, and not recognising who this was inhabiting my husband's skin. The Invasion Of The Body Snatchers was fiction, right? He had worked solidly and conscientiously for 20+ years building an enviable and award-winning reputation, to now be risking it all for a half-completed job? This was not how we did things. This was unacceptable.

I understood he was beyond exhausted, but a work break halfway through a job was not a sound business decision. Why not allocate (more) time between jobs? You cannot ask or expect a client to accommodate such low levels of professionalism, massive inconvenience and flux. By doing so, you will only cultivate a pissed off client, who then gets busy telling all of their friends and associates how pissed off they are. There was a simple rule of thumb Steve and I had always applied: a happy client will gush about you to five people, but an unhappy client will complain about you to fifteen. A reputation truly takes years to painstakingly build, but only seconds of mindlessness to destroy. I couldn't bear to watch. It was like witnessing him strangle the life out of our baby. I was heartbroken. Again.

Then it got worse, as he began telling me he wasn't sure he wanted the business anymore. WHAT?! I wanted to scream: *"But how can you walk away from everything we've built, after all of the years and all of the sacrifices we've made, after everything we've endured?"* – but how could I when he was doing exactly that with our marriage? If he could walk away from us, he was surely capable of walking away from the business too. What a waste. His life's work, thrown away just like that. No wife, no children, no home, no business. All disposable to him now. I felt broken, bewildered and extremely worried about him.

I was in a difficult position, because I really didn't know who I was dealing with here. I didn't recognise this man. To be perfectly honest, he didn't feel like a man before me now, he was behaving like a petulant and entitled little boy, i.e.: This is too hard for me now, I want fun with Helen, so I'm going to throw away everything difficult and not fun; so there! I urged him to go back to the GP and ask to be referred for counselling. He'd had a positive result from grief counselling, following the death of his father, so I knew he thought well of the experience, and this was a safe suggestion to make. I told him, as gently as I could, that I thought he was having a breakdown of some kind, to which he snapped back: *"Ya think? I've been having one for ages, you've only just noticed!"* It was a fair point, he was right. The searing heat of his truth pierced my broken heart, as the tears and regret flowed freely between us. Steve was clearly a man in considerable pain, looking for any port in a storm.

I was sorry. Now. But it was too little too late. He had spent months trying to get my attention, to get me to care about him as much as I had cared for Helen, but all I could see in my crosshairs was her. I was blinded. I didn't understand why or how, but I was. I had told him repeatedly – both implicitly and explicitly – that Helen was my priority. I hadn't cared for him enough, despite my marriage vows to forsake all others.

He had been gradually breaking down for ages, in front of a wife who seemingly didn't care, and now here he was being presented with an opportunity to chase something new, shiny and fun. He had to grab at happiness where he could, because who knew when another opportunity would present itself, and he felt I was drifting away. He felt I was lost to him, so he saved himself with the big soft-landing Helen represented. The risk of being alone – even inside our marriage – was his perceived alternative, which was unthinkable to him I guess, and so he jumped.

Whilst I was now painfully aware of how duplicitously Helen operated, there was no point telling Steve of this, how could I? He had been warning me against her for years, Lauren had been warning me against her for years and had I listened? No. I flatly refused to believe anything negative about her, so why would Steve believe me now? I had contaminated our family with Helen, and Steve was now infected with the same Helen-blindness I had just been inoculated against. I knew it was a fool's errand to try and make him see her for what I knew – too late – to be true. Steve would have to learn his lesson as I had done, the hard way.

All I could do now was wait, prepare the children and manage their expectations of their daddy. For the time being, Steve – *Real Steve* – was going to be Missing In Action, so we were going to have to adjust to our new reality and live without him as best we could. The Imposter had him now, hopefully so Real Steve could heal in the dark recesses of his mind and soul, to eventually emerge into the light again, once awakened from his Helen-blindness. As I had done. I understood this was a process he needed to grow through, and so I've left him to get on with it.

[163]

Finishing our tea together, Steve eventually set off for work (or so he told me) and agreed to still collect Sofia from school that afternoon, as planned. Clearly his client wasn't going to see much of him on this day before he took a couple of days off. This disgusted me. As per school policy, Steve met Sofia outside her classroom door and walked her down to the parking space Helen and I had favoured, all those days back when. Helen had parked there too and was duly waiting for Oliver. She and Steve had a brief discussion, before kissing each other a temporary goodbye, as Steve planned to take the kids back to Helen's for dinner later. This all played out in front of Sofia's widened and horrified eyes.

This was the first time Sofia had seen Steve and Helen together as a couple, and they thought it appropriate to kiss in front of her immediately, without giving her heartbroken, grief stricken, nine-year-old mind time to adjust. Sofia was understandably devastated. Steve brought her home to change out of her school uniform and into clothes that already needed a wash. Sofia then walked up the drive towards Steve's van, where he was busy strapping Alex into his car seat, but he bawled her out before she even got in. This did not bode well, but I kept my powder dry as he drove away with Sofia crying in the back seat of his crew cab style van. His guilty conscience was showing.

Upon their arrival at Helen's house, she had prepared a dinner of turkey burgers, potato wedges and salad, before pushing her hearts and minds agenda. She told Sofia how much she loved her, and how she and Alex were always welcome at their house. Throughout the course of the meal, Helen also thought it appropriate to tell Sofia to cheer up, before kissing Steve again, only this time in front of both of my children. Five-year-old Alex was now wide-eyed and devastated too.

Steve returned the children home at 7.05pm. Sofia was noticeably upset and on the verge of tears. Once Steve left, she told me how unhappy she was about the kissing, how she wanted it to stop in front her, and how seriously unimpressed she was about Steve's belongings having been installed into Helen's bedroom. It was obvious to Sofia that Steve and Helen were sleeping together, and it crushed her. In a few short sharp weeks, her daddy had gone from sleeping in the bedroom next to hers with me, to sleeping two miles away with Helen. This was hard for her child's mind to compute. All that she had known in her nine-year-old life had been ripped away, and daddy kept kissing some other woman who wasn't Mummy.

Appalled by Steve's lack of parental decency and restraint, I sent him the following text message, once the kids were in bed:

"Sofia's asked that you not kiss Helen in front of her. A bit insensitive of you both, don't you think, straight off the bat? Could you not have waited just a little while? What have you to prove and to whom?"

Unsurprisingly, Steve did not reply. This was a measure of who he was now. He'd become a smaller, lesser, meaner version of the giant he had once been. He was now willing and able to hurt and confuse his two young children, simply to make a point, but to whom? A new layer of grief for the gentle bear of a man I had once known, loved and respected, settled heavily onto the critical mass I was already carrying. It's true what they say, you really do become the average of the people you spend the most time with.

Heartbreakingly, when I mentioned to Sofia that I had text Steve about the kissing but had not received a reply, and how he was becoming less and less of the man I thought he was, Sofia responded: *"He's becoming less and less of the daddy I thought he was*". She then went on to ask me why, if she really was the most important person in her daddy's world (as he had repeatedly told her she was), why was he hurting her this way? She also wanted me to explain why, if Helen really did love her as much as she had said she did, was she taking her daddy away from her? This isn't what Sofia had been raised to believe love was. Sofia was clearly disillusioned and confused by these grownups in her world who weren't making sense.

In other news, following a slow and cautious rekindling of our relationship, Paul had completely stepped up and was attentively looking after me. He knew I was struggling to eat, so would send me frequent text reminders to try and take on some form of nourishment. He knew my mind was spinning out and focusing almost entirely on the children and my now dire finances, so he was doing some of my peripheral thinking for me. The thing was, I wasn't hungry and so didn't think to eat.

Obviously, this was unsustainable in the long term, so his gentle prods in the right direction served me well. I ate whatever I thought I could keep down, which was mostly breakfast cereal for their vitamins, iron and the calcium in the milk. He would remind me how much he loved me/us, how strong I was, how resilient and amazing the children were, and that this was all a process that would end one day. His last words to me during our final texts or chats before sleep were: "*Chin up!*" His love got me through, and I was so thankful to have him back. He felt – still feels – like home.

I chatted with Lauren almost every other night, to check in with her and let her know what the day's developments had been. Lauren's counsel is unfussy, grounded, insightful and wise. She was extraordinarily patient with me, letting me think as I talked through what had transpired, whilst grasping for some sense in it all (as I would remain oblivious to the possible Love Bombing machinations for a while yet).

Whilst chatting on this night, it became clear to me for the first time that Steve and I had grown apart, but I couldn't leave him, in part, because who would look after him? Perhaps Helen had done me a favour, like the buyer you sell your car with a dodgy clutch to? Perhaps I'd been released, not dumped? Perhaps Helen should have been more careful and specific about who and what she had coveted? Perhaps Helen had delivered herself directly into the path of the oncoming karma bus? Who can say for sure?

All of Steve's problems were the same as they had ever been, only now they had big, hairy new ones to keep them company. Despite 24 years of me earnestly trying to help him, there had been zero to marginal growth or progress. I had tried all manner of deliverables, often implementing the solutions and suggestions of others to create a breakthrough, but nothing ever worked (for long). After our decades together, it was clear to me I could not encourage or stimulate the necessary growth from Steve, for us to grow together. Ultimately our paths were diverging. When you put it like that, perhaps this was all for the best? Well, for me personally yes, but not for our children. Or was it? Watch closely to see how this all unfolds.

There is a heavy, self-pitying aspect to Steve's personality, instilled in him (I believe, as an untrained lay person), from the hypercritical, spiteful, hurtful words he endured as a child; which he was seemingly unable to let go of. As the cruel and unfounded taunts continued to inflict pain throughout his young, formative years, he had no way to reverse the damage as an adult without professional help. Therefore, I thought – hoped – Helen's hypnotherapy treatments would be able to dig his childhood issues out by their roots. It now appears I was mistaken because Steve's central issues remained unchanged, much to my dismay. With no other viable rescue mission available, Steve must now find a way out from under the pain he suffered as a child by himself. The children and I wish him every ounce of love and strength for his path fighting forwards, and we sincerely hope he prevails.

Bearing in mind I'm still writing about 2 October 2013. I ended the day by having a short vision, appearing to me in my mind's eye before I slept. I was shown a cross section of a seed in the ground. On the surface of the ground, directly above the buried seed, I was shown two paving slabs. I *just knew* [*claircognizance*] the seed represented me, whilst the two paving slabs represented Steve and Helen. This was something of an epiphany for me and made everything a lot easier for me to accept.

It was clear to me now that Steve and Helen had been thwarting my growth, denying me the light and sustenance I needed to develop into *my* full potential. By focusing on helping them, to the detriment of myself, I had not become more than I had started as. I was still a buried embryo of potential, stifled under the weight of others' needs and expectations. All I had to do now was trust in the process I was so clearly undertaking, particularly when things got worse before they got better. I have learnt these visions aren't given to me for shits and giggles, they're given to me for a reason, and they're always instructive and accurate.

Things needed to change, and the first place they needed to change was in my mind. As I settled down to sleep, I acknowledged that as much as I would miss Steve, and all that we had shared together over the years, this was all so completely necessary for me. Less than a fortnight after Bomb Drop, this was my first fleeting sense of being too relieved to grieve. I fell asleep wondering how long it would be before I considered Steve and Helen's combined betrayal the best thing to ever happen to me. Not long as it happens.

Within another few days or so I noticed an increase in my spiritual abilities, my clairaudient abilities in particular. As I've said, I have always been able to hear voices in my right ear but assumed for the first forty years of my life that I may have been (low on the spectrum) schizophrenic. Now with the sucking machinations of Helen gone from my life, it was like a dam had burst, and a flood of spiritual energy was rushing through me. It felt enlightening, it felt empowering and it obviously felt bloody marvellous. After almost three years of unrelenting anger, manipulation and (faux) high drama, I now felt lifted to a higher plane, light, free and above all, happy.

The same was largely true where Steve was concerned too. I hadn't realised before this point exactly how heavy he had become, how the majority of my pre-Helen-blindness waking thoughts had been about *him*, helping *him*, making *him* bigger, better, stronger, faster. This was liberating stuff. I still missed him terribly, and my heart ached for the intimacy we had shared and the good times we had created, but they had been long gone for a long time. I wondered if he was merely a force of habit I was missing, because I hadn't realised exactly how under a paving slab I had been living, until this point. The vision I'd had days before was powerfully accurate.

If Steve and Helen had to be sacrificed and purged from my life to gain all of this in return, it was totally worth it. Besides, if they were capable of such depraved acts of treachery, they were no loss, but this... oh, but this was worth having. With the counsel and support I was receiving, both into my right ear and out, I felt invincible. I wasn't invincible, just to be clear. I still had some hard lessons to learn, which would further grind the rough edges off of me, but I did feel I could vanquish whatever came at me.

The Wisdom of Sylvia and Fred

You may remember I told you about how Helen and I would frequent spiritual development and guided meditation classes together? Well, we did this via the most wonderful married couple, Sylvia and Fred, who I love as family. Their teachings and wisdom, bound together with hoots of laughter and twinkly gentle sarcasm, makes the time I spend with them my favourite part of any day. Their hearts are so pure, and their desire to heal so strong, that I felt stronger and contented just sitting in the warming light of their company. Their love and energy were given in abundance to nurture and nurse my emotional wounds. They listened to me recount how Helen had rejected the love and light teachings of our faith, to then stab me in the back.

You may be asking – with all this spiritual guidance floating around – why I was not alerted to Steve and Helen's treachery, before it inflicted critical damage upon my marriage, family and business. It's a fair question, and one I asked myself at the time too. The answer is beautifully straight forward. If I had known beforehand that Steve would eventually commit adultery, hurt the children and I, whilst decimating our family and business, I would naturally have tried to stop it. Who would allow that kind of pain and devastation, right?

So here comes the hard-to-understand part for most people: what if that devastation had to happen for my/our greatest and highest good? Hey, I didn't say anything about it being an easy, comfortable, joy; I said for our greatest and highest good.

And where exactly does it say on any of our birth certificates, we're entitled to waft through this life stress-free and unchallenged? How would we grow without tests? How would we become stronger without resistance?

It may help you to think of your devastation as a forest fire. When we're in the midst of a forest fire, all we can focus on is the heart-breaking loss, the heat and the immediate danger. But Mother Nature sends us forest fires anyway, and for good reason. You see, after a forest fire, the burnt and blackened landscape is covered in mineral and nutrient-rich ash, which then promotes new and stronger growth. In fact, some seeds – like those from the Giant Sequoia tree – actually need the fire to germinate, so whilst some organisms are destroyed by the fire, others are born of it.

This is why I wasn't alerted to Steve and Helen's treachery beforehand. If I'd been given advance warning, I'd probably have tried to obstruct their progress, which in turn would have obstructed my own. It is clear to me – now, in 20/20 hindsight – that I needed the fire, that I have been born of the fire, and I have risen from the flames like the proverbial phoenix. I wasn't told beforehand because I wasn't allowed to get in my own way or impede my own progress. Like most people, I would have run from or avoided the potential of pain; only masochists run towards suffering, right? But in truth, there are some things you can only learn when being brave and strong is the single choice you have.

As with everyone, my spiritual entourage is comprised of those who love me. Some I have known in this life, like my Mum, Dad, Nanna and Pop, and some passed before my time, like Grandma Annie and my further flung ancestors; but all of them love me. So, my perpetual challenge, when the life shifts hit the fan, is to lean into those shifts, look for the lessons and growth and trust

[171]

– yeah, TRUST – that I'm being taken of, and it's all for my greatest and highest good. Quite simply, there are things in life that I don't like doing, or wouldn't choose to experience, but they're good for me, nonetheless. Imagine parents encouraging children to eat their vegetables, attend school and revise for exams; it's the same principle, only scaled. So, let's now get back to Sylvia and Fred.

During a visit to see them socially, Sylvia led me to another defining moment of exquisite clarity. From the age of twelve, by one definition or another, I have "looked after" first Mum, then Steve and eventually Helen. I had not put my own needs before anyone else's in over thirty years – since I was a child! Now, in the space of Horrible September, I had first lost Mum, then Steve and finally Helen.

Sylvia asked me to consider the possibility that Spirit had become so exasperated with my inability to set adequate boundaries for myself (thus allowing others to take all they needed, to my detriment), that they stepped in to create a cataclysmic event, from which neither my marriage nor friendship could survive. Such a cataclysmic event would render me incapable of doing anything other than focusing on *my* wants and needs (plus those of my children, obviously); because there was simply no one else to look after.

If this theory was even a little true, this was now clearly my time to discover and advance my full potential, rather than facilitate Steve's and Helen's. This cataclysmic event, or events if you include Mum's passing, was ultimately an invitation to a new life. A fresh lease where I could live out *my* life's purpose, as opposed to merely serving as Operations Manager in Steve's or Helen's. I was now free to realise *my* dreams, rather than spending my finite life equity, facilitating theirs. Oh, how this was just the beginning of Act II in the Life of Karan.

I then theorised further. If Steve had had an affair with an unknown third-party, I'd have still been as devastated, but it would have been Helen to have counselled me through it. Likewise, if Helen had done something worthy of dissolving our friendship, it would have been Steve to support me through the process. The only way I could ever be free from both paving slabs, was for them to do something atrocious together, otherwise I'd still be left looking after one or the other. The only thing they could do to push me past the point of no return, was to commit adultery.

Who can say with any certainty this is what actually happened, or not? But the theorising gave me pause. Steve and Helen's behaviour were so out of character for both of them. Steve had been devoted, hardworking perfection for 24 years. Helen had said things like "... *I love you. Always will* ❤" repeatedly, whilst having experienced the pain of Lee's infidelity herself, so how could she be doing the same thing to me now? I no longer recognised either of them, from who they had been before. Something massive – cataclysmic – had certainly occurred. *Why* is still subject to much debate, however.

A Man Of Doubt

Steve continued to see the kids on Sundays, although now he was starting to slip by arriving late. With his overdrafts already maxed out [*that was quick!*], he had limited options when planning his time with the kids. As a result, he usually took them to local country parks [*free exercise*] and his mother's [a *free meal to offset the duty visit?*]. During a telephone conversation one weeknight, I overheard Alex ask Steve where he'd be taking them on Sunday.

[173]

There must have been some prevarication on Steve's part, because Alex offered quickly and anxiously that they could go to "...*the park, or Nanny's house, or to Helen's, where you live?*" So desperate was he to spend time with his daddy, he'd go anywhere to be with him, he just didn't want to be told "*not this week son*". It made me cry with rage.

Still only two weeks since Bomb Drop and the split, Steve was habitually taking the kids to McDonalds for dinner, something he knew I would oppose the frequency of. With his finances sinking fast, surely it would have been cheaper and more nutritious to cook something homemade at Helen's? Why wasn't he doing this? I never did find out, but he would text me to ask if I wanted him to bring me a McDonalds when he returned the kids home. I didn't, but I thanked him for asking. Although things were admittedly strained and strange between us – how could they not be? – we were certainly polite and civil to each other. It was a bit scratchy, but we were making it work.

One Sunday evening in October, following another visit to McDonalds, Steve brought the kids home with noisy and annoying Happy Meal toys. I made a joke about how quickly the toys would be "lost", which Steve found mildly amusing. I was happy and light in my interactions with him, happy to see the kids happy and chattering with him too. I asked Steve if he would like to stay and bath the kids, remembering how he had loved their splashy playtimes together. He said he hadn't eaten yet and politely declined my offer.

The kids, Alex particularly, asked him to stay and not to leave, repeatedly. This upset Steve visibly, and I believed him to be on the verge of tears, still standing there on the doorstep, not daring to come inside for fear of being overwhelmed, I guess. Both children gave him big hugs, told him they loved him, that he was the best daddy ever (Steve said: "thank you"), and made it clear they didn't want him to leave. Tentatively, for the sake of the children's wishes, I asked him if he wanted to stay for something to eat and he paused, looked sad and said: "*I can't*" before leaving two distraught little children behind for me to comfort and settle before bed. Again.

The Suffering Of Alex

Being only five years-old, Alex's levels of hurt and confusion were reaching epic proportions. His young mind had too much to comprehend. It became too great of an emotional puzzle to piece together, and so his bewilderment began to manifest in negative ways. Within a couple of weeks of Bomb Drop, Alex started to meltdown when asked to go upstairs to the bathroom, to have a wash or to brush his teeth. Even going to the toilet by himself became non-negotiable, as he believed Sofia and I would leave him if he stepped out of our immediate orbit. I loathed Steve for subjecting our baby boy to this extreme level of insecurity and separation anxiety. How dare he harm our baby in this way? How *could* he harm our baby in this way?

Now Alex had graduated to full-time during his Reception year at infant school, leaving him at the classroom door was traumatic for the both of us. As much as I tried to sell school as a massive, big boy's adventure, he had to be peeled screaming off of my legs by the kindly Teaching Assistant, every morning for months. He wasn't upset, he was distraught. My only option was to turn my back, walk away and not look back, all the while knowing Alex would be sure, in his distraught young mind, that I was never coming back.

My anger brewed thick with contempt for Steve, for creating this pain. I did attempt to apprise him of the extreme distress Alex was suffering, so he could perhaps snuggle and talk things through with Alex; to allay and soothe his fears of abandonment. Regrettably however all I got in response was: "*What do you want me to do, come back to you just for that?*" Hmm. There are no words to adequately convey how I felt about this response, so just multiply the thoughts you're currently thinking now by *fucking callous pig*, and you'll be about an eighth of the way there.

I Dreamed A Dream

As I've said before, now Helen had been finally flushed out of my life, my connection with Spirit became a torrent of positive energy and communication. Whilst it was my clairaudience which had been boosted primarily, I was also starting to receive more instructive dreams, akin to the "Get Happy" dream in August.

Steve's dad, Bill, had died twelve years earlier and whilst warm memories of him were common, dreams of him were not. In fact, I had never dreamed of Bill. Soon after the Bomb Drop however, I had my first dream starring Bill. In the dream, Steve and I were discussing the end of our marriage, and I suggested we sit everyone down together, to tell them what was happening. We then went into a dining room where the children, all of Steve's family, plus Helen, Oliver and Emily were seated around a large, long mahogany table. I then noticed Bill sitting in the corner of the room, looking furious [*which hardly ever happened in his 75 years of life*]. I seemed to be the only person in the room able to see him, as no one else even acknowledged him. I sat quietly and still as Steve explained what was about to happen with us, and Bill remained looking thunderous throughout. I woke up shortly after that, so there was no discernible end, just a very clear message. Predictably, Steve dismissed this as *just a dream*. Okay. As you wish.

[176]

Too Far

Sunday 13 October rolled around, and it was time for Steve to have the kids again. He picked them up ten minutes late, which is a big deal when you're an over-excited little boy, having put his shoes on in anticipation about half an hour beforehand. Steve then took them to the secure compound where we stored the caravan. The kids sat quietly completing a jigsaw, whilst Steve completed some non-essential caravan maintenance. He then took them to a kid's activity centre as per Sofia's request, and then eventually on to Helen's for dinner.

When the kids got home, it was clear they'd reached a tipping point of some kind, Sofia in particular. They'd had enough and told me all about it once Steve had left. We then had cuddles in the Big Bed, and I got them giggling with belly flubbers and wedgies, to distract their fractious minds before bed. I made them feel "super loved", safe and secure, before tucking them into bed with even more squeezie hugs and an irrational kissing frenzy each. They went to sleep quite certain I was crazy about them. Because I am.

Once downstairs, alone and seething, I composed the following draft email to Steve, which I believe you will find self-explanatory. I didn't send it to him for another two days, as it had to be filtered through the wisdom of Paul, Lauren, Carrie and Hayley, who left it untouched.

Dear Steve,

Please excuse my writing, but our last couple of verbal exchanges have descended into unpleasantness, which I am seeking to avoid a recurrence of. Having said that, I still have a number of comments I wish to communicate to you.

To begin with, I confirm my wholehearted belief that you and the children love and adore each other and need to spend as much time together as possible. However, I am asking you to think about, and accept, how your actions since Sunday 22 September have shaken their nine and five-year-old lives apart and left them in a state of flux. Everything they believed to be strong, dependable and safe has now either gone, or is questioned. Their once solid foundations have been shattered.

As you are already aware, I have attempted to explain your decisions and actions as positively as I can to the children, assuring them that you still love them as much as ever, they will see you as much as possible, that you're not dead and still very much part of their lives; you're just sleeping somewhere else. This however causes its own upset for them as they loved "cuddles in the big bed" with you, with us all together as a family, and so this becomes another example of something else they have to grieve for.

The decisions and actions you have undertaken in the three weeks since Sunday 22 September, have been taken quickly and dramatically. You said yourself (on Wednesday 25 September and Wednesday 2 October), that Helen is reeling from the speed in which events have unfolded. So, I ask you, if a grown woman, who has been involved in all levels of discussions and decisions prior to Sunday 22 September is reeling, how do you suppose a nine and five-year-old are managing to process the proverbial bomb you have dropped onto their lives?

I am asking you to slow down and to stop rushing and trying to force the kids into accepting your new reality, simply because it suits you, appeases your guilt and your separation anxieties. You left the family home and marital bed on Wednesday 25 September and moved directly into Helen's home and

[178]

former marital bed. Sofia was subjected to witnessing you and Helen kissing each other (twice) on Wednesday 2 October; the first occasion she had seen the two of you together as a couple since our separation, seven days prior. I sent you the following text on the evening of Wednesday 2 October:

"Sofia's asked that you not kiss Helen in front of her. A bit insensitive of you both don't you think, straight off the bat? Could you not have waited just a little while? What do you have to prove and to whom?"

Despite it upsetting Sofia, and despite this not unreasonable request, Sofia was once again a witness to the two of you kissing on Sunday 6 October. Also, on the same day, Sofia was subjected to Emily rushing downstairs upon your arrival at the ▉▉▉ home and greeting you excitedly as "Farshier". This crass insensitivity on Emily's part upset Sofia even further, and rather unnecessarily I feel. Emily has largely ignored Sofia and Alex since the new living arrangements have been implemented, leaving Sofia to feel rejected and confused. To have gone from being Emily's "sister" to an irritating inconsequence, has done irreparable harm to their relationship and hurt Sofia very deeply.

As has been the case since April, Oliver is only ever engrossed in Minecraft and merely tolerates Sofia and Alex at best. At worst and at school and the ▉▉▉ home, Oliver does little else but snarl "WHAT?!" at Sofia and Alex, leaving them both in no doubt he doesn't want to play or integrate with them. Sofia informed you of Oliver's increasingly rude and antisocial behaviour last night, and your only response was "It'll sort itself out". It is exactly that kind of attitude to Oliver's ▉▉▉▉▉▉▉▉ that has left him essentially addicted to a computer game (having spent the entire school summer holidays participating in precious little else), whilst continuing to

[179]

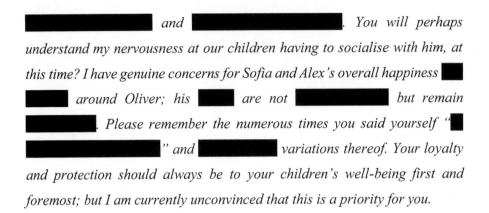

and ▮▮▮▮▮▮▮▮. *You will perhaps understand my nervousness at our children having to socialise with him, at this time? I have genuine concerns for Sofia and Alex's overall happiness* ▮ ▮ *around Oliver; his* ▮ *are not* ▮▮▮▮ *but remain* ▮▮▮▮*. Please remember the numerous times you said yourself "*▮ ▮▮▮▮▮*" and* ▮▮▮▮ *variations thereof. Your loyalty and protection should always be to your children's well-being first and foremost; but I am currently unconvinced that this is a priority for you.*

The fact you are now pushing for Sofia and Alex to stay overnight at the ▮▮▮ *home is too much too soon; please slow down. You stated last night that Sofia needs to spend more time with Helen. That is your opinion, this is not how Sofia feels, nor is it what she wants. You didn't ask her, you told her; imposing your will once again. Sofia has expressed her extreme upset and distaste at the prospect of seeing you and Helen sharing the same bed, which is understandable given that you and I were sharing a bed a mere 26 nights ago. Simply put, Sofia and Alex want to spend more time with YOU!*

Helen has attempted to explain to Sofia that she still loves her and that she is welcome at the ▮▮▮ *home at any time, however, Sofia is having difficulty reconciling Helen's proclamations of love with her actions, to paraphrase "...if Helen really loves me, why has she taken Daddy away from me?" Sofia is astutely aware that if you truly love someone, you do not do all you can to upset and disrupt their life, causing them untold pain in the process. Your attempts to explain your decisions and actions as "I don't want to be here [home] anymore" and "I love Mummy, but I love Helen more" just don't make sense to the children. You were eager on Wednesday 25 September to tell Sofia and Alex your perspective, believing at the time that I had "done a number on them", but here we are on Tuesday 15 October and you still have not explained your actions to them, so that they understand what you have done and why.*

If you had not lurched from their home and family straight into another home and family, the children's transition may have been smoother and easier for them to digest. For example, if you had explained that you no longer loved me, no longer wanted to live with or be married to me and then moved i.e.: into your Mum's or the caravan temporarily, the kids would have had a chance to process this upsetting news first. Unfortunately, however, you have thrown a grenade at their lives and are now expecting them to accept your new readymade family as well. It's too much for them, and far too soon; Sofia is feeling understandably resentful. All Sofia sees is you choosing to spend more time with – and being "Farshier" to – Helen and Lee's children, whilst they barely ever see you; just you. Do you think it would be a good idea to spend some quality alone time together, just the three of you, bonding and healing?

Since our separation, you have had time with the children on four occasions (as opposed to every morning and evening), and only on Sunday 29 September did your time together not involve a member of the ▬▬▬ family; and that was only because they were unavailable. If you continue to impose what you want on the children, before they have adjusted to the new reality, you run a serious risk of it impacting negatively on your relationship with them. Your perfect sheen has already been tarnished in Sofia's eyes, and I urge you not to damage yourself further, because it would be a travesty to squander the love and adoration, she currently still has for you.

I understand that you believe you are in love, and I also believe that the only fly in your ointment presently, is how much you are missing the children.

[181]

However, these are the consequences of your actions and you would be well advised to stop putting your wants and needs before what is best for the kids. Spend as much time with the children as you are able to but stop forcing "happy families" on them; it'll backfire. Give them time, patience, compassion and understanding and they will adjust, and you will enjoy the relationship you ultimately want with them, but it can't be forced, bought or imposed.

You are also aware that there are two sides to our situation, which has left you understandably confused. The simple truth of the matter is that Sofia talks to me and tells me what is upsetting her. I relay her thoughts and feelings to you (as per the kissing text of 2 October), but then when you invite Sofia to open up to you when you're alone, she offers you only "I'm fine" in reply. This exasperates me as much as it does you. I have been encouraging Sofia to tell you directly what she thinks, what she wants and how she feels, but she has so far been unwilling to do so.

I am aware that it suits you well to dismiss everything I say to you as being said out of spite, bitterness and anger etc; after all, it is far easier to betray someone if you're angry with them, isn't it? However, what is actually happening is that Sofia is desperate to spend as much time with you as possible but feels if she tells you what she really thinks, and how she really feels, you will be hurt and/or angry with her, which may result in spending even less time with you. Sofia is terrified – and I am not overstating the word terrified – of your anger, of you being cross with her, and will do or say almost anything to avoid it happening. The scars of Saturday 19 May 2012, (where you punched a hole in the lounge door and threw a glass at the wall in front of her, because she had got out of bed and came downstairs sixteen minutes into the Pink DVD) are still very much in the forefront of her mind.

In short, you frighten her, so when you inform her she needs to spend more time with Helen (or anything else that goes against her thoughts and feelings), she's unlikely to risk provoking your anger or disappointment. You have said yourself many times that she is a pure, beautiful and gentle soul, so please stop imposing what's best for you onto her.

If the children are now treated with kindness, compassion and consideration – and once sufficient time has passed to allow them to adjust at their own pace – there is a better chance you will get what you want without causing them further harm and distress. May I suggest you spend your time with the children (in the immediate future at least), away from the ███████ 's and the ███████ home, by taking them on days out either visiting family or partaking in activities they would deem fun, which would foster happy, positive memories of being with you? Sitting watching TV whilst you play on an iPhone, or being "overly encouraged" to cook with Helen isn't going to foster great memories with you, is it?

I understand your desire to spend more than seven daylight hours with the kids and wanting to tuck them into bed, kiss them goodnight, watch them sleep and have your own morning cuddles, so why not stay overnight at your Mum's, visit Teresa, take them away for a weekend in a Premier Inn, or a break in the caravan (some sites are open year-round)? There are solutions to the current situation, and not all of them require excessive amounts of money; just time, energy and a willingness to be with them and to do what's best for them. You want everyone to respect your right to be happy, so please return the courtesy where your children are concerned.

I hope this has cleared a few of the questions and issues between us and given you a fuller understanding of the situation at home, as no one can operate at their best whilst being kept in the dark. I am more than happy to discuss any areas which may provoke further questions from you, but I wish for those (and any other) discussions to be cordial and civil please, particularly in front of Sofia and Alex.

I hope you enjoy your evening.

Kind regards

Karan.

On the evening of Tuesday 15 October, almost immediately upon having received and digested this email, Steve addressed the contents with Sofia. Sofia duly stood by every word that I'd written, and confirmed how she and Alex wanted to spend more time with *him*, that Oliver was still hostile and bullying her at school etc. Steve responded to her courageous honesty by telling her he was going to have to start bringing them home an hour earlier on Sundays, as he couldn't afford to entertain or feed them. Sofia felt punished, as her fears suddenly became a reality, again. Furthermore, Sofia knew only too well that neither Emily or Oliver were going without food or entertainment, so why should she and Alex?

The problem with Steve's reasoning here is that he was unaware my ever-increasing circle of friends were seeing him, Helen and her kids out for meals, ten pin bowling and spending in excess of £180 in NEXT. Steve and Helen would also be seen regularly having a McDonalds breakfast, once the kids were safely installed at school. The cost of them eating their feelings was catching up on their waistlines, as well as their overdrafts. Is it any wonder I was dreaming about Bill being furious?

Towards the end of his telephone conversation with Sofia, he told her he wouldn't be speaking to her again for another two days, because he was "going out" the following evening. Sofia began to cry and vent her hurt with him, so he hung up on her. Calmly livid [*no, it's not easy*], I rang him straight back and demanded to know why he couldn't speak to the children, at least for a few minutes each, before he went out. I also explained how he was underestimating how much the children looked forward to seeing him every Sunday and talking to him every evening.

Finally, I made it clear that by hanging up on Sofia (who would always speak to Steve first) resulted in a further distraught Alex, sitting wide-eyed and tearful, asking why his daddy didn't want to speak to him. I forcefully suggested that he take his head out of his arse and think about the consequences of his actions where the children were concerned. They were young, confused, hurt and missing him terribly, whilst he was playing fast and loose with their feelings. He needed to grow the fuck up and assume some parental responsibility. This was all the love 'n' light I could scrape together.

Trying to keep the bridge between Steve and his children from disintegrating completely, I asked him what time he was going out, and he said he didn't know. I then told him, in no uncertain terms, that he should establish what time he was going out, advise me accordingly, and I would make the kids available to speak with him at his convenience. I also made it clear that for him to *not call* the kids the following evening, would signal the thin end of the wedge for their weakening relationship with him. How long before he reduced seeing them to once every fortnight, month, every other month, special events, never?

I was working furiously hard [*furious being the operative word*] at rescuing him from an unnecessarily doomed relationship with his children. I appeared to be caring more about this possibility than he was, but then I was the one who soothed them to sleep every night and had to deal with their disorientation and separation anxieties. I vowed to myself not to chase Steve's call the following evening. From now on he had to make and stand by his own decisions. He had gone too far.

Well he rang. True to my word I didn't prompt him to call. I told the children he had until 7.30pm to call, and then they would be going to bed. At 7.25pm he WhatsApp'd to ask if the kids were still up, late enough in the day to bet on me saying *no*. I text back to say they were, and he duly called. As per the norm he spoke with Sofia first, who proceeded to give him a hard time about the night before. She was further enraged when she found out he had been prepared to cancel this call, because they were visiting Mona's youngest son on his birthday. All Sofia heard was: "*I won't be speaking to you or Alex tomorrow, because I will be too busy celebrating Helen's friend's son's birthday, who takes precedence over you*". No, that's not what he said, but it is what she heard.

Sofia then went on to explain how she felt, something he and I (and her counsellor) had encouraged her to do. She outlined how everyone else seemed to be spending more time with him, and this was deeply upsetting for her. Steve responded with what can only be described as a word salad; a combination of "It's hard for us all" and "It's hard for you to understand". He had no real answers for her; lots of words but no sense. There was nothing he could say to defend or justify his position, and nothing which could make her feel super loved, safe and secure. For all his huffing and puffing about me *doing a number on him*, he had nothing, zero, nada to offer by way of an alternative. Duly noted.

[186]

The Trials Of Sofia

The first parent's evening since our separation arrived for Sofia. As parking at the school was likely to be more challenging than usual, I decided to leave early to try and get a good spot. Evidently, everyone else had the same idea, so I had to drive around the block again, to try and capture the free space I'd just driven past.

As I drove past the preferred spot Helen and I used to frequent, I noticed that it too was packed, but also that Helen and Steve had arrived early and were sat waiting. Wait, what? For the 24 years I'd known him, Steve had infuriated me by habitually arriving with no time to spare, or flat out late. He cited his refusal to sit waiting and never accommodated my feelings on the matter, even for special events like the kids' Christmas concerts and sports days etc. Now here he was at school ahead of time and plenty prepared... unbelievable!

I eventually got parked and walked up to collect Alex from his infant's school, who would be released ten minutes earlier than Sofia from her adjoining junior school. As I stood expectantly, waiting for my glorious boy to run into my open arms, Steve tapped me on the shoulder and came to stand next to me closely, as he used to do when we were together. Perhaps it was force of habit on his part, but I reflexively took a step to my right, away from him. I'd done it before I'd even thought about it, and it surprised and enlightened me. Sigmund Freud postulated how the id is the part of the psyche that is the source of instinctual impulses and demands, so basically what you do before you think, is the real you. And I had stepped away, created more distance. I wasn't comfortable being near him.

I looked at him in response to the shoulder tap, and he expressed relief that he'd only just made it. Why lie? I know I should have let it pass, but this was indicative of who he had become, and I hated it. He'd gone from an honourable, honest man his dad used to be proud of, to lying about what he could afford to Sofia, and now this.

My id kicked in, wanting to give him a shot across the bows, to let him in on the fact that I always knew more than I let on, and certainly more than he ever realised. Scornfully I replied: *"So you haven't been sitting talking to Helen in the car for the past half an hour then?"* Stunned, he took a beat – and I could almost hear the cogs in his mind whirring – before he came back with *"I meant I got here just in time"* (gesturing to the playground) a little too slowly to be convincing. It was weak sauce and I turned away in disgust, not recognising who the fuck this was standing near me.

Alex was released from school, saw Steve and ran straight into my arms. *Ooof, that had to hurt!* Consequences Sunshine, consequences. Once I was all hugged out, he hugged Steve and we walked to the junior school together. We waited in the Reception area for approximately 15 minutes, whilst the teachers prepared themselves in the hall, and we didn't speak. I couldn't think of a single, appropriate thing to say to him, in front of Alex or civilised people. Sofia joined us in Reception and barely spoke to Steve either, who was by now looking fascinated with other children's artwork on the walls.

Our allotted time with Sofia's maths and English teacher arrived, and evidently Sofia was doing rather well, academically. The teacher urged Sofia to have more self-belief, because she knew more than she thought she did. The teacher was happy with Sofia's strong work ethic, great results and high-quality homework; delivered on time, every time. Steve barely spoke during this consultation and asked no questions of Sofia or the teacher at all. On the face of it he was there to tick a box, to be seen but not heard. Minimal effort.

Untethered and floating.

Then we met with Sofia's form tutor, who taught all the other lessons. He advised us that Sofia was struggling with the disruptive elements, who were constantly talking, dancing, acting up and disturbing Sofia's concentration, whilst also distracting the class as a whole. Defensively, Steve asked who the teacher was talking about *[he speaks!]*, to which I responded: *"Who do you think?"* Obviously, the teacher could not name names, but assured me the matter was in hand and being dealt with. Sofia had told Steve repeatedly about Oliver's disruptive behaviour in class during numerous telephone conversations, so why this was news to him now? He was clearly agitated and uncomfortable with Sofia's assertions being confirmed by the form tutor, which elicited his defence of Oliver, as opposed to concern for his own daughter's progress.

The parent's consultation was over, and we walked out of the school gates together. I told the kids to kiss and cuddle their daddy because we were going this way, and he was going that way. They all hugged and kissed each other before we walked away. I watched the children closely and they never looked back. Neither did I, so I have no idea if Steve looked back after them, or not. If he did, it would have been painfully enlightening for him to learn where the children's focus was… ahead.

Steve phoned the kids at 6.45pm and began by asking Sofia what she would like for her birthday (in a month's time). Sofia stated that she would really love a long, flowing "Strictly Come Dancing" dress to dance in, and a huge whiteboard to play teachers with. She then tentatively asked him if she could ask him a question, stating she was afraid he was going to get angry and "rip her face off through the phone". Steve assured her she could ask him her question, which was: *"You said that you wanted to leave Mummy two years ago but didn't because of me. Why have you done it now?"* BOOM!

Steve then spent 45 minutes telling Sofia that he had a lot more courage now than he'd had two years ago, that he didn't like me, didn't love me, had more fun with Helen and that she was a nicer person than I am. He also confirmed that he didn't want to live with us anymore. Upset, Sofia insisted she wanted to spend more time with him, but not with Helen, Oliver and Emily because they were mean. Steve said he was sorry she felt that way and asked her what she wanted to do with their time together.

Sofia suggested he could take them to the caravan compound again if he wanted to, but he countered by explaining it was getting too cold for that and was only going to get colder as winter arrived. Sofia then suggested he could play with them at home on the Wii together (whilst I spent time in the office/garden), but he said: "I don't want to", somewhat petulantly. He then cut off further suggestions by informing Sofia that he was working as hard as he had ever done [*err... not strictly true*], and needed to relax at the weekends, rather than taking them here, there and everywhere. THEN WHY ASK HER WHAT SHE WANTED TO DO?

At this point it all became clear, as he introduced the possibility of shared custody as the way to go forwards. He proposed a one week with him and one week with me arrangement. Sofia expressed her rejection of this idea instantly, asking: *"Why would I want to live with the ████████'s, when they are mean to me?"* Steve told her that I was telling her things that weren't true, without offering clear examples of what he was referring to, or factoring in Sofia's first-hand, Mum-free experiences with Oliver at school, and Emily at the ████████ residence. He also maintained that Helen hadn't taken their daddy away from them, whilst she was now living with their daddy. How were the children supposed to make any sense of this?

These were difficult statements for the children to accept as truth. Meanwhile, and unbeknownst to Steve, I wasn't being in the least bit derogatory about him to them; I wasn't following Helen's example of denigrating the father of my children, to my children. Alternatively, I was urging Sofia and Alex to be as compassionate and understanding of Steve's sad mind as they possibly could be, although I now realise what a Herculean task I was asking them to take on. I simply didn't want them walking around with hate and anger in their hearts.

Sofia became so exasperated and confused with Steve's alternative facts and reality that she hung up on him, having been taught this was an acceptable behaviour by the man himself a day or two earlier. Such a wonderful parental example to set. He phoned back immediately, and I answered the phone. He asked to speak to Alex and so I passed the phone over, whilst also putting it onto speakerphone, so I could monitor what he was saying, and how.

He noticed this safeguarding and commented: *"Nice!"*, so I took the phone off speakerphone and went into another room to address his derision; before Alex had had a chance to talk to him. If this was the mindset he was in, he could bloody well snap out of it before upsetting Alex as well. I stated how this was the second consecutive night he had upset Sofia to the point of tears before bedtime, and to buck up so as not to upset Alex similarly, because it was unacceptable. I gave the phone back to a smiling and anticipatory Alex, who was told by his daddy: *"I love you and will talk to you tomorrow night"*, before hanging up. Now Alex was crying! He was confused, feeling punished for something he didn't understand and deprived of his daddy, *again*.

Both children had been sleeping with T-shirts of Steve's, which still smelt of him, as they'd been snaffled from a pile of washing before being laundered. Alex was even sleeping in some of the socks Steve had left behind, in his unseemly haste to get out of the family. These children were desperate for any and every connection they could make with their daddy.

The T-shirts and socks were prized possessions, taken everywhere to cuddle or wear whilst watching TV, completing homework, and to bed to help them sleep; just like Steve had done with the pink onesie, all those years ago. These were now treasured transition garments, because they still needed to feel close to him, despite everything. It was breaking my heart to watch their pain unfold and multiply as time raced on. This sentimentality for their daddy however was not reciprocated, as Steve continued to put his own needs and happiness above even theirs.

Because of the increasingly heated telephone exchanges, Sofia threw her daddy T-shirt out of her bed. To cool things down before bedtime, and to be sure I understood everything as thoroughly as possible from their perspective, I invited the children down to the living room floor and convened a special meeting of Team Mentals. I asked Sofia and Alex how they felt about living alternate weeks with Steve and Helen, in a shared custody arrangement. Neither of them had time to blink before stating unequivocally, and in unison: *"NO!"* Whilst Steve was clearly looking after his best interests, it was up to me to defend the children's best interests. Their unequivocal *NO!* gave me my operational command orders for the mission going forwards.

Where's Psycho Bitch?

Steve's behaviour in the three or so weeks since Mum's funeral, and subsequent Bomb Drop, was starting to severely test my patience. Whilst I was prepared to accept some responsibility for where he was, mentally and emotionally speaking, whatever I may have deserved, the children did not. I was starting to suspect Steve may have been hurting the children (unconsciously) to make my life more difficult and unpleasant. If true, that was appalling and remains his karma to carry. If not true, then I'm happy to be wrong, but you had better prove to me how you are right.

In my youth, partly as a hangover from my furious Noel years, and certainly in the earliest decade of our relationship, Steve had known me to be a fiery psycho bitch when roused to defend those I love. Whilst not exactly fiery or psycho bitch-like now that I am older and wiser, I had still been prepared to defend Helen, Oliver and Emily against the falsely reported tyranny of Lee. I had loved them as my own and so had defended them as my own. During this time though, Helen had seen flashes of intense anger directed at Lee and had peered into the volcano's abyss, to witness a heaving hell lake of fire; molten and seething. Now – rightly or wrongly – I was sensing a push from her to help me boil over and erupt, as per the play she'd called for Lee many times in the past: wind him up and watch him go, but always documenting for family, Police, legal or public consumption. It was not to be.

Here's my advice to you if you're similarly provoked. If people believe they know you well, well enough to think they know which buttons to push to elicit certain reactions, it is imperative you give them what they least expect. Give them the polar opposite of what you've given before; a 180° flip.

Here's an example: Steve, Helen and I once discussed the right age for Sofia to have a mobile phone. A minority of school parents were giving their children phones in Year 4 and 5 (ages 9 and 10), but I thought this was too young. As I was taking Sofia to and from school, she never walked anywhere alone, and was always protected by a responsible adult, why would she need a phone; especially when so few of her friends had one? Who exactly was she going to call? As was so often the case, Helen thought I was being too rigid and overprotective, but Steve agreed with me. Fine.

Now however, as discussions about Sofia's tenth birthday were ramping up, Steve blurted out during a phone call with her, that he was going to get her a mobile phone; she *needed* a phone. Why, when all the variables had remained the same? Ahh, but one key variable had changed, hadn't it? Steve was now sleeping with the enema.

When Sofia told me what he'd said I laughed, but I think I was supposed to be furious. Only a handful of weeks earlier, Steve had agreed with my thoughts on Sofia having a mobile phone for senior school and not before, and now here he was siding with Helen's position. [*Quelle surprise!*] This could easily have been perceived as a provocation, and a licence to rant or behave abysmally, but why give them what they want? Insulting in its simplicity, and entirely bereft of imagination, I do remember thinking: "*So that's how you want to play, is it?*"

I imagined how Helen, via a tug on Steve's puppet strings, was possibly trying to scorch the earth between Sofia and I, by forcing me to defend my no-mobile-phone-before-senior-school policy. If true, and if she was lucky, it would also cause further friction between Steve and I, further solidifying her base with him. Err, no. I just had to game it out. Who had the most to gain if X, and who had the most to lose if Y?

Another key failing on Steve and Helen's part was their chronic underestimation of Sofia's character and intelligence. Sofia was surprised

[194]

when I laughed at Steve's suggestion of getting a mobile phone and asked me to explain. The flaw in this not-so-cunning plan, was that Sofia was acutely aware of how penniless Steve had left us, so I couldn't afford the phone, a contract or top up fees. Sofia also understood my rationale of *"Who you gonna call?"*

We surmised how Steve perhaps wanted a direct line to her, to maybe circumvent me, but Sofia was disinterested in advancing that kind of agenda for him. I had no intention of rising to this bait, if indeed that's what it was, so Sofia and I agreed that if Steve bought her a phone (and was prepared to pay for the contract or top up fees), then more fool him. After all, buying a phone was no guarantee the thing would ever be switched on, was it? Nor were mobile phones allowed in school, so she'd spend most of her time without it. Predictably however, having failed to ignite a tyre fire over this issue, the issue went quietly away. I eventually arranged for Sofia to have a mobile phone and contract when she embarked upon senior school; exactly as I had planned and promised to do. You do not have to attend every argument you're invited to.

By this time, Helen and Emily were all over Facebook, telling the world how happy they *all* were, and how much fun they were *all* having. Having blocked Helen's access to my Facebook account, so in turn I couldn't see the content on hers, these posts soon became the highlight of my day, as new and mutual friends would forward screenshots with hilarious commentary. We marvelled at how they ever found the time to maintain their social media accounts; you know... with *all* the love and *all* the fun they were *all* having *all* the time. The mockery was savage, but it cheered me right up!

If this is something you have experienced, or are currently experiencing, please remember this one truism, no… three truisms: a) you're all grown-ups, so act like it and lead by example if you have to, b) if someone is truly happy, they will be too busy being happy, to have the time or the inclination to tell the world about how happy they are, and c) there's no law requiring you to have a social media account so feel free to unfriend, block or even deactivate. Stop and ask yourself: who are these posts for, *really*? Who are they trying to convince, you or themselves? And why is that? Oftentimes, social media posts like this are as tragic as they are childish. Rise above and remember this one other nugget of wisdom from George Bernard Shaw: *"Never wrestle with a pig, you both get dirty, but the pig likes it"*.

You must disengage and let that shit go. Would you ever chase a turd around the U-bend, trying to get it back? No. Why not? Because it left you for your own good. Had it stayed, it would have been a no less than toxic substance in your world, infecting everything with noxious nastiness. Some things are better flushed away than held onto. Leave those willing to live thigh high in shit to get on with it. You need to focus on getting sunshine on your face, and the sweet smell of freedom, success and freshness into your lungs. Now, where were we? Oh yes...

Once again, these transparent playground tactics were indicative of something far greater than their surface message; their guilt, insecurities and lack of critical thinking were showing. This was like feeding spinach to Popeye for me. I drew strength from every foot-stomping insistence they were happy, and duly grew in mental and emotional power as each new day dawned. Eventually my friends stopped screenshotting the posts to me, as they were getting tiresome and repetitive, but it was already too late. Helen and Emily had already empowered me. Any residual grief or disbelief concerning their actions had been pressure-washed away. Now I felt clean, clear sighted and invigorated. This would not bode well for Helen going forwards.

Now it was confirmed I was dealing with those swallowed by emotional decision making, it was clear what I must do; the opposite. Don't get me wrong, I was still struggling with my complicated feelings of "undeserved" grief for Mum, and the feelings of hurt from Steve's departure were often unbearable, but I resolved to make any and all decisions using critical logic alone. It wasn't easy, but with determined effort and practice, it became second nature. You have got to train your mind to be stronger than the emotions you're feeling, otherwise you will lose the battle every single morale-crushing time.

Of course, anger was one of those feelings I had to navigate carefully, so I started to visualise my anger as something more than just hot and undisciplined and was therefore able to use it differently. Want to know how? Okay. I am sure you can imagine what my hypothetical Psycho Bitch behaviour would look like: wild fury, thrashing about, lashing out, causing (criminal) damage and generally letting myself down. There would be red-hot anger, verbalised almost exclusively in expletives that'd make a sailor blush. This is not how I was raised to behave. As a Spiritualist I am aware of my ancestors watching over me, and they most certainly would not approve of such undignified shenanigans. My Entourage are tacticians, so I would have to raise my game and engage my brain.

First, please imagine my anger and Psycho Bitch behaviour as a huge thick branch of a tree: solid, heavy, too huge to manoeuvre with any degree of finesse or precision. The only result this type of unrefined anger would be able to generate is a blunt force trauma, which would exhaust me in the process of wielding it.

Now think about what happens if you take that huge and unrefined tree branch (anger) and whittle it down into a great many spears and arrows (critical thinking, planning and patience). Now you're agile enough to penetrate defence systems. Now you're able to inflict multiple wounds on your adversary's strategy. Now you're capable of surgical precision, which won't unduly exhaust your resources. Now you have more opportunities to engage in [*strictly metaphoric!*] mortal combat, which your opponent is less likely to see coming, or be able to defend against. Oh, the perfectly legal and moral possibilities are endless when you apply intellect, over blunt force brawn.

This is how I channelled my anger, not by huffing and puffing and telling them how I was going to blow their house down. Why would I telegraph such a thing and give them advance notice? If they knew what was coming and when, they could easily apply preventative measures, which in turn would neutralise the full effects of what I wanted to achieve. People incapable of being quiet and letting their results do the talking, are allowing their ego to run their lives, and you can't afford an ego! Ego needs the oxygen of attention to survive, so these people are more concerned about being seen doing things, rather than being effective doing things.

Yes, you may indeed feel some temporary relief by venting your spleen, but you also reduce your overall chances of success in doing so. Ask yourself: ***This is what I want now, but what do I want more?*** Once you have the answer to this question, steer all of your decisions towards the desired outcome. And I mean all of your decisions, not just the ones that suit you, or are soft and comfortable to effect. If you're not in it to win it, you'll lose.

I went quiet, very quiet, which may have been somewhat disquieting for Helen. I doubt she was actually hearing the cello riff from Jaws in her head, as I swam beneath the surface of her world, but she remained emphatically happy on Facebook, bless her. I believe she was desperate to gauge my thinking and to establish where I might surface next, so I denied her those insights. Helen's apparent desperation to read me only served more spinach to my inner Popeye, and I deprived her provocation of its oxygen by sheer self-mastery. Which wasn't easy.

Self-mastery is simply knowing that you can but deciding you won't. My self-mastery versus Helen and Steve's emotional thinking wasn't even sport, and it eventually led me to victory. You must control yourself before you can control the events around you. You must not allow yourself to become your own worst enemy, or to get in your own way with emotional outbursts or unresourceful thinking and behaviours. If you want to prevail you cannot be the same – as *them*, or who you have been in the past; you must be better!

My War Council came into their own during times like this. They kept my mind focused on the mission objective and filtered my options through several layers of wisdom and strategy. This allowed them to challenge my thinking, to stop me going off on tangents, and to rein in any emotional responses which may have seeped through undetected. It also allowed them to keep me on a path of love and light, with harm to none. As you can imagine, this was tricky for them at times, but they wanted a successful outcome as much as I did, so continued to guide me wisely. Can you now see why assembling your own War Council is nothing less than essential? For me, the body count would have been way too high without my War Council, and ain't nobody got time for that!

With my quick realisation that all decisions had to be made with surgical precision, I only spoke – politely and devoid of emotion – when there was something to say. I didn't offer more information than was necessary. I didn't expend any superfluous energy on fruitless pursuits, which didn't guarantee my desired outcome. This was now a battle of wits I was determined to win.

Because of my teenage experiences at home, combined with my past career responsibilities, I have developed strong strategical thinking skills, and the ability to game out scenarios when I go *into my head*. With Steve and Helen distracted by their emotional immersion into each other, I was at a clear advantage. I must now make this count. Surprise would be another of my signature moves, because both had assumed, they knew me so well. Perhaps they had, but I am not who I once was. They had only known Beta Karan, who was now obsolete and upgraded. Their actions had birthed Alpha Karan, and it wouldn't be long until they wished they hadn't.

So, with every decision being carefully calculated, I wouldn't be surprised if Steve and Helen had begun to wonder: *"Where's Psycho Bitch?"* Why hadn't I shredded the contents of Steve's wardrobe, slashed his tyres, or spray painted the sides of his van? Why wasn't I demonising Steve in the eyes of his children, family and clients, some of which Helen had done with Lee? Why couldn't they provoke the fiery arsehole they'd once been so sure of? Seriously, where was Psycho Bitch? They *needed* Psycho Bitch. Which is precisely why they couldn't have her. Well, not in the mode they were expecting her at least.

Sun Tzu teaches us, in The Art of War, that: *"Open warfare will trigger overpowering resistance. Thus, the key to victory is the ability to use surprise tactics"*. Psycho Bitch was alive and well, champing at the bit to prevail, I can assure you. My greatest challenge throughout all of this was continually having to restrain Psycho Bitch's wildest instincts, and then channelling her monumental energy into whatever was going to bring me triumph. Psycho Bitch's energy was increasingly harnessed through self-mastery, and she smiled wickedly when the games began. Steve and Helen would never see it coming.

The Move That Changed My Life

This was still technically within my October Rest Fest window. You know, the massively generous 31 days I'd given myself to rest and recover after losing my Mum and husband in the space of three short weeks. I did however still need to act. Whilst I had given myself October off from making any major decisions, there was one critical area I could not afford such a time-sensitive luxury; the house, our home.

You may remember me telling you how, as an apprentice Steve had bought a house, which his father helped to finance initially? Well, that house was now our home, and had been for 24 years. The mortgage was paid, although there was one small home improvement loan left outstanding, and Steve's bold vision had paid off handsomely. He was now 45 years old and essentially mortgage free. Steve had bought this house in 1988, before we met, and so naturally his was the sole name on the title deed. He had initially planned to flip it and create a property empire going forwards, but then we met, and he became embroiled in my combustible relationship with Mum. This in turn led us to living in the house when I could no longer live with Mum.

As time went on, we never got around to putting my name on the title deed, despite my salary paying the mortgage, as I supported the fledgling business for many years. I was never motivated to own this property. We were forever, so what was the point of spending out on legal fees to split the equity? Well, now was the point. Please don't make the same mistakes I made. This is exactly why I'm documenting my mistakes for you, so you can learn from them. Everything changes, nothing lasts forever, and please don't dare believe anything else. I hope your relationship proves me wrong, but you MUST safeguard yourself, and particularly any children, as a priority.

I know it's a bit bleak to think a relationship *could* end, but then it's a bit bleak to think you *could* crash your car, but you wouldn't drive without insurance, would you? Same difference only scaled: hope for the best, but plan for the worse. It's the only sensible, grown up thing to do. If you have these security measures in place and never use them, well that's fantastic and good for you. Far batter this scenario than ignoring my advice and ploughing through what I had to plough through. Please do read on through my cautionary tale.

On Friday 18 October 2013, and feeling insecure inhabiting Steve's property, I made an appointment to meet with a family law solicitor, Terri. The appointment was made for 30 October 2013, and I asked Lauren to come over and look after the kids, as the appointment was set within their autumn half term holiday. Obviously, she didn't blink before agreeing to help me, or to pounce on an opportunity to spoil the kids for an hour or so. This appointment with Terri was going to cost me £90 (a discounted introductory rate), which I couldn't really afford, but I couldn't really afford not to either. The children's safety, security and stability took precedence over everything else.

Terri confirmed my worst suspicions. As the house was in Steve's name only, he had the legal right to sell it from under us. Whether he would or not was now up for question. Had you asked me just 40 short days earlier on the likelihood of Steve selling the house from under the children and I, I would have scoffed derisively. Now however I didn't know who the hell he was and wouldn't put anything past him. I also had to factor into the equation the possibility of Helen's unquenchable thirst for money and *stuff*, which had contributed greatly towards Lee's eventual bankruptcy. She knew of the vast equity sum in our mortgage-free home – because I had been stupid enough to tell her [*facepalm*] – so I suspected Steve may now be enthusiastically *encouraged* to sell it.

As a side note: Dawn only ever refers to her as *Lady Helen*, because she seemed [*past tense, not so much now*] to need a degree of grandeur to supplement her self-esteem. Having contributed towards Lee's bankruptcy, by i.e.: insisting they own Land Rover Discovery TD5's when they really couldn't afford it, he had become worthless to her. Now however she had Steve, a successful, fit, handsome man with his own thriving business, a 6-berth caravan [*which I hated but she loved*], a Jeep Patriot to pull it and other assorted goodies and assets. She had "upgraded" the man in her life [*her opinion, not mine*] and now she potentially had our equity to plunder too. If you tilt your head and squint, you can almost imagine how Helen's ship had come in; *ker-ching!*

To safeguard the house, Terri advised me to complete an HR1: Notice of Matrimonial Interest. This would curtail Steve's ability to evict us, now the marriage had broken down and he was essentially our landlord. By completing the HR1, my interest in the property would be recorded on the title deeds. This means that had Steve walked into an estate agent with a view to selling, the agent would not have been able to sell until the HR1 was removed. It essentially rendered the children and I sitting tenants; or at least, that's the way I understood it. As I am not legally trained, I really must insist you seek current, professional and independent legal counsel of your own.

Way back in 2013 though, Terri advised me that to help reduce costs, I could fill in the HR1 myself, but I would need the title deed number to process it efficiently. I had no idea where the title deed documentation was, so I went online to the Land Registry website and paid £6 for a downloadable copy; easy. The Land Registry blurb also told me that any successful application of the HR1 to the title deed, would result in a copy of the revised title deed being sent to the registered owner; Steve. *Fine with me!* Steve had failed to adequately update the title deed, and so his registered address was his parent's former home in Middlesex. *Bummer.*

The only way Steve would find out about my HR1, is if he had tried to sell the house from under me... or, what actually happened... which I can't tell you about just yet, as you have to learn about it in context and sequence. Bear with me, it's worth the wait I promise. Let's just say, the £90 I spent on Terri's advice that day was the best money I have ever spent in my life. Terri is a remarkable solicitor; kind, patient, warm, compassionate and a thoroughly decent human being. I cannot thank her enough for her wisdom, professionalism and generosity.

The Tide Turns

Steve spoke with the kids later that evening and, as was customary, he spoke with Sofia first. He told her how busy he'd been before she told him what she and Alex had got up to that day. She did not however choose to disclose how Lauren had visited, or that I had gone out: "*It was none of his business*". Fair enough, couldn't argue with that.

When Steve spoke with Alex however, it all came tumbling out. Not that this was a problem for me. I have never asked the kids to tell/not tell Steve anything, but Steve was angry with Sofia's omission. Why? He asked to speak to Sofia again, once he'd finished speaking with Alex, and then promptly told her off. Poor little thing had waited excitedly all day to speak to her once darling daddy, only to be bawled out when she does. She must have been wondering what she had to do to catch a break with him.

The core of Steve's ire was essentially: *"You tell Mummy everything, don't you? There's no need for secrets Sofia, why didn't you tell me?"* Sofia clammed up, her little body crawled up into a ball and she said: *"Because"*. Steve then went on to ask her which of her friends she had told about the separation. Sofia said she had only told a carefully selected few, but Steve encouraged her to tell all her friends, because he thought it would help. Sofia then parried, saying she only told people she trusted what she wanted them to know [*zing!*], and that she talks to me about her feelings; tacitly implying she didn't trust him. Well why would she?

Sofia then proceeded to get a lot more upset, notably about the possibility of her upcoming birthday being ruined. It wasn't fair in Sofia's eyes, because Alex had had Steve and I together as a couple for his birthday, but now our family had been decimated in time for her birthday. To add insult to Sofia's injury, Steve had initially promised her that he would sleep over at our house for her birthday weekend. They had planned to camp out in the living room together, on air beds with sleeping bags, so that Steve would be there when Sofia woke up on her actual birthday (a Sunday).

As the post-Bomb Drop days ticked by however, Steve actively began back pedalling, adjusting Sofia's expectations on a downward trajectory. He had tried telling her he would arrive at our house "very early" in the morning of her birthday. Now on this day (the day when she had refused to tell him about my trip to the solicitors), he suggested she spent her birthday morning with Alex and I, before spending the afternoon and evening with him and Helen.

Sofia ruptured, emotionally brutalised and trying desperately to prevent another open wound of disenchantment. She told Steve she wanted to spend her birthday with her Mummy, daddy and brother, the three people she loves the most. Now Steve was saying this was never going to happen because: "*Mummy's being mean about Helen*". Yep, this once devoted father, who had slept with a pink onesie under his pillow, was now denying his baby girl a simple birthday wish, because I was "being mean about Helen". Hmm, let's unpack this shall we?

First and foremost, Helen destroyed her own reputation in the instant she chose to sleep with my husband. There had been no gun held to her head, she knew we were married, she knew we had children, and she knew I loved him deeply. However dissatisfied I/he/we may have been, these issues were ours to resolve, and certainly not a licence for Helen to come between us; so it was a deliberate choice. Steve didn't trip and fall into her or anything. These were two mature adults, making calculated decisions, about committing premeditated adultery, either now or in the spring of 2014.

Secondly, all I had done was tell my friends about her conspired infidelity with my husband, whilst seeking their comfort and wisdom, in the throes of my world collapsing. I can see how Helen might not have enjoyed being subjected to the same intense scrutiny and judgement she had allegedly levelled against Lee's Other Woman, but oh… how indigestibly rich of Helen to play the wretched victim now. *Purleeeease.*

Now Helen was no better than her own opinion of Lee's Other Woman; she knew it, she felt it and she hated it. For her part, the Other Woman duly threw her head back and laughed; thigh-slapping and hearty. Helen had failed her own purity test. Her holier than thou Crown of the Cheated Upon was now down around her knees, and it truly was a magnificent display of self-sabotage. And this is why Steve was denying Sofia her birthday wish. *"Sometimes people don't want to hear the truth because they don't want their illusions destroyed"* – Friedrich Nietzsche

Eve Rides To The Rescue

Eve and I hadn't spoken since the night of Mum's funeral, not because anything was wrong, just because we had lives to attend to. Obviously, I had been swamped with all things Steve and children related and hadn't really thought about going through it all again with Eve. Then, in the middle of October, Eve text me from out of the blue to see how I was.

I returned her text promptly, briefly explaining how and why Steve and I were separating, and that I'd be fine once I'd had time to process my new reality. I was tacitly and politely suggesting she give me the time and space to process, but before my thumb had left the Send button, my phone started to ring. I could almost hear her *"Oh hell no!"* from 150 miles away. Evidently, I had evoked the pissed off and protective instincts of my barely older family elder, who insisted on all the details. Once I'd finished telling her about Steve's sordid little affair, Eve told me what had happened to a couple she cares deeply about, which went a little something like this…

Jayne and Mark had been married for approximately 25 years. They had two healthy, bright and beautiful, grown up children, who were progressing well through university. They owned a retail business together, a holiday property in the mountains, and were to all intents and purposes living an idyllic life together as soul mates. When Mark got into his mid-forties however, he embarked upon a three-month affair with Carol, a sales representative from a supplier of theirs. The affair burned hot with intensity, and Mark became completely infatuated. This caused him to move out of the family home and initially back in with his parents, with a view to eventually moving in with Carol. Naturally, Jayne and the kids were devastated.

Mark's family were beside themselves with concern about his unusual, erratic and self-sabotaging behaviour. What they saw in him now bore absolutely no resemblance to who he had been before. Jayne had actually uttered the words I had thought myself: *"It's like he's been invaded by The Body Snatchers"*. Obviously, Eve had my rapt attention as she went on to tell me how one of Mark's nephews is a criminal psychologist, who advised Jayne how Mark's behaviour bore all the hallmarks of a midlife crisis. Jayne baulked at the midlife crisis term as an excuse for bad behaviour, but her nephew-in-law confirmed earnestly it was a clinically recognised condition.

Eve told me to Google and read about the six stages of midlife crisis. Prior to this I was in complete agreement with Jayne; a midlife crisis was merely the excuse of weak men to behave badly. However, reading about the six stages of midlife crisis was like reading Steve's autobiography; I was stunned. It's also worth noting that women are equally as likely to experience a midlife crisis as men, so the advice here is applicable to all. Midlife Crisis (MLC) favours no race, gender or sexual orientation.

As for Jayne and Mark, things resolved in an unexpected way. Mark had become truly obnoxious to Jayne, screaming an inch from her face about how he didn't love her, didn't like her, wanted to be with Carol, and that she should find someone new. For her part, Jayne attempted to follow the six stages guidance, but after a couple of harrowing months of continuous abuse and apparent hatred, she was almost on the brink of giving up on Mark. There is only so much any of us can take... or *should* take.

At the beginning of one particular week, Jayne was fraught at the prospect of having to work closely with Mark on the Wednesday, due of staffing shortages. The thought filled her with dread; how could they possibly work together with his rampant and poisonous levels of hostility towards her? How could she respect and be outwardly civil to a man who had recently stood up in their beautiful family home, with their two healthy and accomplished children, with a property in the mountains, a roomful of devoted friends to count on, plus a thriving family business and declare with complete conviction: "*I have nothing!*" This man clearly had everything but couldn't see it. How can you reason with this illogical logic? Answer: *don't!*

On the Monday morning, Mark had once again screamed abuse into Jayne's face and, with the imminence of them having to work together in 48 hours' time, Jayne spent some time alone to ponder the mechanics of giving up. Events conspired however, which brought to Jayne's attention the not-so-insignificant matter of Carol having been recently fired from her job. Deploying her womanly ninja skills, Jayne was able to ascertain that Carol had been fired for theft. *Shit!*

Jayne had been following the six stages guidance and had not made any sudden movements which could possibly have spooked Mark. This meant,

[209]

amongst other things, she hadn't insisted on separate bank accounts. Jayne was still fighting for her marriage, so their joint account was still existing and operating as it always had. This was the account from which all their bills and the mortgage payments were being paid. This was also the account Mark still had a debit card and authority for, and now he was fraternising with a thief. Jayne was concerned about Carol's potential access to the debit card, and therefore the funds in the account.

Jayne had no choice but to safeguard her finances and secure their joint assets as best she could. She asked Mark if they could take some time to speak civilly to each other, as she had an urgent issue, she wanted to discuss with him. Mark complied reluctantly. During that discussion, Jayne told Mark how Carol had lost her job due to theft, and that she wanted to apply for new debit cards, as she was concerned about Carol's access to their shared funds. Plural. She wanted to apply for new debit cards for herself and Mark equally. She didn't want to lock him out of their shared account, but she did insist Carol should never have access to his wallet and bank statements etc. Surprisingly, Mark took this onboard and consented to Jayne's suggested course of preventative action. This all happened on the Tuesday.

Wednesday arrived, and Jayne woke with a heavy heart and an impending sense of doom. She had every reason to believe this day had nothing but carnage to offer. Needs must, so she got up and went into work, steeling herself for god awful with a side order of arse gravy. But then *her* Mark arrived at work. No, I mean *her Mark* arrived at work; the kind, loyal, loving, caring soul mate she had married; not the arsehole Imposter he'd been parading around as for the past couple of months. Mark broke down in front of Jayne, telling her he couldn't believe the things he had said and done, that he was desperately sorry and begged her to forgive him.

Jayne was dumbstruck and not entirely sure what to believe or think. Her instincts told her this was indeed the man she loved and married; she certainly recognised his energy again, and she tentatively felt joyous, albeit confused. Mark told her he had felt under some kind of influence, which he found difficult to explain. He likened the past couple of months to being trapped in a self-inflicted bubble on a fast-flowing river. On one riverbank was Jayne, their children and their lives together, whilst on the other riverbank was Carol and all the shiny, new fun she had represented. The problem was, inside his bubble on a fast-flowing river, Mark was completely unable to steer, stop or even slow down his transit along the river. He knew he was doomed if he stayed this course, but he felt powerless to stop it.

By all accounts it was Jayne's calm and collected request to apply for new debit cards, along with the verified news of Carol's thievery, which somehow dropped the veil from in front of Mark's blinkered, *Carol-blind* eyes. Mark said he felt like he had woken up from a bad dream, asking himself: *"Where am I? Who am I? What have I done?"* By Thursday Mark was back at home hanging out laundry on the washing line, as Jayne's head continued to spin. Not once had she let loose her inner Psycho Bitch. Not once had Jayne allowed herself to be less than her best self, and she had won back what she had been fighting for.

This is not the happy-ever-after ending to Jayne and Mark's story, it was only the beginning of their new beginning. Equally committed to putting their family back together again, they embarked upon innumerable and arduous hours of talking about what happened and learning why it had happened. There is no point me going into these details with you now because they are exclusive to Jayne and Mark's relationship. If you are going through a similar set of circumstances and get to the same point Jayne and Mark are at here, then your discussions are going to be as exclusively relevant to you, however similar some key points may be.

Whilst I remained convinced my marriage to Steve was irretrievably damaged because of the adultery, Jayne and Mark's story did teach me about how Steve may be suffering within the confines of his heart and mind. Mark's description of being in a self-inflicted bubble on a fast-flowing river, unable to stop, steer or slowdown was precisely how I had felt during my Helen-blindness. It seemed to me that Steve may now be suffering the same fate. Whilst I was undeniably hurt by him, from someplace deep inside me – which I hadn't previously been aware of – I felt sorry for him and his suffering. I had recognised so much of Steve (and myself) in the six stages of midlife crisis, that when I took a highlighter to everything I'd seen in him so far, the pages turned almost entirely yellow.

From this moment on I resolved to treat Steve as gently and as compassionately as I could. That didn't mean I was going to allow him to ride roughshod over my children's hearts and minds, but neither was I going to unleash my darkest potential on him. I knew he had been battling depression since 2001. I encouraged the children to think of him not as a bad man, but as a good man with a sad mind. Now, if his depression had truly taken hold to this new extreme, and Steve was trying to save himself (justifiably in some cases), then unleashing my dark potential wouldn't be fair. It would be an abuse of power and may result in consequences I still can't even bear to think about. If Steve needed to leave me, to find any respite or happiness he thought Helen could offer him, then I had to let him go and try. He needn't however be hurting my babies. That was a red line he had better not try to even cross.

Eve encouraged me to be his friend, his calm in Helen's inevitable shitstorm, and to be the adult clear thinker in the relationship. She urged me not to take anything personally because Steve didn't hate me, he hated himself and his life, and had merely tried to instigate a change, however cack-handed. Whilst undeniably hurt, I was already starting to enjoy my new-found freedom; my wings were starting to spread for the first time in my adult life. Without Steve's permanently exhausted, depressed energy all around me all the time, I felt lighter, freer... tentatively great! These were still dark and heavy days of misery for the children and I, but I was certainly getting glimpses into what my life could eventually be. This was not the end; it was just the beginning.

He Strangled The Business

Steve and I started the business in 1992. It was started without even a bank loan and operated from the boot of my hatchback Chevette [*remember them?*]. It wasn't long before Steve built a trailer to hitch to a tow bar, and to carry his ever-expanding tool kit. The trailer came complete with a domed lid and was finished in a mahogany stain. He honestly looked like he was towing a coffin, but we were young and allowed to make do in this way. Mischievously, I was tempted to have a brass plaque engraved with the company name screwed to the lid as a joke, but we really couldn't afford it. Every penny we had went either towards the business or the house, which was essentially a building site at this point.

Kept financially buoyant and fed by my accelerated career progression, we devoted everything to the business. We operated a policy of extreme customer service and continuous improvement; always looking for ways to become bigger, better, stronger, and awesome. Our mission statement laid out our plan to become the benchmark by which our competitors were judged. Although young, we were desperately serious about the business' name and reputation.

The business grew slowly at first but began to pick up in pace as Steve's name became synonymous with perfection and professionalism. In the early years, particularly before 2009 when we went online with the website, it was only word-of-mouth recommendations that kept us busy. We had dabbled with advertising in the Yellow Pages with little success, which is why you young 'uns are now asking: "*Yellow Who?*". Our customers became our sales force, so much so that we thought it only fair to operate a commission policy for all recommendations which led to a deposit payment. This in turn led to even more recommendations, and so the pattern repeated profitably for all involved.

Towards the end of 1999 and staring down the barrel of a lot of orders on the books and Steve's imminent knee surgery, we decided I would work with him, following my redundancy from a motor racing company. Within six months we were able to employ a full-time apprentice, so I could go back to fulfilling what I thought was my destiny. Turns out it wasn't my destiny, but the job I took afforded me a great salary and enviable experiences I could not have gotten anywhere else. The business and my career were booming along parallel lines.

This job was based in Buckinghamshire, well over an hour away from home and quickly became a nightmare, largely because of the insane and unsociable hours I was frequently required to work. Thankfully I was made redundant as the company went into administration after thirteen exhausting months, so that was clearly meant to be. It was now 2001, and the business needed my undivided attention daily. The business continued to grow, hitting every target I set. We took an initial hit like everyone else during the 2008 recession, but we found a great many of our customers were investing in, and adding value to their properties, because the interest rates for their savings and investments were so appallingly low. This meant our commitment to excellence was now actively bailing us out of the national economic downturn.

We were soon able to take on larger premises, which had the potential to house the showroom Steve had longed for since the beginning of time. Publishing the website in 2009, to counter the recession effects, boosted our revenue like a match to methane. Now we were exceeding our goals, even the goals once deemed too whimsical to take seriously. We were booming, but Steve was flagging. With two young children and a voracious energy consuming business, Steve hit The Wall and arguably sought refuge in a midlife crisis. I can see – all too late – exactly how he got there, and I am sorry for him. I am sorry for us.

Once the affair with Helen had been revealed and the separation formalised, Steve seemed to embark upon a mission to destroy the business. It's important for me to note here that I am only able to comment as a spectator from the side lines at this point, because I was evicted from the business at the same time as I was evicted from our marriage. All that I say now is from what I have been able to glean, not what I categorically know. I was shut out and banished. I was thrown overboard and discarded; surplus to requirements.

If I tilt my head and squint, I can see why Steve would maybe want to punish and drain the business, because it had punished and drained him. It had taken all that he had to give, but had always wanted more, and could never be satisfied. The business had become a monster, and from his (unconscious) perspective, he may well have felt like he was in a kill-or-be-killed death roll with it. He had given the business everything, and it had given him burnout. This I can see from his perspective, but what I had gone blue in the face telling him for years was, it never had to be this way. If only he had implemented just a few of the work smarter systems and processes I had researched, learned and suggested, his workload could have easily been halved.

I accept unconditionally how our inability to find even remotely competent craftsmen to work alongside us was a major strain, but there was still much Steve could have done to help himself. He lacked the focus and discipline to get things done, in a healthily organised manner. He didn't have whatever it takes to do whatever it takes, to create the reality he wanted. Don't get me wrong, Steve could work fiendishly hard like a machine, but if the energy expenditure is not focused in the right direction, it's a waste of time and energy. Imagine digging out the Channel tunnel. You could start hammering away at the rock in Dover like your life depended on it, but if you're pointed towards Denmark, you're never going to reach France, no matter how hard you hammer. It's true what they say; an inch is better than a mile in the right direction.

This is why, when they dug out the Channel tunnel, they were guided by a Tunnel Boring Machine (TBM), which was responsible for tracking and positioning in the 3D underground working space. Construction engineers were hammering away in the dark but used systems and processes to ensure they never strayed off-course. This was the hypothetical model I tried relentlessly to get Steve to adopt, but he was headed for burnout, due mainly to his exhausted, fight-or-flight, panic-riddled brain fog.

We are all likely to make easy and expedient decisions when we're bone tired and stressed, simply because we're too exhausted to consider, evaluate and imagine more suitable alternatives. We're all more easily attracted to quick fixes when we're knackered. How many of us have bought a takeout because we've been too tired to cook after one hell of a day? It's the same principle only scaled. This is why we must frequently and meaningfully rest, pace and recharge ourselves. Anything important should only ever be completed whilst rejuvenated. Fraught and exhausted is no condition to be making decisions, ever.

Steve was convinced that if he just worked harder, then harder still, then harder than that, he would eventually make it. The problem was, The Law of Diminishing Returns disagreed with him, and I couldn't help Steve understand he was on a hamster wheel. It didn't matter how fast he ran or how hard he worked, he was going nowhere until he changed something he did daily; most notably his thinking and processes. He needed to change his thinking to change his reality, and this represents my greatest failure, that I was unable to convince him of this. After 24 years of giving him everything I had, plus backwards and in heels, I was ultimately unable to save him from himself. I could not shift the damage inflicted upon him as a boy, which still torpedoed his thinking and self-esteem to the day we separated.

Now in the full flush of infatuation with Helen, the business was the last of Steve's concerns. Why would he want to go to work, when he could be having fun with her? You should know that Helen personified the *"life's too short"* philosophy during my years in close proximity to her. I may be seriously wrong here – because I can't possibly know for sure – but I believe Helen is likely to have further tempted Steve away from his responsibilities, by whispering seductively how he didn't need to work so hard, that life is for living and enjoying the finer things in life. She's not wrong, and this is a perfectly good philosophy if – IF – there's a plan for financing such comfort, fun and hedonism. But there certainly didn't appear to be because everything was becoming more problematic in Steve's world.

Whilst evicted from the business, but still connected to its email account (as webmaster), and receiving the daily banking updates, all I could do was observe impotently from the side lines as various organisations started making demands for outstanding monies. It became quickly apparent that Steve was strangling the lifeforce out of the business, by neglecting my key responsibilities.

Getting rid of me was one thing, but the work still had to be done; suppliers and contractors still had to be paid, RTI PAYE still had to be processed and paid, VAT recorded, calculated and paid, quotes compiled, and customers and suppliers liaised with. I had assumed that as Helen is AAT qualified, she would have at least picked up the financial and bookkeeping reins of the business, and ensured all vital functions were completed. Less than one month from my expulsion however it was clear my assumptions had been wrong. Very wrong.

It appeared to me – from my remote and isolated position far outside the bounds of the business now – that Helen may have been enjoying the income from the business, without contributing anything towards it. This cash cow was going to starve on their current spending trajectory, and so I started to grieve for our business. More unnecessary waste, more fury.

To sum up, by March 2014 the website I'd strived to create, and the business landline we'd had for over 20 years, were gone. By May 2014, the showroom had been ripped out and Steve was actively and aggressively downsizing. He'd become a jobbing tradesman, working for former competitors he'd disparaged in the past. It appears our enterprise together was too much for him, I was too much for him, and so he accepted lesser, smaller, safer and comfortable – which of course is his right to do. Let me state for the record though, that I only ever expended so much time, energy, passion and vision on what he told me his dreams were. He sold me his dream, which had become my dream, and we worked to create it together and make it happen. To a degree, Steve got what he wished for, but was unable to handle the success. Otherwise, why has he seemingly blown himself up?

Well, it is my strongly held belief that the root of Steve's confidence and self-esteem issues can be traced back to his formative, imprinting years, when he was wickedly and erroneously told as a young boy that he was "...*thick and stupid and would never be anything*". Steve is not stupid, never has been. Yes, he's done some stupid things recently, but that doesn't make him intrinsically stupid. This is true for us all.

In fact, it has been well documented how amazingly intelligent, creatively gifted, hardworking, imaginative, conscientious, insightful, kind, loving and thoughtful Steve is. He was/is a deep, methodical and critical thinker and, quite possibly one of the world's most extraordinary problem solvers – but he was infected with poisonous negativity as a very young boy and was unable to shake it off during my lifetime with him. I genuinely hope Helen has more luck helping him blossom into his full potential, but it doesn't look like it from the little I can see on the outside. Steve would be truly unstoppable if he could just erase those cold, critical, despicable words uttered to him in his childhood.

Once Steve was on the threshold of a higher greatness, those words of spiteful discouragement that had been gnawing away at him forever, finally bit, and he submitted (unconsciously) to their self-fulfilling prophecy. He had always been told he would never be anything, but here he was about to become something. His reality was conflicting with his imprinted beliefs, so he hit the self-destruct button to make it all reconcile, especially when his burnout fuelled an inner panic. But hey, this is me merely speculating out loud as a lay person, this is not necessarily how things were. What do I know? I'm not appropriately trained in the mental health profession, I'm merely reflecting on our years together, and what I believed to be true at the time; many, many years ago. This is nothing more than very old supposition on my part, but...

I had spent 24 years trying to repair the damage he suffered, but I lost the battle. If Bill and Mike's kind words of pure, unconditional love for him had failed to neutralise the venom in real time, how in the world could I expect to help him? I refused to accept defeat though and kept battling to rescue him from the historic hurts, until of course he evicted me from his life. And as for those souls who foisted their ignorant, hurtful words onto a sweet, innocent and beautiful young boy all those years go, I hope you roast in... [*love and light Karan!*] ... somewhere unseasonably warm.

Skint

So, Steve had left me and forced me out of our business, which left me without money or an income to pay for bills and food. The only saving grace in all of this was Steve said he would continue to pay the mortgage and didn't ask me for rent. Not that I could have afforded it on my £77 per week Jobseekers Allowance. Thankfully, the additional Child Tax credits and Child Benefit gave us a little more to live on, and I was still holding onto the hope that Steve would give me something towards the children, once everything had settled down.

The only way I could make ends meet was by creating a household budget spreadsheet. Because I had at least 50 plates spinning in my head at any one time, mentally grasping and mastering my finances wasn't as easy for me now, as it had usually been. There was only so much RAM in my mind, all of it now dedicated to settling the kids and adjusting to our new reality. Remembering when the gas bill was due was beyond my memory capabilities now, so the household budget helped to ensure everything got paid on time, every time.

If this is your life now, and however great you once were with financial matters before your Bomb Drop, please don't assume you'll automatically be as capable at keeping the same plates spinning now. Accept your mind has more important matters to attend to and create yourself a safety net, which will both support you and catch the things you drop. It is of paramount importance for you to keep up your payments and commitments. I'll show you how well it served me, to help validate my suggestion.

Bearing in mind this can also be achieved on lined paper, my digital spreadsheet is very simple. I have a heading comprised of six vertical columns (Day, Date, Payment Description, Money In, Money Out, Running Total) but you can always tweak this to suit your own needs. Whatever happens though, and as with all things in life, don't overcomplicate it for complications sake.

Let's say you're going to start your household budget today. In the first horizontal row beneath your heading, enter the day (of the week) and the date. Then write the words "Opening Balance" in your Payment Description column, and whatever your current bank balance is, insert it into the Running Total column. Now you need to go through your old bank statements and enter what goes out on a regular basis and when; notably your direct debits and standing orders.

Even though my finances are much improved from where they were post-Bomb Drop, I have got into the habit of maintaining my household budget for a couple of reasons. Firstly, the numbers you focus on improve. Secondly, when I was in the depths of poverty and having to raid the children's piggy banks to buy food, the budget forecasting prevented me from missing vital payments to utility companies etc. By realistically predicting the money coming in and out of my account, my forecast would predict the likelihood of my account slipping into the red. This would then give me a chance to do something about it, i.e.: spend less, amend payment dates, or contact the payee to explain, or set up an alternative payment arrangement. Burying my head in the sand when times were financially tough was not an option, because I was mindful of my credit rating – which we will discuss in more detail soon.

Going back to your household budget, let's say your opening balance is £50. Your first entry is today's monthly TV Licence payment of £12.50, so you leave the Money In column blank, but add £12.50 to your Money Out column. Now, in your Running Total column (£50 - £12.50 = £37.50), enter £37.50, and this is your new balance. When i.e.: Tax Credits or your salary is paid in, add the amount (example: £100) to your Money In column, leave the Money Out column blank, before adding (£100 + £37.50) £137.50 into the Running Total column; and now this is your new balance – and so on.

For me, because funds were so low, I had to budget £60 per week for the grocery shopping, and I tended to shop on a Thursday. I would also have three months of budget forecasting on the go at any one time, to help predict potential payment problems. This means I entered "Estimated Shopping" to every Thursday for three months, with £60 in the Money Out column. This allowed me to predict the Running Total with a high degree of accuracy.

Obviously, the actual shopping bills were never £60 exactly, which is why I made a point of updating my household budget every day with the precise amounts, which in turn would affect the predicted Running Total. With daily attendance to the budget, I was also able to add any unforeseen expenditures as and when they occurred, like when I had to replace a tyre urgently. Admittedly, this required me to delete the predicted amounts detailed in the Running Total column, before recalculating them again, but it was a labour of love to keep us out of financial jeopardy, so I did whatever it took.

One other teeny-weeny tip, should you feel so inclined, is to add one optional extra column next to the Running Total column. I created this untitled column to be wide enough to accommodate a big, bold and orange coloured "B" (for Balanced) in it. Why? Because it gave a me jumping off point for updating the Running Total if I'd left it more than a couple of days to refresh the information. Let me explain. If today is Tuesday, and I haven't tended to the budget since Thursday, but I know my household budget and online bank statement reconciled on Thursday (because of my big, bold, orange B next to Thursday's entry), then I need only recalculate from Friday to today. It's only a suggestion, but why not see if it works for you? If it helps you, keep it. If it's a complicated or unnecessary hassle for you, then dump it. Running an accurate household budget though is essential because it helps to focus your mind.

By focusing on my household budget for a few minutes each day, it also helped to maintain my spending discipline. I also have another handy trick I can pass on, which is admittedly labour intensive, but it ensured we ate better than we might otherwise have done. I know there are some great no-frills supermarkets around these day (Lidl, Aldi, Farmfoods), but they're not currently online and they don't offer a Delivery or Click & Collect service.

What I would do is, create a meal plan for the week ahead. I'd begin by seeing what I had in the fridge, freezer and cupboards, and establish how many meals I could generate from what was in stock.

My shopping list would begin by adding any bits and pieces I would need to supplement those stock ingredients, followed by seeing what was on special offer that week and creating the other meals accordingly. Once I'd established the seven evening meals, I then established what I needed for our (school) lunches and breakfasts, before listing secondary items like personal care, cleaning and laundry products. Now I had my shopping list, and now came the comparison evaluation.

I created a basic shopping list spreadsheet [*no, this book is not sponsored by MS Excel, but I can see why you ask*], with four vertical columns: Item, Tesco, Asda, Saving. I would pull up the websites to Tesco and Asda, to see how much each item was being sold for that week; the cheapest price was then entered into either the Tesco or Asda column, with a note of the saving value in the final column. Here's an example: a bag of apples is £1.39 in Tesco but is on offer this week at Asda for 45p, so Asda gets the sale. I add "Gala apples" into the Item column, leave the Tesco column blank, add £0.45 to the Asda column, before adding (£1.39 - £0.45) £0.94 into the Saving column.

Once I've repeated this exercise for all of the items on my shopping list, I would simply AutoSum the Tesco, Asda and Saving columns to establish how much my shopping in each store would come to, whilst calculating how much I have saved overall this week. If the overall Grand Total (of Tesco + Asda) exceeded my £60 budget limit, I would simply start deleting things off the list.

Tesco was my primary supermarket, because of the added value Reward points (which I would later rely upon to buy the children's birthday/Christmas presents and school uniform etc), so if my overall Asda savings didn't add up to at least £2.00, I accepted the additional cost versus Reward points trade off and shopped at Tesco exclusively that week. This hardly ever happened though, because most weeks I was saving a minimum of £10 by splitting my shopping in this way, which amply offset the tiny amount of additional petrol necessary to drive to the second store.

If an online or Click & Collect service is not important to you, then no-frills supermarkets are definitely a great idea. As I would eventually be trying to build a business within the confines of school hours, I needed to optimise those school hours by working, not shopping. This is why I did my shopping in this manner, utilising the free and expedient Click & Collect services available; time is money and all that. There is obviously a lot of scope for you to tailor this technique to suit your personal requirements, you just need to give it some thought. I hope my outline here is of service to you.

Another thing I would urge you to seriously consider is, optimising and/or protecting your credit rating. I took advantage of a 30-day free Experian trial in January 2014, to find out where I stood. My credit rating didn't set the world alight, but it was healthy, and it was okay. This wasn't good enough for me however, so I took some advice about how I could improve it. The two biggest things I could do for myself was to get a credit card, (because I'd never owned one), and detach myself from Steve's name. Don't get me wrong, Steve's credit rating was A+ at the time, but with his increasingly erratic choices and self-destructive behaviours, I had no guarantees how long this would last. Besides, we were all over as a couple bar the shouting, so now was as good a time as any to detach, so I did.

The problem I had with not owning a credit card is that the credit companies (who feed the credit ratings) didn't know me, so stuck me with a *meh* rating. Because they didn't know if I was responsible enough to lend money to, or not, they hedged their bets. This meant I was likely to get credit if I wanted it, but not at the best interest rates; which equalled more expensive repayments for me. Then I made another big mistake.

Ordinarily I would have known better, but I was still wading through mental pea soup, so fell into an obvious elephant trap. I'm telling you now, so you don't follow suit. Regrettably, I ran headlong, without thinking it through, into applying for a credit card with three different companies but, because the APR was unacceptably high, I kept looking and applying. This had a disastrous effect on my already *meh* credit rating, so don't make the same mistake. Nowadays, credit card companies offer you a risk free "check before you apply" service, to prevent exactly this kind of avoidable blunder, so please be sure to make full use of this facility if needs be.

My second mistake was getting a credit card from my bank, and then not using it. Nope. Credit card companies want to see you using it and paying back the debt efficiently. Every now and again let them earn a little bit of interest off a tiny debt, following a minimum payment, because they're in business to make money. Apparently, your credit rating is based as much on how well you repay debt, as it is about how much money you make them. If you don't allow them to make a little tiny something off you every now and again, it is possible to lose a couple of points off your rating.

I had a couple of months where I'd pay for petrol using the credit card, but then pay it all off in full when due. I thought this would boost my credit rating, but not-so-much. Then I made a larger purchase, forwarded the minimum payment when due, and let them charge me a piffling amount of interest on not a lot of debt and... bingo! I played their game and it seriously boosted my credit rating. This is the advice Experian gave to me in 2014, but you really should investigate for yourself, as rules and algorithms change all the time. This advice may now be dangerously outdated, so don't just take my word for it, go out and learn for yourself. Knowledge is power!

The next thing to maybe consider is subscribing to a couple of credit reporting agencies. These are free services and will give you a monthly update on your credit status. You're also alerted quickly if a problem develops (i.e.: identity theft) and they will spotlight where you might have problems (i.e.: fraud, missing electoral roll data, problematic linked names), before helping you overcome them.

Experian helped me to detach my name from Steve's, but I couldn't afford their monthly subscription (at the time), so I jumped to one of their free competitors, before eventually adding another, for their interpretation of my credit status. It's a good idea to subscribe to a couple of these companies because they all score differently. Working this way gives you a broader picture of where you are across the board, and there's no such thing as too much information, is there?

Over the years, particularly since Steve left me, I have looked after my credit rating, and now my credit rating is looking after me. This is why I am so dedicated to my household budget, and ensuring all financial commitments are paid on time, every time. By forecasting up to three months in advance, I can predict any potential problems and adjust my spending and saving accordingly. I can keep track of what these credit agencies think they know about me, and then be well positioned to correct any errors immediately, before they become onerous and troublesome. Whilst I'm still fighting to remember to use my credit card from time-to-time, the benefit of having a glowing credit rating is preferential and cheaper APR rates, should I ever want a loan, a mortgage or finance in the future.

There is a lot more to consider and talk about where credit ratings are concerned, but this book is not about that, and I am certainly no expert on the subject. I've written about the key areas which affected my life at a particular time, but not all that's available. If you want to know more about how to improve your credit rating, and how to avoid numerous elephant traps like the ones I fell into, then either do your own research or speak to an independent financial advisor as soon as you can.

Condemned

These were harsh times to live through, as the nights were getting cold and I couldn't afford to heat the house overnight. The timer on the old boiler had died, so I would snuggle the kids under piles of blankets for sleep before turning the boiler off. I would then sit in several layers of clothing during the evenings, before enveloping myself in a 15-tog duvet at bedtime. I fashioned myself into a human sausage roll to keep warm and slept in a tube of duvet loveliness. My alarm would go off at 4am for me to leg it – swearing under my breath à la Mutley – to switch the boiler on, before thawing out again in my duvet sausage roll. This continued throughout the entire winter and it was brutal.

Over the Christmas period of 2013 we suffered extremely high winds over a successive number of days and nights, which resulted in the flue for the boiler being blown off the side of our house. For those who don't fully appreciate the inner workings of a boiler flue (which included me in 2013), it's essentially the exhaust system for the boiler. The flue expels waste gases, produced by the heating processes of the boiler, safely out of the house.

As it was his house, and I knew diddly squat about fixing boilers and couldn't afford a Gas Safe engineer to fix it, I informed Steve of what had happened. I had collected the various flue components, which had been liberally strewn across the garden, in the hope that Steve may have been able to reattach the flue. He said this was possible and he'd do it soon. This was also the time the boiler decided to develop internal pressure problems, which Steve had to talk me through repeatedly to fix. I have no idea if this was a missing flue related problem, but in addition to my 4am brass monkey leg it sprints, I was now seriously pissed off with this boiler and wanted something done.

I'm now going to scoot you towards May 2014 for a brief moment. Long story short and somewhat unsurprisingly given who he was now, Steve never did get around to fixing the flue. This left us with a large gaping hole on the side of the house for five months, where the boiler's exhaust system should have been. If the wind blew in exactly the right direction it would blow the pilot light out, resulting in my showers running cold more times than I care to remember (the kids had baths).

I was back on the precipice of fury again for having to live like this, but I flatly refused to vent my feelings. Instead, I exercised my self-mastery and detailed everything in my contemporaneous journal. I tried to purge my fear and loathing this way. So perhaps you can now see how things often work out for the best, when you patiently bide your time? No, it was never my intention to write about my life initially, but when I changed my mind I was furnished well. Like I've said: if you do your best in every situation, it puts you in the best possible position for the next situation.

[229]

As you may recall, I started exploring the possibility of applying for a government grant to replace the boiler, now I was in receipt of the necessary benefits, in September 2013? It had taken until now to find a company not oversubscribed, and willing to conduct a site survey. A gas engineer, Warren, attended our appointment and before he even set foot inside the house, asked me about the large gaping hole, directly beneath the eaves.

Naively, I explained about the flue being blown off during Christmas week, and how my ex hadn't gotten around to repairing it. Horrified, and with as much patience for my naiveté as he could muster, Warren looked me straight in the eye and told me he would have to condemn the boiler immediately. He had to switch it off and disconnect it from the gas supply without delay. This would leave us without heating, which wasn't a big deal in May, but more importantly without hot water. *Shit!*

Unable to fully grasp Warren's reasoning, because we had been existing adequately well until now, I asked if it was entirely necessary to condemn the boiler; couldn't he just replace it ASAP? No, that was out of the question because he was legally obliged to shut it down on safety grounds. Warren explained to me that for five months, noxious gases had been flowing back into the house, because the flue was not there to expel them.

Furthermore, we had been beyond lucky that no birds, bats (which we had in the attic) or any other significantly sized critters had flown, hopped or crawled into the cavity and boiler mechanism, because the consequences could have been lethal. Of course, I mean *more lethal*. I stood listening, blinking and processing what Warren was saying in complete disbelief, initially.

Rage boiled up from the soles of my feet, and I had to take a moment to ensure I didn't unleash it on Warren. My rage was directed at Steve who, although not a registered Gas Safe technician, had worked with enough of them to understand the jeopardy he was putting his children into. The fact he was willing to see me barbequed by a gas incident is one thing, but WHAT ABOUT HIS FUCKING CHILDREN?! I was speechless for several minutes as I tried to compose myself. Warren seemed to understand something was amiss and waited patiently for me to grab a hold of my horses. We then went inside the house, where he duly shutdown the boiler and measured up for the new one.

At the end of the survey Warren told me he needed Steve, as the owner of the property, to consent to the work being done, and to agree to a £90 charge for an extra-long length of copper pipe for something plumbing-related. Not trusting myself to speak to Steve, I gave Warren his phone number and they spoke. Warren agreed to meet Steve at the workshop to obtain his consent signature, because Steve flatly refused to come to the house. I wonder why?

When Warren arrived at the workshop, Steve signed the consent form stating dismissively, and positively loaded with hostility: "*She can pay the fucking £90*", whilst handing back the clipboard. Warren phoned to apprise me of what Steve had said, and to ask if I was prepared to pay for the chargeable essential extras, otherwise he'd have to cancel the job.

I had a choice: argue the toss with Steve, which would likely result in a delay of the boiler installation or find a way to pay the £90 myself. I referred to my household budget and finagled a way to pay it myself. If I reduced our grocery shopping budget from £60 to £45 per week for six weeks, I could finance the £90. I had no other expenditures I could cut back on. I only used the car for essential travel, so I couldn't cut back on petrol any further as I was already operating on fumes. The grocery shopping was my only leverage point, so we endured a grim six weeks of pasta and rice and little else.

Thankfully, Warren and his team arrived the next day and installed the new boiler. Warren had witnessed for himself what I was up against with Steve and had been so horrified that a father could be willing to put his children in harm's way. He clearly pulled some strings for me, to get such an immediate installation date, and I was truly thankful to finally be safe. Thank God for the kindness of strangers eh?

That night I took the unusual step (because we were on a water metre and I was mindful of the cost to myself as well as the environment) of having a long hot shower, to try and wash my disgust of Steve off of me. In all the years that have passed since this misadventure, I *still* haven't washed my disgust of him off of me. Steve did me a huge favour in the long run though. Because of the decisions Steve made, the children and I benefited from a new boiler sooner than we would otherwise have done. My energy bills were significantly less too, due to the new boiler's higher efficiency, so *thanks Steve!*

Unemployable

Unbelievably, following our short excursion into May 2014 just now for the boiler debacle, we're still in the October 2013 Rest-Fest, in respect of my story. *I know!* Can you imagine what it felt like to live it? #Endless*!*

One of my obligations whilst claiming Job Seekers Allowance was to seek a job, funnily enough. My HR friend, Paige, had helped me to compile a killer professional CV, which I then dispensed liberally throughout the county. I also signed up with a few employment agencies, whilst also having to attend the Jobcentre Plus every fortnight to sign on. Whilst my days signing on were some of the bleakest and most soul-destroying times of my life, the universe blessed me yet again by assigning me to Andy. Andy is a big bear of a man, but he's not big enough to contain the vast treasures of his generous spirit, as his inherent kindness leaks out everywhere! He looked after us.

My problem was that as I'd essentially been working for myself for 12+ years, I didn't have any employment references to offer. The company I had worked for directly before joining the business full time had gone bust, and a reference from the employer before that would have been more than 14 years old. There was no one other than my estranged, strange and bastardised ex-husband-to-be who could vouch for me. Evidently employers couldn't countenance the risk, and so I became largely unemployable for the jobs I was qualified to do.

That didn't stop me trying though, as I continued to wade through the shitstorm that was my life, still trying to settle the kids and make ends meet. The jobs I was qualified for were in the higher salary bracket, which would obviously require those references as a matter of due diligence. These jobs however would also require me to work 60+ hours a week for said high salary, but the kids needed me front and centre for the foreseeable future.

The outlook was bleak, but I had Andy, who is softly spoken, has a rapier wit and was uncommonly compassionate and understanding. Andy sympathised with my dilemma and counselled me gently and wisely, and I will forever be in his debt for the care he took of me, advice-wise. The last thing I needed was more pressure, and he knew that.

Andy asked me if I would ever consider mentoring new start up entrepreneurs. I scoffed and dismissed the idea, stating I had no mentoring experience. He then pulled out my CV and noted the 21-year experience I had accrued with our start up since 1992. This was valuable information to anyone starting out on their own now. Hmm. This gave me pause. It's true I had read acres of small business and personal development titles, attended numerous sales and marketing training courses, compiled reams of notes at leadership and productivity seminars, whilst having learnt to manage RTI PAYE, VAT accounting and all manner of other business processes. This information was now being squandered inside my head, not seeing the light of day. If Steve didn't want the benefit of my acquired knowledge and experience, new start up entrepreneurs would jump at the chance to mine my mind.

The question was now how could I mentor these start up entrepreneurs? Andy suggested a couple of organisations I should consider approaching, with a view to helping them, most notably a local social enterprise scheme. Spurred on by Andy's encouragement, I approached the company who ran said local enterprise scheme with an offer to volunteer my services because a) I wanted to reciprocate *something* for the financial support I was receiving from the government (it was important for me to pay it forward), and b) I wanted to help other people – Rescuer that I am – in addition to c) finding out how good I was at it. Napoleon Hill teaches us in Think & Grow Rich, that we can have anything we want in life, so long as we help others achieve what they want. Here was my opportunity to do just that. Following several meetings with influential people and some hugely targeted and beneficial mentoring training, my new mentoring career began. Unsurprisingly, I quickly fell in love with helping dynamic and extraordinary entrepreneurs.

If you will indulge me, I will now jump us forward to November 2014 for a few moments, when I was about to exceed the limit of Jobseeker's Allowance available to me. Even though I was volunteering as a mentor, I had still been unable to find a job due to my employment reference issue, so now what? My year visiting Andy had resulted in him getting to know the measure of me; who I am, how I operate, my high integrity and insane work ethic. Based on all of the character traits he had observed, Andy offered a suggestion: *"Why not go self-employed?"*

Rendered speechless for a moment, as the cogs inside my mind raced to find a plausible excuse not to, Andy began to verbalise his reasoning, whilst I listened intently: I had already run a business for 20+ years. I already had 20+ years of sales, marketing and revenue generation. I had already co-founded and overseen the explosive expansion of a once thriving small business. I had already hired and fired employees, in addition to processing contracts of employment, RTI PAYE, maternity, sick pay and disciplinary procedures. I had sufficient VAT accounting and bookkeeping experience to have adhered to the law, and to be able to furnish accountants with the collated material, competently.

I had already created and managed multiple social media platforms, built a website whilst maintaining and continually refining its SEO. I had already administered a couple of blogs, with regular new features and a newsletter, whilst understanding the importance of consistently fresh content. What could there possibly be, that I hadn't already experienced and mastered, for me to trip over if I went self-employed? What could there possibly be that I couldn't eventually master, given my character, skill set and overall modus operandi? *Well when you put it like that!* My only limit, as Andy so astutely observed, was me.

It was true, he was right. My confidence had taken three direct hits since September 2013, and now my vulnerabilities were showing. I was questioning my own judgement, character and capabilities. I felt like I was swimming in a latrine. What if I hadn't been so fearful and stubborn and phoned Mum, would she still be alive today? When arguably given a couple of forewarnings (the Gypsy's message, the "Get Happy" dream, the crow visitation), what kind of person doesn't err on the side of caution and take the chance to say goodbye? How could I have been so blind and/or stupid, not to have seen Helen's true colours, especially when she had shown them to me, repeatedly? And as for Steve, where do I start? Who the hell had I become, in the fathoms of my Helen-blindness, to be capable of hurting such a vulnerable and gentle bear of a man? Andy was right, I was hobbling myself by perceiving myself unworthy and incapable of starting again.

I went inside my head, argued with myself for hours and then submitted the topic for discussion with my War Council. We all agreed with Andy. We all agreed that I should get over myself, harness the years of experience life and the business had afforded me and to "pull an Adele". Unless you've been living under a rock, you will know who Adele is, surely? Adele has an outstanding voice and song writing ability and has largely founded her career on songs about various heartbreaks. One of my favourite songs is Rolling In The Deep, particularly the lyric about turning her sorrow into treasured gold and how they'll pay her back in kind and reap just what they sow.

So, it was decided I would become self-employed. This allowed me to shift out from under the expired Jobseekers Allowance, and into the realms of Working Tax Credits. Then the real work began as I built a website and created the new social media platforms for my beloved new work project. The Tax Credits office wanted assurances I was working a minimum of 30 hours a week on the business, so I sent them all that I had done, which could be independently verified by my online presence, and all that I planned to do. My dreams and goals were vast. I had gone "lock on" [*extremely focused and driven*] and was working the six hours a day whilst the kids were at school, and then up to another four hours a night when they were in bed. Evidence of my lock on was there for anyone to log on to, and so the DWP agents were satisfied.

Something had awakened in me. A sense of lightness and freedom was growing stronger, and an excitement for the future was starting to fizz. I loved my work as a volunteer mentor and was blessed to meet some of the most wonderful people on that journey. I revelled in their company because I was able to learn as much as they did, because we all have different strengths and gifts. There were tears of struggle and joy, there were goals smashed or courses corrected, there was mental, emotional and even spiritual growth – and all for the greater good. It was wonderful, and I was finally in my element, not Steve's.

Then came the paid clients, and my soul just soared. Making a positive difference to hard working, talented and honourable entrepreneurs, and private individuals who are chipping away at their goals, continues to be my honour and privilege. The vision, passion and energy my clients were bringing to our sessions was powerful, and needed only direction, focus and momentum. One of my earliest clients was a joy to behold, because when we met it was like our session was winding a key in her back. By the time she came back to me for another session, she'd left an entrepreneur-shaped hole in the goals we had set before, which she had relentlessly crushed. In fact, I found myself playfully trying to out-read this particular mentee, because she had an uncommonly voracious thirst for knowledge. I lost, she won and if you're out there reading this Crazy Lady, please bring the book to me and I'll confirm it's you in your copy.

Following the principles of continuous improvement, I have pursued my quest to be bigger, better, faster and stronger than I was the day before. I don't compete against my competitors; I compete against my own personal bests. This keeps me focused on what I'm doing, and where I'm going, rather than on what they're doing and where they're going. This philosophy was further reinforced by Alex's athletics coach, who taught him to never look over his shoulder when approaching the finishing line. To look over your shoulder distracts your focus away from your goal, and ultimately slows you down.

Besides, just because your competitor is doing a thing doesn't mean it's right, or right for you. Always do your own thing. Only ever run your own race, as well as you can. Just as Alex's eyes are firmly fixed on the finishing line, my crosshairs are focused on the attainment of my goals. Every decision I make passes through a now automatic thought filter of: is this moving me in the direction of my goal? If it is moving me closer towards my goal, I continue with it. If it moves me away from the achievement of my goal, or even holds me statically in place with no advancement at all, then I don't do it. I must have forward momentum. If it doesn't evolve me, it doesn't involve me.

Reality Bites

With my wildly optimistic October Rest-Fest now over, November rain began to trickle down for Steve and Helen, cold and bitter. Five weeks into their affair and reality was biting. Whilst it may have felt fairy tale-esque to them in the beginning of their infatuation, with hormones inflaming their adulterous loins, and rose-tinted spectacles colouring their view, there was one small matter they'd overlooked. Have you ever noticed how there are never any bill payments and bowel movements in fairy tales? No, because fairy tales are detached from reality, they are make-believe; merely an illusionary story created for light relief.

Whilst missing the relationship I'd once had with Steve, whilst struggling and infuriated with the financial and emotional hardship he had plunged us into, having mentally accepted we were over made things so much easier on one level: schadenfreude. Schadenfreude is the pleasure derived from another person's misfortune. Don't get me wrong, he was still the father of my children and I wouldn't want to see him hurt or in serious jeopardy, but I did enjoy him struggling without me. He had discarded me so callously and dismissively, like I was nothing. I was disposable after once being indispensable, so he'd better have at it and create something out of the freedom he'd sacrificed everything for. But after only five short weeks of living actively against me, Steve was starting to realise just how much I had done, without ever knowing how I did it. He was now working without a net.

One Sunday morning, as he was collecting the kids for another scintillating day of washing his van at the workshop (in the cold), before buying their snack-based lunch at Farmfoods, Steve asked if he could take the fence sprayer from the shed, which he did. We then became engaged in a three-hour long discussion about all things financial. From my perspective it was simple, I was skint, had no room for manoeuvre or error, but as long I as coloured inside the lines, we would be okay. Things were more tense for Steve and Helen though, by all accounts.

He started the conversation by asking me what I was going to do with the Jeep Patriot. I made it clear I was looking into getting rid of it because a) it was like driving an armoured vehicle and was massively over spec'd for the school runs, b) it was insanely expensive to fuel and insure, and c) it sure as hell was never going to tow the caravan again. I hated the caravan, despite its comparative 6-berth luxury accoutrements.

I had never wanted a caravan, but it had been a long-held ambition of Steve's, so we got a sodding caravan *sigh*. From my motorsport enthusiast's mindset, I could never understand why you would want to tow a tin box – *slowly!* – for the privilege of paying an extortionate fee to shit in the woods. Yes, we had a miniature, flushing chemical toilet, but was this really what my life had come to? With an injured back, sleeping on a bed compiled of sofa cushions was literal agony for me, and took me until lunch to feel my feet again!

Steve's dream of owning a caravan was heightened in the summer of 2011, when we visited Helen and Lee's caravan set up 17 miles away from their home. Yes, you heard me... 17 whole miles away from their home. What exactly the point was, was never explained to me. You would think however, if Steve was trying to sell me on the pleasures of caravanning, he'd have taken us to the Lake District, or somewhere equally picturesque, but no. I had to physically restrain myself from proclaiming "*I can see my house from here!*"

on the caravan steps every morning.

On this morning though, Steve broke the news to me that he was going to have to sell the caravan, and I'm not sure what he was expecting from me by way of a reaction. Barely contained delirium was what he got, as I fought to prevent an incendiary smile spreading across my face. He then asked me for the business debit card reader I used to make online payments with. He had cancelled my business debit card, and associated account authority, and was now trying to fulfil my broad-spectrum responsibilities himself, without my knowledge, training or experience to guide him. He didn't ask for help and I didn't offer. Dissatisfied with "having nothing to show for his life", he was now clearly trying to carve something out for himself. I stood aside to let him try, in much the same way as I taught the kids how to brush their own teeth. I knew it would end in a big mess, but how else were they ever going to learn? They can't be dependent upon me forever.

Whilst Helen is AAT qualified, she had been employed for 24 years in a two-bit accountancy firm, with one dusty computer to its name. The work Helen and her colleagues compiled therefore was all completed via paper ledgers, with adding machines and pencils; it was all very 1980's. In fact, Helen had even asked me to teach her how to use Excel and create spreadsheets, but we never got around to it; what with all the sex she was having with my husband and all. She had administered Lee's business in this antiquated way too and had obviously never considered teaching herself the dark arts of Excel; preferring to stay inside her comfort zone, I guess. Oh well, a smooth sea never made a skilful sailor, and all that.

Apparently, the Department of Work & Pensions had stopped all of Helen's benefits, as a result of me opening a new claim the day after Bomb Drop, whilst also reporting Steve's new living arrangements. I didn't do it for this reason. I did it to secure whatever income was available to me, to feed and provide for my children, but if my actions resulted in financial hardship for Helen too, well then that was just a happy accident.

To be honest, if Helen had reported her Change of Circumstances within one month of Steve moving in – as she was obliged to do – they would have ended up in the same financial position anyway; only without any penalties for failing to report. This is why I always do my best in every situation, because it puts me in the best possible position for the next situation. Of course, the reverse is true, as Helen was starting to find out.

The problem for Helen was, whilst I reported the change in my circumstances, apparently Helen had not and was duly punished. In turn, Steve lashed out and punished me for their financial hardship by flatly refusing to pay me anything towards the children. He was happy to leave the children existing in a perpetual state of lack, whilst continuing to tell me he was paying for the house. Please remember that whilst Helen's benefits may have been stopped, they were still in the enviable position of living off the business. Or so I thought. I wouldn't learn until much later, the degree to which Steve had let the business slide, and how quickly.

Steve told me he had a meeting scheduled with a mortgage lender, to find out how much he/they could borrow. This sent shockwaves through me, and I became instantly more alert to the possibility of danger for the roof over our heads. How was he going to do this? As the sole legal owner of our home, was he going to try and put the house on the market, with a view to swiping all the equity he was not likely to share with me? He didn't mention my newly decreed HR1, so I assumed he was oblivious to how legally hobbled he was, without my distinct cooperation. I didn't volunteer this information; I didn't want to spoil the surprise. Besides there are three things you should always keep to yourself: your love life, your income and your next move.

During this conversation I urged Steve to remember the £11k capital investment I'd put into the business, and how I would want that back, now he'd shot our future together out of the sky. He asked if I would accept the £11k within my 50% share of any house equity, and I said no, I would now want it in addition to my 50% share. He looked dismayed and highly stressed, but these were the ill-considered consequences of his impulsive actions. My sole priority was the children, and I was going to guard their interests and well-being with the ferocity of a Mamma Bear leading a troop of rabid baboons strung out on meth.

Steve was most unhappy with my refusal to accept anything less than 50% equity + my £11k investment; he thought this unfair. Yes, really. I reminded him he'd been the one to end our marriage and working relationship, and was solely responsible for the difficulties we now found ourselves in. He bucked against my stance with: "*What about all the money I've put into the house and business?*", and I parried with: "*Our assets are only going to be carved up now because you have chosen to leave the marriage and provide for someone else's children instead of your own*".

He then resorted to telling me how he had been the one with the balls to end the marriage, that he'd been unhappy for two years (since my friendship with Helen began), and that I'd only invested the £11k through choice, because I believed in him. This was all absolutely true, but now he'd moved the goalposts and had run off with the sodding ball. I could no longer invest in him, because I no longer believed in him. I no longer knew who he was.

[243]

Besides, look where investing in him had gotten me, I was down to counting pennies to feed the children. I no longer had a choice; I could only ever invest in myself from now on.

Lower Than A Rattlesnake's Belly

Steve then sank lower, trying to make me feel as bad as he was feeling, I guess. He told me how warmly he had been invited into Helen's family, and how lovingly embraced by Emily and Oliver he had been. How lovely for him, but I still couldn't see how they were worth liquidating his life's work of 25 years for. No doubt they are loved by at least some of their blood relations, but Steve had made derogatory remarks and observations about each and every one of them, so he would have to excuse my incredulity now he believed them to be great. His wilful ignorance was leading him into a world of illusion, denial and eventual pain, and all I could do was to stand aside and let him learn the same lessons I have.

Steve then sank lower still, telling me he'd be unable and unwilling to continue phoning the children every night. Apparently, these calls were negatively impacting their mealtimes where he lived and were just awkward on every level; particularly on nights he had client consultation appointments. Predicting the emotionally explosive effects this would have on Sofia and Alex, I told Steve he could tell me in advance which nights he had appointments, so I could manage the children's expectations gently, rather than him just announcing it to them coldly when they could next expect to hear from him.

He also took this time to tell me that him having the kids every Sunday would have to stop, as he needed to rest. Seeing his children for seven hours once a week wasn't restful, poor lamb. His priorities were emerging, and they didn't include the kids, or any kind of consideration towards their love for him, and their desire to spend time with him. Something snapped quietly inside, and I decided I was not going to soften this blow on his behalf with the children. I told him, as civilly as I could muster, that he would have to look them in the eyes and tell them himself. He would have to see the pain and hurt in their beautiful, innocent faces and (hopefully) hate himself for that anguish he had brought to bear. This discussion was now getting heated.

He blurted out how annoyed he was at me for "...*saying mean things about Helen*". It's true, I had exercised my freedom of speech and expressed my low opinion of Helen. I had called her an opportunistic _____ repeatedly, but only for the lack of a more accurate phrase. Steve's mid-life reprogramming was clearly complete, as he played out his *Defender of Poor Helen* role like the windup toy soldier he had become; in my place. He was also operating under the mistaken impression that I gave a single flying fuck about whether he was annoyed with me or not, or that Helen's feelings were hurt. Had either of them considered my feelings? Had either of them ever considered Sofia and Alex's feelings? No. So his approval had lost all currency in my mind. He could seethe away to his little heart's content. Have at it, big boy!

Besides, what else *do you* call a woman who proclaimed to love her friend like no other, who pounces on a weakened marriage, who moves in with a depressed and mentally vulnerable husband of said friend, less than a week after the funeral of said friend's Mum? It's opportunistic in its timing and she's a _____ for going through it, particularly whilst decimating the hearts of two young children in the process. Madeleine Albright (former US Secretary of State) said it best: "*There is a special place in hell for women who do not help other women*", so where exactly am I being unreasonable in

[245]

this assessment of her? I understand how Helen might not like being called an opportunistic _____, but please gaze upon my field of fucks and see that it is barren!

After being annoyed with me, Steve then went on to tell me how annoyed he was with Sofia, for not disclosing Lauren's recent visit, or my excursion out a couple of weeks earlier (to the solicitors). Still thinking about it then. How insightful. How he thought this was any of his business remains a mystery, but he felt Sofia was withholding information from him, and being unnecessarily secretive.

It's true, she was withholding information from him, but not unnecessarily so. He had decided he didn't want to be part of my life any longer, so why did he have a right to know, or even an interest in knowing, how and where I spent my time? I think he may have expected me to tell him where I was that day, to help exonerate Sofia's close hold on the information, but it really was none of his business. Besides, he'd find out when the time was right, exactly as I had done in respect of his affair with my "friend". Methinks he was nervous. Methinks he was right to be nervous, because my Master Plan was starting to come together.

Don't worry about what I'm doing.
Worry about why you're nervous about what I'm doing.

I made clear that Sofia's trust in him was broken, because she felt he had left her, and because of his numerous actions before and since our separation. I told him his perfect sheen was now tarnished, to which he responded petulantly, by pointing to the internal door he'd punched eighteen months earlier and saying: *"Well it keeps being thrown back at me, it's been years! I keep saying sorry, but it keeps being thrown back at me!*" The problem was, Sofia was eight when it happened, and he had frightened her. Now this god's gift of her once darling daddy, was reduced to sleeping with Helen and living with Emily and Oliver instead of us. In Sofia's young mind, he had chosen – and continues to choose – raising Emily and Oliver over her and Alex. He chooses them every day, and everyday Sofia's love and respect for him dies a little more.

We then spoke about Sofia's imminent birthday and agreed upon the following. Steve would attend the birthday party at a local health and beauty spa. Helen, Oliver and Emily were not invited or welcome, in accordance with Sofia's birthday wishes. After the party, the four of us would visit Mallie's, where we would meet up with Teresa, Len and possibly their adult daughter Jess. Then, on the Sunday morning of Sofia's actual birthday, Steve agreed to come to the house early in the morning, so he could be part of the present opening excitement. We would then go to the cinema, before having a meal at a restaurant of Sofia's choosing, together. Together was the operative word for Sofia, which she kept repeating.

As for presents, because I didn't have two buttons to rub together, Steve agreed to buy a laptop from the both of us, whilst I would buy a selection of smaller items from her Birthday Wishlist (like a box of Coco Pops and some felt tip pens). When I first suggested a laptop as a present, Steve baulked and suggested she have his iPad mini instead, so he didn't have to spend out. I pretended to think about it for a minute, before confirming how Sofia would require an actual laptop for her increasingly demanding homework assignments. This was entirely true, particularly now senior school was on the horizon.

Reluctantly, Steve agreed to pay for the health and beauty birthday party, and to buy a laptop. As something of a technological Luddite, he let me research which laptop he should buy, which I was more than happy to do. I knew if Helen was involved in his decision-making processes, Sofia would probably have ended up with a second-hand 1970's Etch-a-Sketch or something. I duly researched the best available model for her and emailed him the Argos link and product code, with no alternative options. He was then concerned Sofia would read too much into our joint present and time together on her birthday [*ooh, what an ego!*], but I assured him she was crystal clear on the reality. All Sofia wanted was to spend time with the three people in the world she loved the most, which isn't unreasonable for any child to request, is it?

As for Christmas, I confirmed to Steve that the kids and I would be spending it at home, as we had always done. Steve and I had operated a "Home At Christmas" policy since the kids were born. We didn't want the obligations of having to be somewhere else for dinner to ruin the morning fun. If we wanted to stay in our pyjamas playing all day, then we wanted to be free to do just that, and this year would be no different. One of the most important things I had to provide for my children right now was stability and as much consistency as I could rescue. They had always known Christmas to be a home event, so there was no way I was going to change it this year, of all years.

I told Steve he knew where the children would be, and the ludicrous time they'd be up and at 'em, so it was his choice when he arrived to join in. I confirmed he had a choice: to spend all day with us, part of the day with us, to pop in for a cup of tea when it suited him, or not to spend any time with us at all. I was setting no restrictions, he had to act his conscience. I also offered him the chance to stay for Christmas dinner, quite certain in the knowledge he would decline, because Helen is a far better cook than I am. Whatever he decided, I had to be able to tell the children I'd invited him, that I had tried everything to give them what they wanted, despite him making my skin crawl. He said he would probably arrive for the present opening mayhem, and then go back to Helen's for dinner; finally accepting the fact the children never want to see Helen again. This was progress.

Strike 3 Looms

By all accounts the meeting with the mortgage lender didn't go so well. Steve had seemingly damaged his credit rating and, along with only a projected 50% less £11k share of any equity from the house, his mortgage options were as bleak as they were limited, especially after the subprime lending consequences of 2008. Neither could he rely upon Helen to bring any financial assistance into this equation because a) Strike 3 was looming and the repossession of her former marital home was now imminent and b) her credit rating had been poor for a while. The reasons why Steve represented such a great catch for Helen were innumerable, but never more so now she needed a place to live and somewhere to house her children.

Painfully aware of their impending homelessness, Steve spent days (some of which were with Sofia and Alex) driving around looking for somewhere to live plus, a landlord prepared to rent to them with three adult Labradors. Steve told Sofia they were looking at four-bedroom properties, so she and Alex had somewhere to sleep when they stayed over "...for weeks and weekends". Urgh, this again? Steve was now floating the possibility of shared custody to Sofia. Not with me, just to Sofia. It mattered not, as he got the same resounding "*No!*" from Sofia, as he would have had from me.

When he first floated the idea to Sofia, she became highly emotional, stating

"I never want to see any of the ███ *'s again!"* Steve responded by telling her to stop giving him a hard time, outlining, again how she would always be welcome to stay with them. He told her, again, how Helen and her kids loved and adored her (and Alex), resulting in Sofia crying harder, before shouting that she didn't feel loved by them. Steve cut her off and asked to speak to Alex because: *"I'm not getting anywhere with you"*. Sofia said: *"I don't understand how you don't want to be with someone as special as Mummy"*, to which Steve replied coldly: *"Helen is more special"*, before telling her he'd be round soon to take more of his belongings. Sofia felt punished. Again.

As for the new rented accommodation, one of Steve's workshop neighbours bailed him out of imminent homelessness, by leasing a rental property to them for a period of twelve months. It may have been by the skin of his teeth, but Steve had saved the day and was earning his keep. Steve is an incredibly handy bloke to know, and Helen was profiting handsomely. The Steve versus Karan choice was paying off for her, as she and her children would now have a roof over their heads. A roof she and her poor credit rating could not have provided for them otherwise. Well, she could have provided a roof, via social housing, but it was easier and more desirable the have Steve sort it out. Plus, he could afford bigger and better than social housing, which probably meant she could continue playing *Lady Helen*, for a while longer.

Steve then took the opportunity to play silly buggers by not revealing to me where they were moving to. So, let me get this straight: he'd gone from insisting the children spend time with him at Helen and Lee's marital home, to floating the idea of shared custody, to withholding his address from the mother of those children? FFS, I was getting seriously tired and bored with his childish games. It was only when Alex started karate lessons in January 2014, and I had to put Steve's emergency contact details on the registration forms, that I was able to drag the address out of him. I suppose I didn't *have* to include Steve on the form, but I was doing all I could to keep him involved in the children's lives, exactly as I had promised I would do. This was fast becoming a one-sided tug of war, because Steve wasn't even trying; tugger that he was.

Kicked Out Kicked Off

Evidently the mortgage lender Steve had met with was Nationwide, which made perfect sense because he'd held an account with them since his adolescence. When we decided to move in together in 1990, I joined this account whilst maintaining the Nationwide account I'd had since adolescence, which became my secondary. The bills for the house were still being paid from the joint account, whilst my benefits were being paid into my secondary. I'm not as green as I am cabbage looking.

Shortly after our separation, Steve had opened a secondary account of his own, but had only recently become aware of how valuable a longstanding bank account would be to his credit rating. Steve now wanted his original account back and asked me to remove myself from it. I complied with his request quickly, wanting to throw myself clear of any financial crash he may have been steering into.

We agreed I would transfer the utility direct debits over to my secondary account, and he would sign things like the TV licence over into my name, so I could administer it properly and ensure its payment. Sadly, I would not have put it past him to tell me he was paying for it, but to then be fined for non-compliance following detection. I could no longer afford to take Steve's word for anything and needed everything under my sole control.

Another huge benefit to walking away from the joint account was leaving the debt behind. As I had not been able to administer Steve's wages from the business, and I had not been paid by the business for a couple of months myself at this point, the joint account was significantly overdrawn. Seemingly Steve had taken his eye off this ball too, and as I was locked out of the business account, there was nothing I could do about it, by way of transferring funds.

Referring back to my household budget and noting the various payment dates for each direct debit, I made the transfers actionable from the following month, giving me a little extra financial leeway with less to pay immediately from my secondary account. I was able to create a nice little financial cushion, whilst smiling and complying with Steve's request for me to leave the joint account.

If this is mirroring your life right now, please remember this: there is nothing more devastating in circumstances like these than a smiling assassin. Had I unleashed Psycho Bitch when Steve kicked me out of my life and off the bank account, he'd have been more alert to the possibility of me pulling a fast one on him. Neutralising my ego, whilst outwardly soothing and understanding Steve's need for a longstanding bank account, sympathising with his position and being perfectly reasonable, no alarm bells went off in his head. This allowed me to swim beneath the surface arranging things to suit me best. Here's another of my favourite quotes from The Art of War: *Feign weakness, then conquer.*

Steve candidly told me that the loan outstanding on the house was screwing with his ability to get another mortgage. That and being 45 years of age couldn't have helped. Astoundingly, he asked if I would consider buying him out of the house; with all the buttons I was sitting on presumably? I reminded him of how all of my nest eggs had gone into the business, that I had always invested in him, his training and equipment, and now I was penniless with his two children to care and provide for, scrimping an existence from government benefits. Steve reiterated how the house was screwing him over, and how he hated the idea of having to rent. Poor lamb was really having his nose pressed up against the mirror of consequences, but there was nothing I could – or would – do to help him.

Concerned about the stunts he could pull in respect of Sofia's upcoming birthday I asked him, in front of her, if he was still happy to pay for her health and beauty party. He said he was, but he couldn't afford the cinema trip and subsequent meal afterwards, as money was exceptionally tight. You know that Oprah Winfrey quote I keep quoting: "*If you do your best in each situation, it leaves you in the best possible position in the next situation*"? Well, the reverse is true, and now it was Steve's turn to start finding that out: dish shit out, get shit back.

Fissures

Bearing in mind Steve and I had told the children their time with him would be only slightly less than usual, that he was just choosing to sleep somewhere else, that he would talk to them every night and see them every Sunday. Yeah, well now he was starting to walk that back too. Now he wanted to lessen the number of Sundays from every week to a couple of times a month, just as I had predicted; *dammit*. He was complaining because he and Helen hadn't spent an entire weekend together and made clear he was putting her ahead of the children, again. This fact was not lost on a heartbroken and frequently weeping Sofia.

To his credit though, Steve did indeed attend and pay for Sofia's health and beauty birthday party; even allowing Sofia and her friends to paint his nails and give him banana smoothie facials. It was like Sofia had flashes of her Real Daddy back again, now that he was unchaperoned. From there we went back to Mallie's as planned and then out to dinner. It was awkward and stilted, but civilised. Everyone worked hard to keep it as light and enjoyable as possible for Sofia, and obviously someone else paid the bill, for which I remain truly thankful [*sincere apologies for not knowing or remembering who*].

The following morning was Sofia's actual birthday and Steve was several hours late. I tried to distract her by busting out my embarrassing Mummy moves whilst playing Dance Party on the Wii, but she still ended up spending endless tearful hours just staring out of the window, waiting for him to arrive. There was no explanation when he did arrive either, but he had bought her the laptop we discussed, so she smiled at least once before he left quickly again to be with Helen.

Christmas wasn't a lot better. He arrived with a lot of tat wrapped up for the kids, along with a sumptuous Christmas bouquet of deep red roses [*an old Christmas Eve tradition of ours*] and a £15 iTunes gift card for me [*another Christmas tradition, WTF?*]. I was stunned, confused and stated without apologising that I had nothing for him. Any funds I had been able to cobble together had gone towards the children's Christmas presents, and our Christmas dinner. In fairness however, Steve understood this and was perfectly gentlemanly about it. Huh, another unchaperoned Real Steve flash. How curious.

Steve spent two hours with the children on Christmas morning before choosing to eat his Christmas dinner sat next to Helen's chain-smoking elderly mother. How lovely. To this day I don't understand where *my Steve* went, although I obviously have my suspicions. The same Steve who detested smoking and reeking of cigarettes. Oh, how *my Steve* had fallen, to choose this personal nightmare over his once beloved little children. How compromised can one man be?

I pitied him. He was about to endure his own private hell, for however many hours, and for what? He would be appalled by the stench on his clothes and in his hair, whilst he waited for his turn to shower once they'd all gotten home. Urgh, what a horribly expensive price to pay, to make Helen happy; but that's the nature of infatuation folks. It's a shame he couldn't, or wouldn't, sacrifice himself even a fraction of the same amount to make his children as happy, but it remains his loss.

During the evening on New Year's Eve – Helen's birthday, don't forget – Steve had an emotional breakdown on the phone to Sofia, sobbing his heart out and promising to make everything right. Sofia had never seen Steve so much as tear up watching The Lion King, much less experience this level of deep emotional pain and anguish.

Their conversation started normally enough, with him asking what she'd been up to that day. Then Steve started talking about our Big Ben midnight ritual, telling Sofia she could ring him if she wanted to, if she was still awake. Sofia crushed him by replying that she just wanted 2013 to be over and didn't want to see the New Year in. She went on to say how 2013 had been the worst year of her life, as Steve started getting tearful, saying he was sorry for ruining her year. He progressively got more upset, openly sobbing in places, saying how it was all so hard and he wanted to sort something out, so he could see them more. Sofia was certain, for the first time in a very long time, that she was talking to another flash of Real Daddy. This led to Sofia breaking down in floods of tears too, missing the deep closeness they had once shared in abundance, which was now as delicate and as fleeting as a butterfly's kiss. Was Real Daddy breaking through The Imposter's grip? Was this a bug or a feature?

I wasn't at all sure what to do for the best. On the one hand I was satisfied Steve was experiencing some of the pain he'd inflicted on the children, but on the other, my love and compassion for him wouldn't let me sit on my hands and not try to do something kindly about it. I opted to text him: "*Sofia's upset and has said you're upset too. Please feel free to come around and see the kids if you need to x*"

It took Steve about 20 minutes to reply: "*No I won't make it any worse for the kids I'll talk to them tomorrow*". I didn't respond to this, as I'd expected as much. How in the world could Steve leave Helen's house during her birthday and likely New Year's Eve party, to come and see the children? His life wouldn't have been worth living. It would have been histrionics a-go-go if he'd even thought about visiting Sofia and Alex on this night. What did make me smile quietly inside though, was the distinct possibility Steve's distress would have marred Helen's birthday. There's always a silver lining somewhere.

The Bastard's Back!

Early on Sunday 5 January 2014 Sofia was rushed into Casualty with suspected meningitis. Terrifyingly, she had many of the symptoms, including a rash that wouldn't blanche under the glass test. She was in extraordinary pain, significantly weak and frightened in the Paediatric Assessment Room. I was out of my skin afraid but trying to feign nonchalance... and to quell the overwhelming urge to throw up. I knew both children would be looking to me for their cues again, on how serious this all was, and I assured them both I would tell them when it was time to worry [*a shameless lie, because that was never going to happen*].

At 10.08am, once Sofia had been triaged, I sent Steve the following text message with an accompanying photograph of Sofia looking frail, pale and stoic in her hospital bed: "*Morning. Don't panic but we are at A&E for Sofia, initially as a precaution for several meningitis symptoms, many of which have been ruled out. There's still a rash, intermittent photophobia (aversion to light), muscle pain/stiffness/cramps in neck, stomach & legs + severe headache with nausea, no vomiting (yet). She's okay in herself & it's more precaution than anything. Waiting to be seen by a doctor, will keep you informed. Signal may be erratic & I may have to turn phone off, so bear that in mind*".

At 11.37am I sent this follow up text, having not received a reply from Steve: "*They're keeping her in for observation*". Still no response from Steve.

Once seen by a doctor, and once an assortment of test results had come back, Sofia was eventually discharged at around 1pm, now famished. The doctor had been able to rule out meningitis and could only conclude Sofia had some kind of viral infection [*isn't that what meningitis is?*], which I could treat with a combination of Calpol and Nurofen at home. Feeling better than she did when we arrived, but still very poorly overall, Sofia was more despondent by the distinct lack of daddy to cuddles whilst in A&E. Of course, Alex and I had been cuddling and making a fuss of her, trying to make her laugh and feel better, but this daddy's girl had wanted her daddy too. With her eyes brimming with tears, head bowed, and heart crushed, we made our way back to the car.

I assured her repeatedly that I had text and WhatsApp'd Steve twice with updates but hadn't had a reply yet. I had deliberately covered all bases, but knew they had Wi-Fi (to facilitate the WhatsApp service) and lived within a strong signal area (to facilitate the mobile phone and text service). Obviously, this didn't make Sofia feel any better, as she knew full well that he would be with Helen, Oliver and Emily, when he should have been with her. Why hadn't he come to her? What father, in his right mind, would deny comfort to his baby girl, who was afraid and in pain?

Whilst the WhatsApp messages had remained "unread", I was all but certain the text duplicates had been read. This gave Steve plausible deniability later, when excuses for his absence beside his ailing baby girl were called for. My guess is, Steve may have been convinced this was nothing more than a ruse to get him around to see us, because I was in the habit of sneaking my children into Casualty at stupid O'clock on Sunday mornings, to have their painted pale faces photographed in hospital beds for shits and giggles. Nothing made me feel more alive than abusing NHS resources in this way [*sarcasm!*], but Steve would not be budged from his precious alone time with Helen.

[258]

I tried to distract Sofia by asking her what she fancied to eat. As she'd felt nauseous all morning, which was now subsiding, the trick is to eat anything you fancy, and Sofia fancied croissants. This would require a pit stop at Sainsburys on the way home, where I would endeavour to pick up anything else she fancied, just to encourage her to eat something. Besides, she'd had a bloody horrible morning in pain, being poked at and prodded, with bloods taken and the humiliation of peeing into a thimble, she deserved a treat.

So did Alex for that matter, who'd been ripped from his sleep unfed, in my haste to get Sofia to hospital. None of us had washed our faces or brushed our teeth, we were minging. Alex hadn't eaten and hadn't complained about it all day. He was *Mummy's Big Handsome*, and had looked after Sofia, getting her books to read and toys to play with, cuddling her and being generally adorable, kind and wonderful.

This beautiful boy needed a treat too, but offered to share Sofia's croissants, because he knew I didn't have much money. My heart burst all over him in the shape of a million tear-soaked kisses and a big squeezie lift-up cuddle in the middle of Sainsburys. He gave me his *"I know you love me, but please stop doing that because people are watching"* smile before they chose their croissants and pain au chocolat treats. My credit card willingly took the hit.

We arrived home and Alex helped Sofia get comfortable on the sofa with a drink, as I put the oven on to ~~nuke~~ err... gently warm the croissants. Once appropriately heated, and not in the least bit charred or overdone, we all settled down together to eat, cuddle and recover from what had been a distressing morning. At 1.26pm I received the following text and WhatsApp from Steve: *"I have only just seen text sorry, how is she now?"* Realising this was likely to result in a phone call, I made him wait eleven minutes, to finish eating and cuddling, before responding at 1.37pm: *"We're home now. They ran a million tests, ruled out meningitis, although she was symptomatic, and determined "it's a virus". Meningitis can also be viral, which is why they were so worried. They found they could bring her temperature down with Calpol and Nurofen (i.e.: what I have at home) and discharged her. If I can't control her temperature, I'm to take her back to A&E pronto".* To which Steve responded: *"Okay, that's good, poor Sofia! Keep me posted please and give her a big hug from me".*

I didn't respond to this text at all because I was barely able to hold onto myself, and Sofia was my priority. Unleashing Psycho Bitch would have achieved nothing more than making Sofia feel worse, and that was unthinkable. My anger and disgust with Steve were locked away, with a solemn promise to unleash them one day, when the time was right. I couldn't believe he wasn't going to visit his little girl, who was unwell enough to warrant a trip to Casualty.

His baby girl who'd had blood taken and her body examined whilst in immense pain and feeling nauseous. She was ten years old, and only four months into trying to adjust in her life without him. Could he really not come and see her for himself, to hold her close and make her feel better, as her beloved Real Daddy would have done? Why couldn't he at least phone her to tell her how much he loved her and wanted her to feel better soon? Seriously, who was this creep? I did not update him further and waited to see if he phoned the kids later in the day, as promised during their last conversation on Friday night.

Sure enough he phoned just before 7pm, and Sofia asked him straight away why he hadn't been to see her, as she had really needed a daddy cuddle. He stated, as predicted, that he had seen the texts too late to visit her in hospital, although he said at one point he was going to come and collect Alex. Hmm, curious. If the first he'd known about the whole saga was post-hospital discharge time, then why was he going to come and collect Alex? Alex would have been on his way home with us? CLANG! Steve had just dropped the bottom out of his own excuse. Thinking about coming to get Alex, whilst Sofia was in A&E, clearly demonstrates he'd read the texts in the time before her discharge. My theory about them protecting their weekend time over Steve tending to his poorly daughter, was holding water. Sofia missed this, but I seethed.

Sofia however bit down on another angle: "*So you'd collect Alex, but not me?*" She then asked why he hadn't visited her, in the 5½ hours she'd been home, to which he actually replied: "*...because I was spending time with Helen*". Yep, theory confirmed. [*BASTARD!*] Openly weeping, Sofia said: "*Well that just confirms how important I really am to you. You chose to spend time with your replacement children instead of with me when I was poorly!*". At this point The Imposter appeared to step in and take charge of Steve's fragile psyche and told her defiantly that he wouldn't be phoning tomorrow night: "*...because these calls are so negative now*".

This was Helen's vernacular, not Steve's. I can only surmise she had been instructing him on what to say. This isn't how Steve spoke, and it wasn't who he'd previously been; callous and self-centred. He felt lost. He'd clearly lost sight of the fact he was the grown up in his relationship with the children, and that it was his responsibility to ensure the phone calls were, or remained, positive. Sofia had called him out for his atrocious decisions and choices, which he could not justify even to himself, so out came The Imposter in all of his obnoxious, childish splendour.

Teresa's Lip Curled

Steve's older sister, Teresa, phoned later that evening, to ask if the kids and I – plus Steve – were available on Friday night, for them to take us out to dinner. As we'd had Christmas at home, Teresa and Len wanted to visit, so they could give the kids their Christmas presents. Teresa also asked if it was possible to come with me to collect the kids from school, which we duly arranged. I explained to an otherwise oblivious Teresa why, after Sofia's meningitis scare, I didn't want Steve to be invited. I simply didn't believe I could resist pulling his arsehole over his head and didn't want to make a public spectacle of his rectal re-engineering. Teresa said she understood completely and was outwardly disgusted with Steve's behaviour, choices and priorities.

Teresa agreed to make alternative arrangements to see Steve whilst she was in the county, even if that meant visiting Helen's house again. Teresa had only visited Helen's house once before and didn't appreciate the three large adult Labradors either sitting on her feet, or sleep-kicking her legs and farting next to her on the sofa. Not once was her comfort assured whilst a guest. Once back at Mallie's, where they were staying overnight, Len went to greet Teresa at the door with a hug, but Teresa pushed him away until she'd had a bath; she felt filthy and was covered in dog hair apparently.

This surprised me because Steve had always been highly considerate in matters like this in the past. Teresa generally likes dogs, but she doesn't appreciate being subjected to them on this level; she felt it rude. You see, Teresa is a masterful and generously accommodating hostess when you visit her home, so she was perhaps expecting a similar level of etiquette and care whilst a guest in Helen's?

[262]

Teresa's impression whilst visiting Steve, was that he was trying to force his relationship with Helen onto her and the rest of his family. At one point he grabbed Helen's hand almost defiantly, and held it as if to say, "*So there!*" Positively child-like. Teresa also felt Helen was trying too hard to play happy families and said that it was all really rather awkward; not at all natural or authentic.

Teresa would tell me in the months to come how, after the funeral service of their Uncle Don, Teresa had offered Steve and Helen a lift to the post funeral reception. To her surprise, both Helen and Steve got into the back of her car "*...and started snogging*", as Teresa recalled. Understandably stunned, Teresa tried to jokingly tell them: "*Hey, cut that out you two!*" only to be told by Helen to "*Just shut up and drive!*" Yes, really. Obviously, I wasn't there, but I have no reason to disbelieve Teresa, who's never lied about a damned thing to me in all the time I've known her. If the truth would be too inflammatory, Teresa would now prefer to say nothing at all, or to skirt the issue with genial obfuscation than lie. How tragic of these two middle-aged adulterers behaving like devil-may-care teenagers. Boy, didn't they have a point to prove, bless, 'em? I feel kind of sad for them.

Okay, I'm over it now.

A Word In My Shell-Like

After a long and hectic day running the gamut of human emotion in Casualty with Sofia, I needed a soothing act of friendship before sleep, so I phoned Lauren. I apprised her of Sofia's progress following the A&E trip, of Steve's descent into deadbeat daddery [*new word!*], and of my conversation with Teresa. As is her way, Lauren listened intently as I spoke, before breaking open the vault of wisdom. She advised me how she had felt on numerous occasions that I had shied away from confronting Steve, and this was another of those occasions. Lauren believed I should have gone medieval on Steve's arse, for failing to come and comfort Sofia. Lauren's point wasn't without merit, and from the outside I could easily see how my choices were perceived in this way.

However, as my spiritual connection had strengthened, particularly since being severed from Helen's heavily weighted influence, I have come to trust my instincts and spiritual guidance implicitly. So much so, that prior to making any significant action or decision, I ask my Guides to help me say and do all the right things, at the right time. This will then invite a word in my shell-like (my right ear), telling me to shut up and be still, or to say something specific, or to take a particular course of action. The more I have listened to, trusted and implemented this guidance, the easier my life has become, and the better things have worked out for me. The only time I get myself into trouble, is when I ignore or override the guidance I've asked for. That little voice in your ear, that gut feeling you get in the pit of your stomach, should be listened to – with one important caveat.

IMPORTANT CAVEAT: That little voice in your ear should never tell you to hurt yourself or others. If the little voice in your ear tells you to harm yourself or others, please seek professional, medical attention immediately. Spiritualism is only ever about love, light and healing. Instinct is only ever about survival and growth. There must be harm to none.

So, back to my chat with Lauren. Whilst I understood her point of view about me shying away from confronting Steve, I was asking for and applying the guidance I was getting from my spiritual Entourage. I explained how I sympathised with Steve's predicament, how I accepted a degree of responsibility for where he now found himself, and didn't want to compound his misery, or make his situation worse. Whilst Steve had no compunction about making my life more difficult, that was going to be his karma to carry and eventually deal with. My priority was to lead my children into a bright new positive future, with as clean a karma as possible, so we could fully enjoy the fruits of our labours when we got them.

To hit back at Steve, every time he hit me [*figuratively speaking*], would only have escalated the war between us. I had to stay focused on my goal, which was for him to ultimately come back to himself and father these babies; because that's what my babies wanted. One of us had to be the grown up and, whilst Steve didn't appear to be in his right mind right now, that grown up had to be me. I had to walk the walk, spiritually speaking. I had to live what I professed to believe in. I had to rise above it all – in love and light – and to take the blows; some of which I richly deserved.

There was also another aspect to why I resisted chewing Steve out in a blaze of anger, notably I was still in a healing phase of energy repair and conservation. The children were rightly taking the lion share of my attention and energy, and so confronting and fighting with Steve, would have left me dangerously depleted. These babies needed me more now than ever, so I couldn't waste my energetic resources on such a low value entity as Steve. I had to guard my energy like gold. The energy I saved by avoiding unnecessary spats with Steve, I spent loving and repairing my babies during the day, whilst thinking and strategizing at night. I had become so much more

[265]

aware of what was really worth my energy, and now I had to put that learning into practice.

One final point. Do you remember the George Bernard Shaw quote from earlier in the book: *Never wrestle with pigs, because you both get dirty and the pig likes it?* Well, be under no illusion, Steve and Helen needed to feed off my energy, as they had always done, so why would I spoon feed it to them now? They needed to point to any Psycho Bitch clap back from me and use it to justify their betrayal and adultery. Granted, when no such Psycho Bitch behaviour materialised, they lied about me having an affair (...which led to them getting together blah, blah, blah), but again, this is their karma to carry, and they can have at it! At the end of the day, it's always the ones with dirty hands who are pointing the fingers.

By doing my best in every situation, by rising above every heinous provocation, by accurately recording every detail and corresponding piece of evidence, instead of shouting it out for the townsfolk to hear, I put myself in the best possible position in all subsequent situations. Just watch how this plays out. No, it wasn't easy. Those bastards tested me every day, but I continued to rise above them. I can't tell you the number of times Paul, Lauren, Hayley, Carrie or Eve had to talk me down off a ledge, but they soothed me by reminding me of my ultimate mission. This world is nothing without friends, aunts and brothers like these, and there's no growth without challenge. Although tested every day, I could feel myself changing, getting stronger and wiser, and growing into who I will eventually become. I was beginning to emerge from my chrysalis.

By rising above their provocation, I gave Steve and Helen nothing to throw back at me, other than their lies of course, and the truth will always out, so

I'm not worried about that. If the people around them, notably Steve's family, truly believed I was capable of having an affair and betraying Steve in this way, then they never really knew me and are no loss to me now. If you're in a similar battle just remember this: **every time you engage with stupid, every time you respond to provocation, every time you accept an invitation to an argument, you are essentially handing your opponent ammunition to fire back at you.** Don't do it! Silence is a powerful and vastly underutilised response, so maintain your dignity. Why? Because your opponent(s) can't decode silence, and they most certainly can't misquote you to serve their own agenda. The more silent I was, the harder Helen worked to try and tempt me into surfacing, so she could know what was going on in my head. Hmm. No thanks. Access denied.

Not knowing what I was thinking was a major problem for Helen when we were friends. Now, knowing how dangerously my mind can operate when provoked, she was desperate to know the direction from which I would attack her. Ahh, but I don't attack anyone – love and light baby – but because she was judging me by her own standards, my refusal to engage confounded her. The art of war is always to destabilise your opponent, so give them what they least expect. In my case, this was silence and stillness, because I can be somewhat red hot and blustery when pissed off.

The problem for Steve and Helen now was that I was so far beyond being merely pissed off, because my babies had been hurt. Now I was white steel and icy, whilst quietly digging the ground out from beneath their feet. My plan was to tend to the children before all else; love them, settle them and make them strong. Only then would I turn my attention to Steve and Helen, and not a minute too soon. No one knew when that would be, including me, but evidently it worried the bejesus out of Helen.

Dinner With The In-Laws

So, Friday 10 January 2014 arrived, and Teresa and Len duly travelled from Berkshire. They stopped en route to collect Mallie, which I wasn't thrilled about, but I was trying to keep the family channel open for the kids. We all went back to our house after the school run, where the kids opened their belated Christmas presents, and Alex was particularly thrilled with the Superman costume they'd gifted him. The costume went on in a flash and he was chuffed to bits, keeping it on in the restaurant and throughout dinner, cape flapping in the air as he zoomed.

Whilst Mallie was in the loo, Teresa apprised me of how Mallie had recently chided Steve for being short and impatient with the children. Even she had noticed a change in him. Good God, I almost fell out of my chair! Steve had always been Golden Bollocks to Mallie and could do no wrong. For Mallie to have noticed he wasn't himself, things must have been worse than I thought. According to Teresa, Mallie had told Steve to go back to being the daddy he used to be, and that everyone in the family had been disgusted he hadn't seen the children since Christmas morning.

Real Steve could not have gone a single day without holding them tightly and telling them how much he loved them. He would then go into "Pest Mode", where he would flubber (blow raspberries on) their bellies, give them wedgies, or stick a wet finger in their ear. The kids would object loudly, but they loved every second of it. The glee in their eyes and their infectious giggles would light up our lives and swell our hearts to bursting point. They also loved being dangled by their ankles, thrown up on his shoulders to see higher, and held like a baby whilst he stroked their cheeks and ran his fingers through their hair. He used to be so fun, loving, kind and nurturing to them, and it still breaks our hearts to remember him this way. Where did he go? We all still miss this version of who he was. The children still love him deeply, despite how he now chooses to stay away from them.

I told Teresa I would never hurt Steve and was trying to be as compassionate and understanding of his (possible midlife crisis) condition, but his treatment of Sofia over the meningitis scare was sailing dangerously close to unforgiveable. Teresa said that if Len had done to her what Steve was doing to me, he wouldn't still be walking. I nodded my appreciation of this support and explained my love and light philosophy. I didn't want Steve to suffer, or to bring suffering to him, as that would have eventually brought it back to either me or mine, with the power of three. Ancient wisdom instructs us: "Before embarking upon a journey of revenge, first dig two graves", because revenge will claim you too, and of that you should have no doubt.

Whilst Teresa may have broken Len's legs in similar circumstances, I decided I needed to prepare for battle against this worsening version of Steve. I reluctantly accepted it was necessary to continue retaining, collating and recording all future communications with him, to defend against any claim for shared custody. He was being far too inconsistent for me to trust him. One day it would seem like he'd accepted the children's wishes about never seeing Helen again, but in the next breath he would discuss shared custody again. He could ramble on to his heart's content, I cared not what he said, but if he made a legal move, I had to be ready to decapitate it without breaking a sweat.

Teresa also went on to tell me how her daughter, Jess, was not inviting Helen to her upcoming nuptials in April. I had informed Teresa in November that I wouldn't be attending the wedding and was respectfully stepping aside to allow Steve to attend without controversy, in his capacity as Jess' blood uncle. This was despite Jess knowing me as her aunt since she was four years old. Steve had repeatedly intimated to Teresa and Jess that he had wanted Helen to go, but it was Jess' big day, and what she wanted overrode any new interloper's thirst for the limelight. Teresa gently suggested to Steve that he took the kids, as a polite way of standing Jess' ground re: Helen. Apparently, Helen had gone down like a lead balloon within the family, but they smiled and tolerated her for the love of Steve. Who'd have thunk?

The rest of the meal passed without an international incident, which was as much as anyone could have realistically asked for. Steve text at 6pm to ask if the kids were ready for their chat, so I informed him we were out, and that I would let him know when we were home, at approximately 7pm. He replied that was fine, and he'd ring again between 7pm - 7.15pm. All very civil. We didn't get home until 8.30pm however, and the kids were sleepy. As Alex had been unbelievably difficult to settle at bedtimes since Steve's departure four months previously, I decided to strike whilst the iron was hot and just put him to bed, without speaking to Steve.

The problem was, I couldn't guarantee which Steve the kids were going to get: Real Daddy or Fake Daddy. Either way was going to enliven and upset them one way or another, so I made an executive decision to let them try and get the best night's sleep possible. Fully anticipating a ferocious push back from Steve, I put them to bed anyway. I then text him to explain we had been out later than anticipated, knowing full well he would soon learn we'd spent the time with his family, but I certainly didn't offer that information. I explained, again, how Alex had been difficult to settle for sleep since Steve had left, but he was sleepy now and I wanted to capitalise on this, so he could bank some serious sleep hours. Surprisingly, Steve text back saying he understood, and thanked me for letting him know. Huh, civil again? So, it could be done?

Alex Draws A Line In The Sand

Steve phoned the kids the following evening and all was going well until Sofia asked if he was going to collect them the following day. Bearing in mind they hadn't seen him in over two weeks at this point, plus he'd refused to comfort Sofia during her meningitis scare, so the children were no less than desperate to see him. He told her he wouldn't be collecting them because they were packing to move to a new house.

Desperate, Sofia asked if it was possible to see him for just half a day, to which he replied flatly: "No". Now desperately hurt, Sofia snapped back through outraged tears: *"Enjoy your time with your new family! It just goes to prove how unimportant we are to you now!"*, before hanging up. He didn't call back to either make things right with Sofia, or to speak with Alex, he just ran away like a frightened little boy. Again.

How do you explain to a five-year-old boy that his daddy doesn't want to talk to, or see him? Alex has these beautifully huge blue eyes, which just looked up at me as they filled with the tears of more heartbreak. All I could do was explain how they were clearly moving to a new house soon, that the old house needed packing up and his daddy was busy, but that was never going to cut it. I cuddled them both and told them they had me, would always have me and I loved them enough for the entire world. I then started my campaign to claim Pest Mode as my own, and duly started flubbering their bellies and tickling them to try and take their minds off of their now deadbeat dad.

Later that day I was following Alex upstairs for bedtime when he said: *"I want daddy to come back, but he's not going to come back. Please will you get us another daddy?"* We sat on his bed and sobbed. I had chosen Steve to be the father of my children because I thought he would be the last man on earth to do exactly what he was doing. Alex had just drawn a line in the sand. Something had clicked in his five-year-old logic. All he wanted was to be loved, so if his biological sperm donor wouldn't do it, he was ready to accept a non-biological upgrade. I could have horsewhipped Steve for squandering Alex's love and adoration in this way. It will ultimately be Steve's loss though, as Alex continues to thrive, despite the pulsing unrequited love for his daddy.

As I was tucking Sofia into bed I heard in my right ear: *"He's not enjoying himself"*, along with a vision of Steve packing boxes. Well, in all honesty, who does enjoy packing boxes and moving to a new house? But I think there was a broader point being made. Steve had run away from me, the children, and the business to relax, have fun and enjoy himself with Helen which, as decisions go – and as he must have been discovering by now – was nothing short of a hot mess. For all the stress Steve had been trying to escape from, he'd actually plopped himself into something far worse; like out of the frying pan and into a septic tank. *Oops!*

Alex continued to take my breath away and make me cry with his matter-of-fact pronouncements. One day, aspiring teacher Sofia, was listening to Alex practicing his reading, whilst I was sitting on the stairs, eavesdropping and smiling proudly with his progress. He read flawlessly, but after he read the words: *"Where's Daddy?"* in the book, Alex stopped and said: *"I don't have a Daddy"*, which reduced us all to tears again. I got up from my spy stairs and went to cuddle and console them. We truly are the little family that snot built. A bit gross, but true.

Paul's Woes Worsen

A little background for context. In 2006 Paul was working for a pharmaceutical company, and was crushed between industrial racking in the warehouse, and a reversing forklift truck. As you can imagine Paul was seriously hurt, which has resulted in a lifetime of pain management and incapacity benefits. Paul now has the mobility of an arthritic 90-year-old man, and numerous medical complications associated with the accident.

The pharmaceutical company bore down on Paul like a beast, sending threatening correspondence during his recovery, daring him to take legal action and denying the existence of CCTV footage of the accident. By the time he had learnt how to manage his life changing injuries sufficiently, his wife had left him, and he was physically, emotionally and financially broken. Clinical depression set in with a vengeance. Hurtling towards divorce and unable to entirely fend for himself, he had no other option but to move back in with Mum who, as a semi-retiree, could take care of him. He was 33.

Then in the spring of 2010, the Department for Work and Pensions (DWP) unilaterally decided Paul was fit for work and rendered him not entitled to the Personal Independence Payment (PIP), which he and Mum now depended on. This plunged them way beneath the poverty line and significantly into debt almost overnight, as bills were paid with savings and then overdrafts. The situation got so bad they resorted to transporting the single toilet roll they had in the house upstairs at night, and downstairs in the morning. Paul was able to reclaim his PIP on appeal almost a year later in 2011, but significant financial damage had been done.

In November 2012 the DWP did it again, claiming Paul was fit for work when it was well documented by numerous medical professionals he wasn't. They revoked his PIP again. This plunged Mum and Paul back below the poverty line and further into debt, having not fully recovered from the last time, just over a year ago. Paul tells me now this had a devastating effect on Mum mentally.

This was the straw that broke her spirit and, whilst still helping Paul to fight and appeal the decision, Mum was kind of broken by a lifetime of ceaseless heartbreak and struggle. Mum became combative and insular, understandably seeing threat and peril everywhere. This was not how she had imagined her golden years to be, and she became bitter and hardened. Evidently it was this version of Mum I had unknowingly slammed up against when making my final attempt at a reconciliation before she died. We were truly doomed.

It was Mum's strict household budgeting model I would later adopt in the years to come, as she and Paul would discuss how little they could get away with eating each week. This is one of the single biggest reasons for Mum's significant weight loss (in addition to the advanced and undiagnosed liver cancer), and why Paul looked the way he did, when I saw him for the first time in years, on the day of Mum's funeral. His overcoat looked like it was hanging on a clothes hanger, if you remember. He was skeletal and so frail, and still only 40 years old at that point. He had spent almost seven years in unrelenting agony, two of which in unrelenting starving agony. That kind of suffering etches itself indelibly onto your face, I can tell you.

From my adorable, blonde-haired and blue-eyed angel of a baby brother, Paul had now become a hunched and shuffling crippled man, barely able to walk even with a stick. He had become too weak and demoralised from the seven bells of shit the DWP, his ex-wife, life and the death of his beloved Mum had kicked out of him, but he vowed to fight the DWP – *again!* – for all he was worth. The alternative was certain death by either starvation or incapacity and misadventure, once Mum was no longer around to look after him. The stress and anxiety from fighting the DWP however almost killed him too, but whilst Mum was gone, I was now on the scene, and no one treats my brother like that and gets away with it. I was ready and willing to suit up for battle, but Paul was waiting for the results of his appeal, so I could stand down for now.

On Friday 20 September 2013, the day after Mum's funeral, Paul dragged himself slowly to another DWP Appeals Hearing in the centre of town and won. Again. Now all he had to do was wait for his claim to be processed and the backdated funds to be released. This took months. Months where the nights were getting colder, and he couldn't afford heating. Months of starvation, because he couldn't afford enough food. Months of living in unhygienic conditions, because he couldn't afford help or do it himself. This man struggled to wash, to feed himself and needed a coat hanger to help him get dressed. This man's mobility was shot to hell and with no chance of parole. His injuries and his condition were for life, but the DWP kept trying to insist he was fit for work. What work was he fit for exactly? No, no one ever could satisfactorily answer that question.

On a day in January 2014, whilst waiting for his PIP to be backdated and processed, Paul asked me if I could lend him £10 because what little benefits he was still getting were gone, and his heating had run out (they'd had to install a prepayment metre when the utility bills had become a debt). I asked him if he had enough food, and he hadn't so I sent him £30, which is all I could cobble together. No, I couldn't afford it either, but he wouldn't survive the winter nights without heating or food, so more sacrifices were made, and my household budget finagled it.

Neither of us had enough of anything, but what we did have we shuffled between us, depending on whose need was the greatest at the time. This is what family is to us. We'd had to pull together to make ends meet like this when we were kids, when Noel was having his foreign affairs and not sending his salary home from Canada or Japan. Mum was working as many hours as she could (around our school hours) in the local chemist, which was never quite enough. I watched her plan out her income versus expenditure with stress etched upon her face. I helped her with the second job she took, of packaging greeting cards and gift bags at home, but we were barely treading water until Noel returned home. Our childhood and past experiences gave Paul and I the tools we needed to eventually deal with the challenges of adulthood, and we stood unified in the face of adversity. Not strong, no, not yet, but definitely together.

That's not to say we didn't feel sorry for ourselves, of course we did, because both of our lives had imploded at exactly the same time. It felt unfair and way too much to handle, all at the same time. We would regularly wallow in our little pity parties, but after a certain amount of wallowing, we began to realise the wallowing wasn't actually getting us anywhere, so we began to focus more on what we wanted, than on what was wrong. We found that if we replaced *"Why is this happening to me?"* with *"What is this trying to teach me?"* everything shifted.

When panic or anxiety hit either of us, we would stop and ask each other: *"What can you do about this now, RIGHT NOW?"* If there was something we could do right now in that instant, we would go and do it without further delay. If there was nothing we could right now, but could at a later point in time, we would diarise it and do it then as a priority, no excuses. If there was literally nothing that we could do about it ever, we worked on our ability to let that shit go. No, it wasn't easy – it never is – but with relentless practice, we're both now experts at it.

Lessons Repeat Until Full And Learned

Here's a little exercise we use, which may help you. We visualised the issue(s) we had zero control or influence over as two gigantically large, overstuffed and heavy suitcases. We then imagined ourselves trying to lift or shift these massive suitcases, even an inch without success, and endeavoured to *feel* the pointless redundancy of our endeavours, as vividly as possible. When our fruitless pursuit became painfully apparent, we were more easily persuaded to let it go.

There is truth in the wise old maxim: *The act of worrying is like a rocking chair; it gives you something to do, but it doesn't get you anywhere.* We could have pushed and pulled on the suitcases all we wanted, but we were never going to be able to carry them. For that matter, we could equally attempt to shoulder barge the white cliffs of Dover, in an effort to shove them into Derbyshire, but they ain't ever gonna budge. Worrying is just as futile. If there's something you can do, do it, otherwise let it go.

The times I have over thought a thing to exhaustion, trying to address every variable, only for the one thing I hadn't considered to actually happen instead. The hours, days, weeks and decades I've wasted doing this, *urgh!* Do you know what I do now, now that I have matured and learnt from being burnt? Well, in the first instance and as a matter of habit, I always do my best in every situation, because it puts me in the best position for the next situation. Come on, you must have seen that one coming?

Seriously though, if I live my life in the default setting of honesty, integrity,

[277]

hard work, humility and love and light generally, I have no lies to remember or shady practices to defend. It means I won't have anyone coming after me looking for money, revenge or reparation of any kind. This equals less stress and a life lived in inner peace, which in and of itself is priceless. Then, should an unforeseen situation present itself, I do...

1. What I can, whilst avoiding denial
2. When I can, avoiding procrastination; and I always...
3. Do my best, avoiding laziness whilst staring down all fear

These three modus operandi require extreme self-awareness and honesty. You must be aware of when you're lying to yourself and denying reality, and then having the will and strength of character to stop and course correct without delay. This means accepting you make mistakes, that you're not perfect and will forever be a work in progress. It means accepting personal responsibility for everything that happens in your life, good or bad, and dealing with it. Yes, I know it sounds kind of obvious, but not everyone can do this, or is willing to do it. I'm writing this book for those who can and do.

Nowadays I only play the cards on the table in front of me. Whilst there are many cards in the pack, they're not necessarily meant for me, so I play the cards I get, rather than fretting about those I might get (and equally, might *not* get). I explore this hypothesis more fully in the Nine of Diamonds chapter later, but for now, you need to know how I am mindful and protective of my energy levels; conserving them ruthlessly. I have to justify my physical and cognitive energy expenditure before spending it, so I don't waste it as I have done in the past. Let me tell you another true story.

When I was 17 years old, I was living with Noel in the pub he and Mum had once managed together. Mum and Paul had moved out, and I felt like I was holding down the fort all alone. It could legitimately be argued I was living with an "under siege" mentality. My relationship with Noel was toxic nuclear waste, but I seemed to thrive off the energy. Rather than let the smallest of transgressions pass by, I would ramp up the animosity to DEFCON 1; possibly still trying to make him pay for all that he'd put Mum through.

Just before UN peacekeepers were called in, Noel's assistant manager, Neil, stepped in and took me to one side to share his wisdom, which I will paraphrase for you now. He said something along the lines of: *"You're 17 now and so full of anger, it's not healthy. You're in danger of getting to 35, looking back and lamenting the time you've wasted on these issues; which you probably won't even remember the details of, then. Let it go and get on with your life. Enjoy your youth and stop wasting your time and energy"*.

I scoffed at Neil and thought him a fool, certain in my youthful arrogance that I would always have the energy and inclination to fight all comers. No. Nope. Not even close. As time marched on, I began to realise how wise Neil's counsel had been, and that I had been the fool all along. Looking back now, I can see how I squandered too much of my youth and vitality on things that just didn't matter or were in defence of others whilst I took on their battles. This had been the pattern of my life since the age of twelve. I hated injustice or emotional carnage of any kind, so would seek to sort it out and make it better. To this day I feel compelled to help others. I just can't help myself helping people; but I digress.

Shortly after Steve's departure, my mind's eye showed me the movie of my life to date, which echoed Sylvia's wise words of spiritual counsel closely.

From the age of twelve I had been fighting Mum's battles (Noel, Maggie, anorexia, financial distress). From the age of 18, I had been fighting Steve's battles (the hypercritical imprinting, subsequent low self-esteem, grief, depression) and facilitating his dreams (the business and sodding caravan ownership). Then from the age of 40, along came Helen whose battle against Lee I gradually became involved in, like a frog in a pan.

For the uninitiated: if you throw a frog into a pan of boiling water, it'll jump straight out, reflexively. However, if you place a frog in a pan of tepid water and slowly heat, the frog won't realise it's being boiled alive until it's too late. Where Helen was concerned, I was that frog. By the time I realised what she'd been up to, whilst pretending to be my friend, it was too late I was a goner and had been evicted from my life. Make sure this never happens to you by simply stopping to take stock of who you are, what you want, what you're doing, why you're doing it and what your genuine levels of happiness are. Don't sleepwalk through life as I have done, because one day you will open your eyes and won't recognise who you are, where you are, or how you got there. Believe me.

Can anyone here point to the phase in my life where I was fighting my own battles and working to achieve my own goals and dreams? Hmm, no, neither can I. I had allowed myself to be swept up into the goals, dreams and lives of other people, with no thought of following my own. With Mum, Steve and Helen now gone, here was my chance to change something.

You see, life is a series of lessons and those lessons will either stay or repeat until they are full and learned. Clearly, I had not learned my lesson from Mum, and so it repeated with Steve. Then, when I hadn't learnt my lesson via Mum and/or Steve, Helen was sent to deliver the smack across the chops necessary to wake me up from whatever stupor I had been sleepwalking through.

Now look at my Horrible September from this perspective: First, Mum died and left my life. Second, Steve ended our marriage and left my life. Finally, Helen's treachery and betrayal were revealed, and she left my life. 1, 2, 3, gone within three weeks. Other than the kids (which isn't an apple for apples comparison for obvious reasons), I had no one whose successful transit through life was now more important than my own.

Yes, Paul has his challenges, but part of his journey has been learning to navigate them himself, without relying upon a strong female influence in his life (Mum and Rhea) to lean upon. I had been freed and gifted an opportunity to make Act II of my life better than anything that had gone before. This epiphany compounded my realisation that I may just be too relieved to grieve.

Do you ever ask yourself: *"Why does this keep happening to me?"* Okay, that's common, but the better question you could be asking yourself is: *"Why do I keep allowing this to happen?"* Are you sleepwalking through your life, not recognising your life lessons for what they are; or even worse, denying them? Are you churning over the same situations time and again through force of habit, rather than mindfully slowing down or stopping long enough to take stock? As Ferris Bueller said during his infamous day off: *"Life moves pretty fast. If you don't stop and look around once in a while, you could miss it"*. Wise words for a truant!

Can you see the difference between *"Why does this keep happening to me?"* and *"Why do I keep allowing this to happen?"* The first is taking an extrinsic position, you're viewing the situation as something being done to you. It is external and outside of your control or influence, it negates and surrenders personal responsibility. This will only feed your victim persona and heighten your sense of powerlessness. It's weak sauce. It's what you'd say if you operated within a "poor me" control drama [*read: The Celestine Prophecy by James Redfield for more on control dramas*].

The second question is strong, intrinsic, self-aware, honest and courageous. This question is posed by life's perpetual students, with inquisitive and open minds, willing to absorb or at least consider new information, techniques and theories. This question is posed by those who are unafraid to be wrong, to be taught and to be endlessly smoothed and enhanced by the Sandpaper of Life. This question is posed by those who reflect and think deeply about substance and consequences, and who pull problems up by the roots, rather than skimming over them with a lawnmower. The weeds skimmed over in the name of expediency and short-term gain will grow again (in the same place and ever more resilient), in the same way lessons will repeat until full and learned.

Emotionally Illiterate

As Steve was starting to plead poverty and was reluctantly complying with the children's wishes to never see Helen again, he had few places to take them on Sundays. So, he took them to Mallie's, where it was warm [*and by warm, I mean the central heating was on*] and she cooked them a Sunday roast.

During these visits to Mallie, without Helen and her brood, Sofia had Steve more to herself (sharing him with Alex wasn't an issue), and so she would cuddle him voraciously. These cuddles were lovely and soothed her troubled soul, to begin with. The closer to home time they got however, the deeper Sofia's sadness began to sink, knowing she would soon have to give him up again, until some undetermined time in the future. Sofia's heart was breaking, as she tried to absorb every last ounce of her Real Daddy's love and attention; she looked sad, because she was sad.

Mallie's reaction to witnessing Sofia's gradual decline into emotional pain and sorrow was to blurt out bluntly: *"What's the matter Droops?"*, or some other hurtful variation on the Droopy Drawers theme [*and I dare you to Google the literal meaning of Droopy Drawers*]. Wasn't it fucking obvious what the matter was?

This was a ten-year-old child still wrestling with the separation anxiety she was feeling for her once beloved and darling daddy. This was the little Daddy's Girl who had waited weeks for this moment of love and attention, where she didn't have to dilute him with the contrived energy of others, which was now about to end, and you're asking her what's wrong, whilst referring to her disparagingly? This happened every week Steve took the children

[283]

round there, and never once did he step in to shut his mother down.

Sofia asked Steve repeatedly to talk to his mother, and to ask she refrain from the name calling, but no avail. Sofia initially felt that she was wrong somehow, or oversensitive to be feeling sad as her time with Steve was ending; until I got hold of her and reframed her thinking. I reassured Sofia her feelings could never be wrong, and that in actual fact, they were perfectly acceptable and understandable given the circumstances. I encouraged Sofia to feel her feelings, because masking them or pretending they were something they were not, was unhealthy. I clarified that Sofia had correctly assessed the type of person Mallie is, and to not expect her to change now.

Then I gave Steve a stark and forthright ultimatum: either he could speak to his mother to tell her to stop addressing Sofia in this way, or I would, and he wouldn't like the outcome of that. He could either formulate a pleasing sentence structure to get his message across, without causing World War IV, or I would start World War IV in a heartbeat. Sofia simply had too much to be handling for a ten-year-old child as it was, without being exposed to the kind of shit Mallie was spurting in her direction. The rot was to stop here.

Steve vowed to speak to his mother and, whether he did or not we will never know, because he would never take the children to Mallie's again. I would for a while, but he didn't.

The Valentine's Night Massacre

A little background for context. For about a month prior to Valentine's Day 2014, Sofia had had a sense that "something big" was going to happen on 14 February. Not Valentine's Day, the 14 February specifically. She could be no more explicit than that, and so tried to put it out of her mind; but it kept coming back front and centre. We have never been a Valentine's Day kind of family, so there was certainly no excitement about getting a card from her crush at school or anything like that. Valentine's Day was always something other people did, and Clintons profited from. We operated more along the principle of showing and telling each other we loved them every day, not just on some arbitrary date in late winter. I know, romantic huh?

Being as similarly spiritual as I am, Sofia was then shown a non-specific WhatsApp message from Steve in her mind's eye. The message in the vision was blurry, and she couldn't make out what it said, which was frustrating but otherwise par for the course. We did our best to put it out of our minds and duly got on with our lives, until 14 February finally arrived.

Trying to manage Sofia's expectations, I pointed out that neither her spidey senses nor mental picture had decreed which 14 February "something big" was going to happen on. There was no guarantee anything was going to happen this year. This did little to quench her sense that "something big" was going to happen on this day, which was now stronger than ever. I must admit to chalking this up to some kind of wishful thinking. No. Nope. Not even close.

The day of 14 February 2014 was unremarkable. Both kids had great days at school, we had no additional issues to speak of at home and were looking forward to the weekend ahead. Steve was due to have the kids on Sunday, and I had made plans to see some friends, so all was looking as well as could be expected. This was a Friday night, and Steve hadn't spoken to the children since Tuesday night. In fairness though, this was largely due to Sofia having a school disco on the Wednesday night, and Alex attending karate on Thursday night. The kids were itching to catch up with him and to hear his voice again. They wanted him to squeezie hug them, kiss them goodnight and flubber their bellies, but their expectations of him had been lowered dramatically during the past five months. This was their new reality and they were gradually in the process of adapting.

I'd had to prompt Steve at 7.20pm on Tuesday night to call the kids, because it was rapidly approaching their bedtime. This was answered with a "Just finishing dinner" text, so imagine my surprise when I received a text at 5.51pm asking if the kids were ready to chat with him. As I wasn't expecting a message from Steve so early in the evening and was otherwise busy processing the kids with post-school homework, preparing/eating dinner and baths etc, I didn't see his message until 6.42pm. This is our WhatsApp exchange, which I obviously still have saved.

[Steve]: *Are the kids ready?* 17:51

[Karan]: *Yes* 18:42

[Steve]: *I'll call them tomorrow* 19:33

[Karan]: *They're waiting for you!* 19:33

[Karan]: *Why not talk tonight, you last spoke to them Tuesday!* 19:33

[Steve]: *I'll call them tomorrow!* 19:34

[Karan]: *You can try* 19:34

[Karan]: *They both have said they are desperate to talk to you* 19:35

Steve then rang the kids and was openly furious. Apparently my 50-minute delay in responding was unacceptable to him, but he had clearly not factored in how much I had to do every day, that the kids had stuff to do and I had things like dinner to prepare. Why was he texting so bloody early anyway, when I'd had to habitually prompt him to call gone 7pm most other nights? *Ahhhh......*

In that moment it dawned on me, it was 14 February and, more importantly for Steve and Helen, it was Valentine's night; their first Valentine's as a couple. But had he really wanted to get his call with the children out of the way as quickly and early as possible, because they had romantic plans? Surely, he would have engineered his Valentine's night around his call with the kids, especially as he hadn't spoken with them for three days. Besides, who on earth goes out on a Friday night, for a Valentine's dinner, the cinema – whatever – *that* early?

Sofia had been aware of our WhatsApp exchange, and my initial struggle to get him to talk to them. When he did finally call under sufferance, she let him have it, in direct accordance with her counsellor's advice. Sofia's counsellor, Sam, had advised her to express her feelings freely, but to carefully channel them in the right direction; at the source of her anger (Steve), and not at Alex or her friends. Sofia made it clear he had hurt her feelings again, by making her feel not as important to him as Helen obviously was. He was her daddy, and he should love her more than anyone and anything (excluding Alex, obviously). He was failing her, and he was hurting her.

Steve tried to defend himself by saying he thought they went to bed at 7.30pm, which was largely true, however this defence left him exposed to an awkward question: if he knew the kids usually went to bed at around 7.30pm, why was he leaving it so late to try and talk to them ordinarily? Was he leaving it so late, to limit the time available? I honestly wouldn't have put anything past him at this point.

As it was a Friday night, and as the kids hadn't spoken to him since Tuesday, I was prepared to offer a little bedtime leniency – all in the name of trying to hold their collapsing relationship together. I was running myself ragged trying to maintain Steve's relationship with his children, and now I was having surprise tactics, like this earlier than normal request to speak to the kids, used against me and as a means of hurting Sofia and Alex. My disgust in Steve had never been so profound and palpable. My patience with him was never more threadbare. I was getting dangerously close to the edge of my limits. Again.

If Steve and Helen genuinely had plans for Valentine's Day, it would hardly have been a surprise, so why not arrange an earlier call in advance, to guarantee a successful desired outcome for all concerned? Yes, I can "hear" Steve's defence of his actions as something along the lines of: "*Had we told Karan we were having a romantic Valentine's night, she would have tried to ruin it*". Hmm, well look where not telling Karan got you.

Once Sofia had finished ripping Steve a new one, he hung up on her, and never called back to straighten things out, or to speak with Alex. Again. This time Alex was inconsolable, barely able to articulate: "*Why doesn't he want to speak to me? Why doesn't he want to speak to me?*" between sobs. I scooped him up and took him to the big bed for a Super Cuddle, rocking and soothing him into an eventual calm. Sofia just sat on the edge of the bed, almost catatonic, staring blankly into a space about two feet in front of her, processing what had just happened. Again.

I have a helpful tip for you, should you ever have to console a deeply distressed child, or a child in the throes of a catharsis. This is not a scientific or medically approved method, that I know of. This is simply what I did instinctively – repeatedly – and it worked like a charm. At the very least it will do no harm and will bring a degree of comfort and solace. Ready?

The ultimate aim here is to try and evoke the child's unconscious memories of being safe in the womb and listening to their mother's heartbeat from inside. First hold the child firmly and tenderly (tacitly informing them they're safe and that you care for them), rocking them gently from side-to-side and to-and-fro, whilst their ear lies flat to your chest, directly above your heart. Then you must concentrate on slowing and regulating your own breathing, which in turn will slow and regulate your heartbeat.

Pat or stroke the child's back slowly, gently and rhythmically or, if they're young enough and it's appropriate, hold them and pat their bum rhythmically, like you used to when they were a baby. Start by taking slower and slower, deeper and deeper breaths, and their breathing will eventually sync with yours, calming them. I can't say how long this will take, as every child is unique, but at the end of the day, it will take as long as it takes – your child is in pain and needs you, so focus and be attentive. Do your best because they need you now.

As the emotional energy subsided and the children nestled into our family cuddle, mentally I was composing a *"Your goose is cooked Sunshine"* text. This was a new low for Steve, and I was going to let him have it. But then, in the quiet stillness of my bedroom, with my two babies snuggled in my arms, and a fire of fury silently swirling around in my mind, I heard: *"Stay out of it"* in my right ear.

Wait. **WHAT?!** You have got to be kidding me?

There is no way I could let him get away with this! I tried to fight for my right to rip him a new one, but all I got was: "*Stay out of it*". ARRGGHH! And there's the rub. When you ask for spiritual guidance, you have to be prepared to accept it – whether you like it or not – otherwise what's the point of asking for it? I didn't like this guidance, because it wasn't allowing me to satisfy my basest instincts; it wasn't allowing me to lash out or to unleash Psycho Bitch, which I desperately wanted to do. My temper was in full force, whilst I was tenderly nurturing my children, and it wanted its pound of flesh... NOW!

But the guidance had been given for my greatest and highest good and I had to trust that. This is a lesson I have struggled to learn, and a lesson I now pass on to the kids. One example involved Sofia wanting a particular maths teacher to be assigned to her set in the new academic year. She would countenance no other, no, nope, not ever. She started to wish and wish for this one particular teacher, before I stepped in to advise her to be careful what she wished for, because she might get it.

Sofia wanted Mr Chipping for maths, and Mr Chipping is indeed a fantastic maths teacher for Sofia. What I suggested Sofia do instead, was to ask the universe for a maths teacher for her greatest and highest good, not for Mr Chipping specifically. Whilst Mr Chipping may indeed turn out to be for her greatest and highest good, there is always the possibility that by getting him, Sofia would be plunged into a class of e.g.: unruly kids, which in turn could have a detrimental effect on her progress and results. Maybe, by being assigned to another teacher, Sofia would thrive in a class of like-minded, hardworking students, ultimately for her greater good.

Sofia saw the wisdom in this theory, and duly asked the universe for a teacher for her greatest and highest good. She then had to sit back and trust that whoever she was given, was right for her. It was not easy. It might not always be apparent straight away but give it a minute and all will be revealed in perfect time. What's meant to happen always does, and for what it's worth, Sofia went on to get an even better maths teacher than Mr Chipping, and is positively fizzing and thriving, thankfully.

In this situation with Steve, it would have been the easiest thing in the world to have started a shit-slinging competition, but it wouldn't have been very enlightened of me, would it? Here I was trying to embody *Do your best in every situation, because it will place you in the best possible position in the next situation* but was now actively tempted to slip in my resolve and to send a combative text. No. I decided I had to hold myself to a higher standard because rising above this text temptation, would put me in the best possible position for whatever came next. I reminded myself that I didn't have to attend every argument I was invited to, and that I can't be spiritual only when life is easy. There's no growth with challenge.

Who knows, maybe Steve and Helen were trying to start a conflict with me, to unleash Psycho Bitch, so they could point to her as the reason for his abandonment of the children? I sure as hell wasn't going to give them that excuse. Never give your opponent the ammunition to fire back at you. Think twice and act once with considered precision. Don't be consumed by the minutiae of the minute you're in, because it will change in the next minute; everything is temporary. Breathe. Take a step back and see the big picture. Then respond, not react, there's a difference. A big difference.

Imaginary Judge

Instead, I now started to get deadly serious about quietly compiling evidence against Steve, whilst being extraordinarily careful to not give him anything of the sort in return. It was clear to me that Steve was beyond redemption at this stage and was not going to wake up from his Helen-blindness anytime soon; so, what was the point of arguing with someone who believes their own lies? What I had to focus on now was to guard against any joint custody claim he may try to initiate, and so I developed myself a new little credo to guarantee my desired outcome.

The children had made their thoughts and feelings about spending time with Helen, Oliver and Emily abundantly clear, but some may have assumed I was poisoning the children's minds against them. What they possibly failed to appreciate (or remember) however is how the children had witnessed the depth of love and friendship Helen and I once had for each other. The children used to bask in the warm glow of our deliberately extended family, so they were no less than horrified when Helen betrayed me – us – in the way that she had. Neither child could grasp how she had purported to love me – us – and then hurt us so badly. They had a point.

Obviously, I was at a total loss of an explanation because Helen had completely blindsided me, and I struggled with the same questions they were wrestling with. Sofia and Alex were wholly appalled and disgusted with Helen and had been repeatedly ridden roughshod over by Emily and Oliver, to no longer care about them either. They could all go to hell in a handbasket for all we cared, but Sofia and Alex refused to spend another second with any of them.

If it's not already self-evident, and for the avoidance of doubt, my children have strong characters, high principles and know what they do and don't want. For the likes of Mallie to think they were ever so gormless as to not recognise naked betrayal when they see it, speaks volumes about how little

[292]

she knew them. My children have always been strong, perceptive and independent thinkers, whilst heavy on the spiritual insight. They are my gifts in this life, to be sure, and I am thankful to be able to love them.

Now, if you're going through this, if you're dealing with an acrimonious split with a partner and/or a betrayal at the hands of someone close, here is a handy tip to help keep you on the right track. I'm sure you've seen cartoons and movies where a little angel and an opposing little devil appears on the shoulders of the central character, to illustrate how they're wrestling with a dilemma? Well in my case I have a little imaginary judge sitting on my shoulder.

Before I take any action, or make any critical decisions, I ask myself how I would defend my decision or action in an eventual court of law; I game it out. If I have a solid reason, based on facts and logic (not emotion or assumptions), which is then further supported by buckets of evidence, I go ahead. If I don't then I won't. I always stop and ask myself *"Where's the evidence?"*, and I never do anything I couldn't explain to my Imaginary Judge. Neither do I do anything I wouldn't want to have to explain or excuse on national TV. This simply makes me more trouble repellent, and I urge you to follow suit.

Adopting these simple but effective thought and action filters, for any and all decisions or actions (even those unlikely to require actual legal intervention) will keep you firmly on the straight and narrow. These filters will encourage you to always do your best in each situation, which will then put you in the best possible position in the next situation. I did warn you this would be a recurring theme. Imagine how my kids feel, living with me!

In real terms, I suspected Steve might try and apply for sole or joint custody

[293]

at some point. He was going through a horribly arrogant phase, where his needs were of paramount importance and to the detriment of the children's. He had spent decades tending to the needs of others, to the detriment of his own, and now he had flipped 180° to become the total antithesis of who he once had been. I was concerned that in his mind, he needed the children in his life to complete the Utopian paradise he believed he'd created with Helen. But this isn't what the children wanted.

The children had given me my mission objective, notably that they never wanted to see Helen and her kids again. This was my mission to effect. Yes, the children loved and wanted to spend time with Steve, but it looked to us like he was withholding himself from them until they buckled and accepted Helen. It seemed like he was playing chicken with our children, expecting them to blink first. *Hah!* There was no way in hell I was going to allow their thoughts and feelings to be hammered into submission this way.

I reassured the children their feelings were their feelings and could never be wrong. I taught them how they were entitled to think and feel whatever they were experiencing, and they should not – under any circumstances – bottle up or mask how they felt. This was obviously supported by Sam's wise words during Sofia's counselling sessions, so I was just an empowering echo chamber for much of this stage. I wasn't going to do anything rash or heavy handed, like apply for a No Contact Order against Steve, because that's not what the children wanted either. All they wanted was him, not her, but he wasn't willing to give them that. So, I waited in the long grass, and not at all patiently.

Pre-2013 I was perhaps one of the least patient people on the planet. I am known to tear around like my hair is on fire, wanting eternally to *"Just get on with it!"* It's part of being a Type A personality apparently. Inside my head, this is because I have so much I want to accomplish; I'm a missile on a mission. I figuratively itch with ants in my pants if I'm not achieving something tangible and measurable. When I do eventually kark it, I want to have left this place in a better state than I found it. There has to be a discernible reason for me being here, and I'm not going to be here forever, so can we *purleeease* just get on with it?

Post-2013 I have had to learn to be patient, and it has been excruciating. Can you imagine having ants crawling and biting you all over your face, body and in your hair? This is what it felt like for me to be patient, but you know what? The more you do something, the deeper the neural pathways in your brain grow, and the easier it becomes; practice really does make you awe inspiringly adept; because "perfect" is a myth, obviously.

Hayley and I have grown through this trial together, as we were both impatient nightmares. That didn't stop us telling the other one to be patient on a regular basis, but we just steamed through our rank hypocrisy with a dismissive flick of the *"Do I say, not as I do"*, before laughing at ourselves. We knew it was a bit rich to counsel the other in this way, when we ourselves were so hopelessly impatient, but we accepted the wisdom as truth all the same. My point in telling you this is, if Hayley and I can master our impatience, so can you!

Your Goose Is Cooked, Sunshine!

So, Steve had hung up on Sofia during the Valentine's Night Massacre and failed to speak to Alex at all. This was a Friday night, and I did as I was told, which was to "Stay out of it" and opt against sending the "Your goose is cooked, Sunshine!" text. I waited to see what Steve would do next. After all, he was the grown up, and he had been the one to childishly hang up the phone. Did he seriously believe Sofia or Alex would blink first and call him? No. Nope. Not even close. We waited. Now that's not to say the kids weren't desperate to hear his voice again, or to be with him, but they understood it was his place to make amends, and to accept personal responsibility for his childish actions.

The next item on the calendar was his scheduled day with them on Sunday. I had no idea what to expect. Was he going to rock up to collect the children like nothing had happened? Was he going to ask to come in and talk about it, perhaps even to apologise? Was he going to take the children somewhere peaceful, buy them an ice cream and talk it through to try and take the heat out of the situation? Any of these options were perfectly viable and, whilst I had my own plans for Sunday, I was willing to delay or cancel them if Steve had wanted to mend some fences.

Sunday 16 February 2014 tentatively arrived like a profusely apologetic houseguest finishing the last of the milk, whilst the children and I did what we always did on a daddy Sunday. I got the kids up, washed, dressed and full of scrambled eggs, just in case Steve didn't provide a great lunch. By 11am, the historically agreed upon time for collection, the kids had their coats and shoes on, and their backpacks loaded with the toys and games they wanted to take with them; in case they ended up bored at the workshop, whilst Steve washed his van.

We got to 11.05am and there was still no sign of Steve. The kids were getting impatient, but this was nothing out of the ordinary. One of the things that drove me mad about Steve when we were together, was how he was always one of life's late breakers. He hated to wait, so would only ever leave to arrive exactly on time, or slightly late. We had wildly opposing levels of respect for other people's time, and it caused a lot of friction between us. I thought him rude and he thought me tightly wound. I believe we were both right.

Then we got to 11.10am, which wasn't entirely out of the realms of possibility, as he had been as late as 11.15am before now, but I was starting to get a sinking feeling in the pit of my stomach. I sat with the kids on the stairs in front of the front door, trying to send a telepathic *"Fucking hurry up, Wanker!"* message through the ether, but it appears I need more practice, or he was tuned out.

Trying to distract the kids from the passing of time – it was now 11.20am – started to fail as Sofia wandered off to stake out the front room window, overlooking the drive. I kept looking at my phone, checking for a missed call or text message, but there was nothing. By 11.30am it was clear to Sofia and I that he wasn't coming. She took off her coat and shoes, threw her backpack on the floor and began to cry the hot tears of the forsaken. I hugged her tightly, with nothing positive to say.

Alex remained implacable in his coat, shoes and backpack on the stairs, waiting. Waiting for his father, who had hung up on his sister about 40 hours previously, and who he hadn't spoken to in five whole days. Five days felt like a lifetime to this wee boy, and he was not moving from his waiting stair. It was like his young mind had convinced him that if stayed in place, didn't move, refused to quit or stop believing his daddy would come, he could actually make it happen. His big baby blue eyes, framed by the most ridiculously long and beautiful eyelashes, remained fixed on the front door, forever hopeful.

At around 11.45am I left an emotionally shattered Sofia, crying quietly on the sofa, to help Alex adjust to another new reality; his daddy wasn't coming. Openly crying myself, because I could feel their pain as much as I saw it in their eyes, I gently encouraged Alex to take off his coat and shoes, to which he replied: *"Five more minutes Mummy"*. Sofia heard this and wailed. I heard this and crumbled.

I didn't even get the chance to look round for something to cling to, some excuse or rationale I could offer by way of explanation for their father's unexplained abandonment of them. The pain, grief and ferocious anger boiled from a dark, dark place and I had to battle it back to focus on my broken babies. There was nothing in the world they had done to deserve this, and there was nothing in the world they could have done to deserve this. My children had been repeatedly emotionally brutalised by their father, and it was going to fucking well stop now.

The Silence Was Deafening

In the aftermath of Steve's no-show, the energy at home felt sombre, like someone had died. In many respects Steve had died. The Steve we had known, adored and cherished was now clearly gone. Gone to the Ninth Circle and Pit of Hell, where betrayers of kin are doomed to an eternity of being lodged headfirst into a block of ice, according to Dante; but then he's a big softy compared to what I had planned for Steve. What exactly did I have planned for Steve at this time? I'm going to spare you those details, because you'll only talk about me and cross the road when you see me coming. I caught myself on sharpish though, and restored the balance of my mind, because he's still the biological father of my children, and they still love him.

Yes, really.

So, I did absolutely nothing. Not on this no-show Sunday, not the day after, or the day after that. I did zip, zero and nada, despite hearing a continuous primal scream coming from the inside of my head. I didn't ever say this journey was easy. As was unmistakably clear to a blind man on a charging horse, Steve and Helen were both despicable, awful, hateful people, so what better course of action than to leave them wallowing in each other, and the misery they have heaped upon themselves?

Perhaps they were each other's karma? They deserved each other, and there was no way my children were ever going to be infected by either of them again, so they could have at it. I was done. I would take the children and I would build them a new life without him. Our new life could be anything we wanted it to be; any shape, size or consistency. This is where we got off this godforsaken, terrible and macabre ride. This is where we were thrown clear of Steve's wreckage and, looking back in 20/20 hindsight, I am grateful for the universe's mercy.

Steve and Helen were now free of us. Free to live in their squalid and dystopian reality, clinging despairingly to each other by their fingernails, because they were all each other had. Their reputations, their integrity, their friendships (such as they were), their family bonds were all shredded for some pathetic and shabby excuse of an affair. They had not even been able to rustle up a first date, because their relationship was founded on the wreckage of his marriage, and the broken hearts of his children. We all know the higher you want to build, the deeper the foundations must be, well their foundations are riddled with the cancer of deceit, ruthless self-absorption and empty illicit sex.

I had been told Helen was desperately unhappy about losing my friendship, had wanted to explain herself to me in person, and to have that one last moment of connection with me (per her conversation with Wilkie). I know she rues the day she lost me and has had to make do ever since. I know sounds extraordinarily self-assured of me, but Steve had told me (two weeks into their relationship) that Helen had recognised what she had become, and she didn't like it; she hated herself apparently. Steve told me, during my last day in the office, how Helen was painfully aware that she was no better than Lee's Other Woman, who she has reviled and sought vengeance against for all of these years. And this was just the beginning.

Not Giving In

It took Steve five weeks of living in the deafening silence of his deliberately withheld parental contact to blink first; but this was never a blinking game. In the meantime, I had dropped him like a hot rock. As I've said before, I deserved many of the lumps Steve served to me, because of the choices and actions I made in the past, but the children deserve nothing less than pure love and unconditional devotion. Anyone who can do what he has done to his own babies, deserves the Ninth Circle of Hell, with bells on.

Whilst I'm thinking of it, how could Helen be with a man who would do such a thing? How could Helen, a woman who so relentlessly and erroneously tried to paint Lee as an unfit parent, and went to court to secure a No Contact Order against him, be with a man who needs no such legal documentation to stay away from his children? What kind of woman is she? What kind of mother is she? Why is Steve's behaviour not ringing alarm bells in her head? If he can be so ruthless and self-centred with his own flesh and blood, what will he eventually be capable of doing to her? Remember, what they do with you, they will do to you, which applies to both of them equally.

Now that Steve was about to contact me about seeing the children again, he was also about to become aware of the seismic shift that had occurred in his absence. I'm not saying it was easy, joyous or light, but the children and I had gotten on with our lives, had dedicated ourselves to each other and were adjusting well to our new, smaller family dynamic. Where I was concerned, Steve was about to be introduced to an icy, seething, chess playing Mama Bear, who was going to block his access to the children until he could prove himself mentally and emotionally fit to parent them again; and generally, be worthy of their love. Buckle up because it's about to get bumpy.

On Thursday 20 March 2014 I received this text message...

[Steve]: *I'd like to see the kids on Sunday, what time is best for you?* 13:49

Oh, bless his little cotton socks, did he really think I was going to just let him see the kids again, after five weeks of unforced silence and absence from their lives? No. Nope. Not even close. I was also tickled that he'd had Helen write out the text for him, because this is not his vernacular. Where was his apology? Where was his explanation? Where was his awareness of the hurt he'd caused Sofia and Alex? The children are not pieces in a game to be picked up and moved around at will, only to be put back in their box when it suits him.

I was also mindful of the possibility that Helen had counselled Steve on what to say, how to say it, and would know full well I'd be pissed off with the lack of even a cursory apology. I understood everything I was about to do in response to his text enquiry, could possibly be playing into her hands. You see it suits Helen – in my opinion – to have Steve estranged from his kids, because it's less attention she has to compete for. I remember only too graphically how possessive Helen used to be when we were friends, and the damage she attempted to inflict on my relationships with Lauren and Hayley. So, I was only too aware I could be giving her exactly what she wanted, by impeding Steve's contact with the kids.

What mattered most however was the mental and emotional well-being of Sofia and Alex, who were still recovering from the emotional grenades Steve had thrown at them only six months earlier. They had tentatively found their feet, before being emotionally blown up again (meningitis no-show, the Valentine's Day Massacre and Sunday no-show); they'd been through more than enough. I now had to serve as their buffer, their protector. I couldn't trust Steve to treat their fragile little hearts and minds with enough love, respect or compassion to deserve the time with them. They didn't deserve him, or his recent treatment of them. No. Steve would have to demonstrate to me he was fit to father them, before I could even approach the subject of them maybe seeing him again. And even then, it would depend on what they wanted. The children had been pummelled enough by what Steve had wanted, and they had a birth right to be listened to, loved and respected. This was my mission to effect.

I spoke with my War Counsel (Eve, Hayley, Paul and Lauren) via phone and/or text. Paul, in his exalted position of doting and attentive uncle went absolutely batshit, completely losing his temper. This was most out of character, but he is only slightly less protective of Sofia and Alex than I am. He reared up at the prospect of them being emotionally smashed again and had no earthly idea of what to expect from Steve any longer. None of us knew who he was anymore.

One thing I need to point out here is how Paul had once adored and idolised Steve. Paul was 16 when I met Steve and they became close, often playing pool and snooker together, working together and swapping old survival stories about life with me. One of my favourite memories of the two of them together involved a boys' night out on the beer. Both were lightweights in the beer-drinking department, so it was a comparatively cheap date. They spent the evening at a snooker club, whilst I spent the evening with Mum (pre-kids). When the boys were ready to come home, they called me, and Mum and I drove out to collect them. I think they'd had all of three pints each but could barely stand up for giggling and laughing so hard. Mum and I loaded them into the back of the car, but the five-mile journey back to Mum's house took the best part of an hour. It wasn't because they had to stop the car to be sick or anything, it was because they were both so damned hilarious, I couldn't drive – I had to keep pulling over. This is how they were. They egged each other on something chronic and they had a blast together. This is the Steve Paul was now grieving too.

My War Counsel approved my planned course of action, so at 4.17pm I sent this...

[Karan]: *It's not as simple as that Steve. Before you can see the kids again, you and I are at least going to need to talk. I am free at 9.30am on Tuesday and Thursday next week, please let me know which suits you best.* 16:17

Regrettably for Steve he hadn't amended his phone settings, so I knew he read my message within a minute. It's not a huge leap to assume therefore that he conferred with Helen, before responding approximately 90 minutes later...

[Steve]: *What do you need to talk about? And why can't I see the kids on Sunday?* 17:48

Oh dear, he was still worse than I thought. I didn't reply to this text because I'd already made my position perfectly clear. This text was inviting me to an argument I had no desire to attend, so I didn't. I chose to rise above. I was well within my rights to protect the children's mental and emotional well-being. In fact, it was my duty as their mother to do so, and so I did. This was all so easy to explain to my Imaginary Judge. Steve and Helen could easily have predicted this was the position I'd adopt but had only belligerence to respond with. They sure as hell didn't have a raft of reason and logic behind them, so they opted for harrumphing. You know, like how all the great thinkers do? *Eye roll*

If this sounds remarkably similar to something you're going through now, don't ever back down in the face of belligerence, it's nothing to be afraid of. In fact, it's often a strong indication your adversary's argument has run out of steam, so smile quietly inside and know you have the advantage. And what do you do with an advantage? You press it. The secret to success here though is to take the emotion out of everything you say and do, remain courteous, fact and evidence based, whilst relentlessly focused on your desired outcome. Once you have defined in your mind what your desired outcome is, all subsequent decisions become easier to make, because you pass your options through the "Will this move me closer towards my desired outcome?" filter. If yes, do it. If no, do something else, or tweak it until it will.

Don't arrogantly and dismissively sweep their acts of belligerence aside though, because they often contain clues as to what's coming at you next. So listen, pay attention, keep notes and record everything for posterity. These information nuggets put aside today, might one day create you a nice little insurance pay-out; by one definition or another. Remember, empty vessels make the most noise and, because your opponent is unlikely to have anything in the way of strategy against you, they may try and intimidate you with loud, noisy threats of something else (legal action, humiliation, intimidation,

[305]

financial penalties etc). This is bullying, and we stand up to bullies, because they're often about as substantive as a fart in a fog. Having said that, we may as well try and determine where the next punch may be coming from whilst we're at it.

It took Steve another two days to get back in touch...

[Steve]: *What time can I pick the kids up tomorrow?* 11:15

[Karan]: *I have already answered your question. What day and time are you free to talk?* 11:15

[Steve]: *What do you need to talk about?* 14:11

[Karan]: *Let's arrange a date and time and we can discuss everything. As you've said many times in the past, text is not always the best method of communication. I'm afraid I can only do Tuesday morning now, can you make that work at all, or would you like to suggest an alternative date and time?* 14:11

[Steve]: *I'd like you to explain why I can't see the kids tomorrow (23/3/14), and to avoid any unnecessary confrontation, may I suggest that we communicate via email?* 17:40

[Karan]: *I don't anticipate any confrontation at all. Please suggest a date and time for us to meet. May I suggest we meet in a neutral public place?* 17:40

[Steve]: *You still haven't answered my question. Why are you stopping me from seeing the kids tomorrow? I think the best way to communicate is email.* 17:41

[Karan]: *Then we have a difference of opinion. My position stands.* 17:41

Obviously, I have all the original messages saved, for the avoidance of doubt.

There was no way I was allowing Steve within a country mile of the children, until he could persuade me, they were mentally and emotionally safe within his care. In the recent past he had become consumed by what he wanted, with little or no regard for what they wanted. My October 2013 email had tried to warn him of the dangers of pursuing such a selfish agenda, but it appears to have been disregarded. Now this text exchange had blasted any possibility of Steve atoning for his horrible misdeeds, completely out of the water. I'm aware of the possibility that Helen had tried valiantly to puff out her chest and play with the grownups, but she had only succeeded in sounding childish and petulant, if true. It did make me chuckle though, so I have her to thank for that. I felt like a lioness stomping on a dung beetle.

Whether Helen counselled Steve and typed out what to say, or not, is irrelevant. What's relevant is that Steve agreed to it all. Where I was now taking personal responsibility for the consequences of becoming an errant wife in the final years of our marriage, Steve was equally going to have to accept personal responsibility for the circumstances he now found himself in too. He had only himself to blame, whoever may have been typing out his texts.

Steve and Helen knew exactly why I wanted to meet with and talk to him. I wanted him to explain himself, to explain why he'd made the decision to hang up on Sofia, to not call back and make amends, to not call back and speak with Alex, and to explain his thinking behind the no-show stunt on the Sunday following the Valentine's Night Massacre. I wanted him to express some genuine remorse for his disgusting behaviour, and to obtain his assurances that it would never happen again. In six short months, I'd had to piece my babies back together more times than I should ever have had to, and it was going to end here. I wasn't going to let it keep happening.

By meeting Steve in person, I would be able to read his body language, his eye contact (or lack thereof), his demeanour and the words he didn't say, as much as the words he did. They both knew I would be reading him and his energy from start to finish and would absorb more information than they wanted me to have. They also knew of the guidance I receive in my right ear, and that it's not always from my spiritual family and entourage who guide me. Helen is acutely aware that I too have met with Robert since his passing and had relayed at least one occurrence in which Steve's late father, Bill, made his feelings abundantly clear. Steve and Helen knew only too well they were up against a veritable platoon of disapproving onlookers, and they probably felt vulnerable. And guilty.

Of course, I would have to have met Steve alone, because Helen didn't dare come anywhere near me. It wasn't the threat of physical violence that worried Helen – because that really isn't my style – it was what I would say to her that she'd have no answer for. Remember, she and Steve sneered at me for being "clever with words", but then I guess it is an intimidating quality to come up against when you're not? Helen knew she had no ground to stand on, and that I had captured the moral flag. What could she possibly have said to me that was worth listening to?

The only thing this text exchange resulted in was Steve blocking me on WhatsApp. For a moment I was staggered by his childishness, but then I remembered he'd done much worse, so this was merely bottom feeding now. It appears I had de-fanged them both and left them with only petulance to play with. Whatever dude, we're busy creating a new life without you. Be lucky.

Almost two weeks later however, Steve tried again by initiating this text exchange...

[Steve]: *Please can I see the kids at the weekend?* 11:40

[Karan]: *Have you time for a chat beforehand?* 11:41

[Steve]: *I've got a lot on this week, anything you have to say can be put in an email.* 11:42

[Karan]: *Then we have a difference of opinion. My position stands.* 11:43

[Steve]: *I will be filling in the form for mediation then, you should hear from them soon.* 11:43

Steve didn't appear to realise that he couldn't threaten me with mediation, because mediation was what I wanted and needed to eventually be able to divorce him. With the benefits I was on, the service would be free to me but would otherwise be expensive for him (approximately £130 + VAT per hour). If I had believed for a moment, he'd have been willing to pay and attend, I would have suggested it months earlier. So, I waited him out, until it became his idea. Whilst his last text was probably meant as a mild threat, it was actually a welcome and not entirely unexpected turn of events.

I don't think Steve fully grasped what would be involved though, despite Helen having experienced mediation with Lee. I'm reasonably sure Steve thought the Mediator would side with him against me and give him what he wanted. Not with all that I had to tell them – plus supplementary evidence – they wouldn't. Steve was so far up his own backside, failing to entertain any dissenting opinions, that he saw himself as the sole victim of all that had happened. He was not considering the children's experiences or opinions about what had happened. Oh, how this was going to be a rude awakening for him.

I didn't respond to his final remarks and duly waited for him to make the necessary arrangements, despite having a few retorts locked, loaded and ready to go. It took all of my self-control not to shoot back: *"Looking forward to it already!"* or *"Think carefully big boy"*, but neither of these would have come from my best self, and I could imagine my Imaginary Judge chiding my childishness, so I refrained.

Besides, what if I had text him *"Think carefully big boy"*, and he had heeded my warning and actually thought carefully? My warning, if heeded, would have constituted unintended helpfulness on my part and may even have resulted in better decision making on his part. Why assist his agenda to the detriment of my own? Thankfully, my mindfulness and self-awareness stepped in and shut me down. This one wholly unnecessary, somewhat juvenile, egoic and reflexive text could have been accepted as wise advice, so why in the name of custard would I offer him help like that? I had to stay focused on my desired outcome, which in this instance, was to lead him into accepting and respecting the children's wishes about seeing him and not Helen.

Self-Mastery: Knowing You Can, But Deciding You Won't

Once again, it took everything I had to step away from engaging with him, but self-mastery was the key to my success here. Remember, self-mastery is the fine line between knowing you can but deciding you won't.

As a teenager, glimpsing my first snippet of a televised boxing match, I asked Dad why the boxers didn't just lay into each other. Why did they hold back, why were they so controlled? My Dad chuckled and taught me that boxing isn't about anger and aggression, it's about precisely targeted power, skill and strategy. The first boxer to lose their temper would lose the match, because their precision would be impaired, and a win is determined by either a knockout blow, or on points for accuracy. This left a profound and lasting impression on me: never let your emotions overpower your intelligence and strategy.

Thrashing about wildly without discipline or reason, may make you feel better in the instant gratification moment, or be an interesting spectacle to behold for onlookers, but it's more likely to be detrimental to your overall cause. Think about how a surgeon operates slowly and carefully with the thinnest and sharpest of scalpels for accuracy, rather than with a hedge trimmer; there's a good reason for this. Optimum results are achieved with focus, dedication and most importantly, precision.

People without self-mastery operate in much the same way as a hedge trimmer; lots of noise, lots of mess and an imprecise result. People without self-mastery tend to be rash and impulsive, prone to lashing out, being argumentative and combative. These people are unpredictable, which makes them untrustworthy to those around them. Without trust, relationships are difficult at best. These people know they can and, without sufficient influence over their impulse control, they do. They rarely think about the consequences of their choices, so must then resort to damage control – following a convulsion of impulse remorse – to negate their lack of self-mastery. A lack of self-mastery only creates extraneous, self-inflicted trouble and strife, so why would you? Self-mastery is the challenge of transforming yourself from your own worst enemy into your greatest ally.

Daddy Fool

It would take Steve another three months before he acted on seeing the children again. Evidently this was not a high enough priority for him. Any eventual judge would find this detrimental to his case, but he clearly wasn't thinking things through well enough. On 4 July 2014, I received a letter from Steve's newly appointed solicitor, who implied I had denied him contact with the children. The solicitor asked if I was prepared to re-establish contact willingly, or whether the matter had to go to mediation, and then to court for a Contact Order. The solicitor then stated that if I was willing to re-establish contact between Steve and the children, I was to do so without making direct communication with Steve.

Wait, what?!

In the first instance I was operating under the impression – per his 2 April 2014 text – that he was planning for us to go to mediation. His last words to me were "*... you should hear from them soon*". I was now equally confused and amused by his willingness to pay a solicitor, with money he said he didn't have, to "threaten" me with something he'd threatened before *for free*. Mind boggling for sure, but valuable evidence of their collective idiocy all the same. The expandable file documenting Steve and Helen's unforced errors was padding out nicely and would eventually help to guarantee their mission failure.

In the second instance, let's stop and think for a moment about how this was all supposed to play out, according to Steve and Helen's perspective. We may need to squint and tilt our heads to see this, but here goes. From his texts in March and April, he made it abundantly clear he wanted us to co-parent via email, which got a big "*Oh hell no!*" from me. If he couldn't be adult enough to liaise and co-parent with me in person, then he wasn't adult enough to deal with the children's emotional scars and gun-shy behaviour around him, was he?

He had already developed a nasty habit of hanging up the phone on Sofia when he couldn't argue or reason with her ten-year-old logic. What was supposed to happen if the kids were spending the weekend with him and they got into similar disputes? Was he going to dump them at home with me before running away? What if I wasn't home, then what would he do with them? What further damage would his impaired adulting do to the children's already damaged mental and emotional condition? How low was he prepared to go exactly? Had he even hit rock bottom yet? Why was he prepared to gamble with their emotional well-being just to make himself feel better – what about what they wanted? I didn't have the answers to any of these questions, and I was willing to bet, neither did he. So that was another hard and fast "*Oh hell no!*" from me.

Another question that was just begging to be answered was: Why was Steve so afraid of me? Yes, I had become an errant wife during our final two years together, as my friendship with Helen ignited, but what exactly had I done to warrant not being allowed to communicate with him directly? All contact and correspondence had been courteous and factual. I had made no threats against either him or Helen and had allowed them all the space they desired to pursue their relationship. I had given him everything he'd asked of for, notably the end of our marriage, without any hissy fits, slashed tyres or Psycho Bitch behaviour. Yes, I was working furiously hard behind the scenes to secure our future, but he/she/they wouldn't have known this at the time. And even then, I wasn't planning to hurt him – by any definition – only on securing what was rightfully ours.

In fact, post-Bomb Drop, I had recognised quickly what an opportunity I was being presented with and had just as quickly developed a taste for the freedom he had gifted me. Yes, I was grieving for who he once had been, and what we once had had, but the kids and I had so evidently been thrown clear of his train wreck. I didn't do the pleading "please come back to me" bit, because I didn't want him back. I was perfectly capable of speaking with him, without yearning for his return to my life. So, what was his problem?

Rhetorical question time. Could the problem have been his inability to be near me? Had he processed my departure from his life as successfully as he perhaps thought he should have done? Had he processed the guilt and shame he may have brought down upon himself? After 24 years together, was he missing me (on any level) and finding it difficult to be near me whilst no longer a couple? Who knows, perhaps Helen felt insecure with the idea of him being near me? Perhaps Helen felt diluted when comparing herself against my energy and accomplishments? Rhetorical questions all, but they gave me pause. Whatever the answers, they were his to deal with. My focus, as ever, was the children.

Steve and I finally sat down together with the Mediators, Annette and Beth, on 24 October 2014. As possessive as ever, Helen chaperoned Steve's 20+ mile journey to meet with me but was left to sit in his van in the nearby multi-storey car park. I do hope he remembered to crack a window. The meeting lasted about an hour and got heated in places, despite Annette and Beth's attempts to keep things cool and amicable. The entire process can be summed up in the following couple of sentences. I confirmed to Steve, again, that the children loved him and wanted him, but they didn't want Helen, Oliver or Emily. Steve responded with: "*Well, I'm not prepared to live two lives*". Annette, the lead Mediator, threw her hands in the air and said: "*We can't help you*". And that was that.

Stunned, gutted and furious with the waste of time and petrol this whole process had been, I asked Steve why he had hung up on Sofia on 14 February 2014 and not called back. He said simply: "*I didn't know what else to do*". And there it is. Ladies and gentlemen, introducing Steve 2.0. If this is the kind of man Helen can love, if her self-esteem is so low as to not think herself worthy of more than this, then I wish her the future she truly deserves.

I Wrestled The Obligation Out Of Him

So, Steve had been flatly refusing to contribute anything towards the children's welfare from the moment he left us. He didn't even offer any guilt money. I remember asking him for as little as £20 per week in the days following our separation, but he always rebuffed my requests with: "*I'm paying the mortgage*". I tried to give him the benefit of the doubt for as long as I could, but when I saw the big new house they were renting, the wallet-busting trips to NEXT, and the holidays to Cornwall during peak summer season, I decided to open a claim with the Child Maintenance Services (CMS).

This was not a simple task however because Steve is self-employed, which complicated matters a lot. It took approximately six months for the CMS to pin Steve down and submit his income numbers. Then he had the nerve to ask me to accept Direct Pay, which is where Steve sets up a standing order to pay his contribution directly into my bank account and, because the CMS are not involved, there are no supplementary fees. The alternative would have been for Steve to go onto Collect & Pay, where the CMS would take his payment, plus an extra 20%, keep the 20%, take another 4% and pay me what's left.

As it had taken so long to extract Steve's income numbers in the first place, and then for the CMS to figure out what he should pay towards the children, Steve had accrued arrears. I was informed the arrears would be chunked down and added in instalments to his weekly liability. I agreed that Steve could pay me directly, as another gesture of goodwill so he could save himself the 20%, but on one condition: he had one shot. If he missed just one payment, I would have him on Collect & Pay so fast his head would spin.

He agreed to these terms and also paid me a one-off goodwill gesture of £100, just before Christmas, which was incredibly helpful. Prior to this we were staring at a Christmas of Dickensian proportions. Of course, I mean slightly *more* Dickensian Christmas; but I dared to wonder if relations between us were starting to thaw into civility, because this was a genuinely kind and entirely optional gesture. No. Nope. Not even close.

He Shows His Hand

Very early in January 2015, I received an email purporting to be from Steve, but was so clearly written by Helen. In the sentence or two of text, Steve outlined how he could no longer afford the mortgage, now he was paying CMS. He asked if I would be willing to sell the house, so we both could profit from it.

So, this was his next move was it? I didn't trust him in the slightest. I was also interested to know how he said he couldn't afford to pay the mortgage and CMS, but didn't make any mention of still being able to afford their residential rent and rates, their commercial rent and rates, his van lease payments, fuel and servicing, their expensive restaurant bills, excursions to Covent Garden, and peak summer holidays to Cornwall. And this was all before they'd eaten a crumb, bought premium dog food, switched on a light, kept themselves warm and entertained themselves with cinema and ice-skating trips. No. This wasn't a question of not being able to afford the mortgage, this was a question of priorities; and the children simply didn't make the cut.

I thought about the email and gamed it out in my head. I knew the mortgage itself had been settled in June 2013, so when he said "mortgage" he was talking about a small home improvements loan repayment. As the mortgage itself was paid, there was a lot of equity in the property, so I wasn't surprised he wanted access to it now. The problem I had was, if I agreed to sell the house, how were we going to affect that course of action if I wasn't allowed to communicate directly with him? If he'd have had me co-parent by email, he wasn't likely to accept direct communication for selling the house, was he?

Also, by agreeing to sell the house, the local council would conclude that I had made us voluntarily homeless and would be less obligated (if obligated at all) to re-house us. Furthermore, how in the world could I now trust Steve after everything he'd done against us? My answer was a polite and simple: "I decline your offer to sell the house" and nothing more. I could have written paragraphs, but with every superfluous word I offered, Helen would have had more insight into my thinking, and that wouldn't do.

But Steve had shown his hand, so now I knew it was just a matter of time before this issue would rear its ugly head again. The only thing I didn't know was exactly how or when that would be. Yes, he had telegraphed his intent, but there wasn't much I could do about it at this point. I had his email, and my subsequent rebuff, to prove to the council I had done everything I could to stay housed, which was something. It wasn't just blarney either. The last thing the kids and I needed, after the year we'd had, was to pack up and move to a new house. I genuinely wanted to stay as settled as possible for as long as possible. Besides, I had no money to privately rent, as my business was still in its infancy and not setting any new income records just yet. As it happened, I would have to wait until October 2015 for Steve's plan to fully unfold, which we will get to shortly.

Cancer Must Die

I busied myself building my new business by perpetually refining the website, optimising the SEO, learning more, reading more, writing blogs and obviously tending to clients; both of the paid and voluntary variety. I was still nurturing the household budget like a sickly infant, still exercising my ludicrous grocery shopping protocols and still counting every penny. Our finances were now stretched with no room for spare or error but were otherwise stable. I watched my credit rating steadily blossoming into something beautiful, you know... should I ever be able to afford anything ever again, but it was all progress and on an upward trajectory. We were on the right track, facing in the right direction and certain of success if I only maintained my discipline. I finally had things under control.

Hmm, in my world maybe, but Paul was getting weaker. He felt constantly fatigued, was struggling to maintain his mental equilibrium and had a new assortment of medical difficulties to contend with. Then he noticed a lump just above his right collarbone, and we both shuddered; we both *just knew*. Paul has been known to procrastinate in his lifetime, so I was equally proud and relieved when he quickly arranged to see his GP for an initial diagnosis. Long story short, Paul was sent to a Consultant Haematologist, Dr P., who eventually diagnosed Stage 4 Hodgkin's Lymphoma.

Whilst Paul remained typically stoic, outwardly at least, I immersed myself in research, because that is what I do. I will whittle away until I understand, until I find a reason, a solution, whatever is required. I can't rest until I have a grasp on what's happening. I must have facts, knowledge, logic and evidence. Realising I was worrying enough for the both of us, Paul – after an initial period of fear – seemed to settle into serenity. He told me he *just knew* he was going to be okay. This wasn't good enough for me though. How did I know he wasn't just saying that to try and stop me worrying?

Somewhere in the deep recesses of my fear infused mind, my inner child was terrified of losing my brother, especially after I'd only just lost my Mum and husband (and Dad a couple of years before that). My inner child concluded immaturely, that if I worried enough, I could save him; that my worry would absorb his cancer somehow and make him well again. So, I worried. I worried a lot. Researching his Stage 4 diagnosis only threw petrol on my anxiety fire though, and he and I were about to do battle again, with cancer.

Paul has always stood unflinchingly four-square behind the children and I, every step of the way. As the keystone member of my War Council, Paul listened patiently and compassionately to months of alternating snivelling, self-pitying grief and rage-filled invective, before helping me to steer my thoughts and feelings into something more productive and resourceful. Now it was my turn to stand four-square behind him, as Dr P. recommended 28 courses of chemotherapy, starting immediately. Paul was now in the fight of his life.

Paul met his chemotherapy sessions with a nod of respect, like a boxer eyeballing an oversized opponent before the bell. He knew he was about to be battered before victory, but he joined the fight all the same, like the fierce warrior he is. Franklin D. Roosevelt taught us: *"Courage is not the absence of fear, but rather the assessment that something else is more important than fear"*. Paul was not ready to be beaten by cancer, and had every faith in Dr P., who acquitted herself with a genial confidence which inspired a strong faith in her expertise. He felt blessed and safe in her care, and the compassionately supportive Macmillan nurses were nothing less than angels here on earth; no doubt about it.

I bought him American military style dog tags [*because one of his favourite TV shows is M.A.S.H.*], to empower him through this war he was fighting for us; complete with a personalised message of love embossed where his name and rank should be. I bought him Beanie hats to keep his head warm, once he lost his hair, embroidered with "Sofia's Uncle Paul/Alex's Uncle Paul" to help keep him focused on the love we have for him.

We made sure he never felt alone and sent our love and healing prayers out into the universe when we couldn't be with him in person [*we lived about 25 miles apart at the time*]. Spiritually inclined friends also sent love and healing out into the ether, because "*...there are more things in heaven and earth, Horatio, than are dreamt of in your philosophy*". Sofia was even sponsored to stop eating and drinking chocolate during her Cancer Must Die pledge of January 2016 and raised £263 for Cancer Research. We hit back hard as a family to support one of our own.

I'm not going to go into Paul's chemotherapy experience in too much detail because a) that's more his story than mine and b) I don't want to unduly frighten or alarm anyone else currently on this journey. What's important to know is that from August 2015, through to March 2016, Paul did as he was told by Dr P., dug deep into the reserves of his personal will and came out swinging at his lymphoma. Remember, Paul was not a well man to begin with, physically or mentally, so there is always hope – *always!* – if you just hold on. Fight with every ounce of what you have because: **IT AIN'T OVER. UNTIL. YOU. WIN!**

During March 2016, around my birthday as it happened, Paul went for – what we hoped would be – his final PET scan. This is the Positron Emission Tomography scan which can detect the size, composition and location of cancer cells, and takes between 30-60 minutes to complete. It's not a joyous experience, because it leaves you somewhat radioactive for a while afterwards, but hey, needs must! Once the scan was complete, we then had to endure the interminable wait for the results, which ultimately came back clear.

Paul was now cancer-free. Paul had fought and won the fight of his life, but the fight had changed him. Having lived through a nightmare, and now suffering the horrific and incurable side effects of his chemotherapy (which may have been because of, or exacerbated by, his pre-existing health issues), Paul's perspective on life was different. He was now able to see more clearly what was truly important, and what was nonsensical piffle. Paul would never be caught up in blather again.

Fighting cancer has been the single hardest thing Paul has ever had to live through, and that includes a difficult childhood, divorce and the death of Mum, but he did it. Paul was plunged into the depths of Hell and came back victorious; partly because he always believed he would. For all my fear and worry, Paul genuinely knew he'd survive. Maybe he just decided to survive, but he wasn't making it up to make me feel better. Paul may be a lot of things [*i.e.: a bit of a procrastinator in the past, scarred by the breadknife incident, a lifelong broken toe victim, a Manchester United supporter and unapologetic lover of cricket*], but a liar he ain't. He reminded me gently of this fact at the end of it all, as we hugged, and I made his shirt a bit soggy.

One of the greatest lessons Paul's cancer taught us was this: "*When you're going through hell, keep going!*" This is a quote by Winston Churchill, and perfectly defines what I'm trying to achieve with this book. Yes, I was experiencing grief from the loss of Mum, then I experienced betrayal and heartbreak at the hands of my husband, but some of us are fighting significantly bigger battles than that, and none of us can afford to stop and admire the view. Like my son being told not to look over his shoulder as he approaches the finish line in athletics training, because it will slow him down, we can't afford to look anywhere but ahead when we're in the fight of our lives; literally or figuratively.

By turning our head before the finish line, by wasting time complaining and feeling sorry for ourselves, we are causing a kind of aerodynamic drag on our progress going forwards; we are actively slowing ourselves down and impeding our potential for success. So, what to do instead? How about we take our cue from Olympic sprinters? Watch what they do as they approach the finish line, their eyes are locked on the finish from the start, they operate smoothly and aerodynamically throughout, and they lean into the finish line. In fact, they sprint past the line, they don't slow down to admire the timing beam, they sprint past it and slow down later. This is what you must do: focus, be smooth, do your best during every stride, lean in and keep going! Get what needs to be done, done... and cry later if you need to.

SERIOUSLY?

Karan & The Banshees

On 15 October 2015, I received a letter from a firm of solicitors based far away. Evidently this firm represented Nationwide (Steve's mortgage lender), and they were writing to advise me as the occupant of the property, that they were starting repossession proceedings against Steve. I was to make alternative living arrangements as quickly as possible. In that instant the world fell out of my arse. I got hot, my stomach churned, whilst fear and loathing swirled around like a tempest inside my mind. I felt dizzy, nauseous and disbelieving this could be happening to us. Why hadn't Steve at least warned me this was a possibility?

Like the doomed being maliciously pushed off a cliff, grabbing frantically at the air for something – anything – to materialise and halt their plunge, I was free falling in terror. Banshees were howling *"You have to house the children! What about the children? How could he do this to the children?"* in my head, but they offered no practical solution, only unresourceful fear and noise. Vicious heat continued to spread from up from my chest, acid blistered my stomach and the relentless banshees wailed on and on. I had to stop this process. I had to stop this ride and get off. I had to pull this calamity back into my orbit and back under my control. Panicking was only wasting time and energy. What did I have to do to make this stop? What did I have to do to master these circumstances, to neutralise the atrocity Steve was trying to perpetrate against the children and I? Stop feeling Karan and think!

The first thing I did was to tell myself forcefully and repeatedly to breathe. As simple as it sounds, I needed to be told to calm down and breathe, but as I was alone at home, I only had myself to soothe me. Okay, needs must, so I set about speaking the words "*Just calm down and breathe*" out loud, and as many times as I needed before my unconscious mind finally heard the words and complied with the order. I was in the middle of a fight or flight response, and I needed to convince my instinctive, unconscious mind I was fine and didn't need to fight or take flight. To do this I needed to breathe slowly and deeply.

Our prehistoric ancestors, when confronted by a predator, had two options to ensure their survival, to either fight the predator, or run away from the predator. Either option would require the mind and body to direct all available resources to the body parts responsible for fighting or running away; the arms, legs, heart, lungs, brain. This required non-essential functions like digestion in the stomach to stop, so the blood and energy could be diverted to the essential extremities and organs. This is also why some people urinate and defecate when frightened, because the body is making itself lighter, to better facilitate action. We can override this instinct though by breathing slowly and deeply. From my unconscious mind's point of view this day, if I had the time to breathe slowly and deeply, I clearly wasn't about to become a sabre-toothed tiger's next meal. Yes, our instinctive operating systems really are about 200,000 years out of date, but that's another topic for another day.

Once I had calmed down and started breathing slowly and deeply, I set about engaging my logic to further quell the panic. I reminded myself how I had been expecting some kind of self-serving play from Steve, since he showed his hand in the January email, inviting me to sell the house. I then thought about how this letter actually helped my cause, because now I was being involuntarily evicted, and would be entitled to social housing, eventually. This is why it pays to stop and breathe, because first impressions can be wrong.

Following some research, I knew I couldn't afford to privately rent on my Tax Credits and miniscule new business earnings alone, so social housing was my only option. A mortgage was now also out of the question, because it didn't look like I was going to get any equity from the house, and I had no idea how big a debt Steve had racked up. I guessed the debt was three months of missed payments, but had he taken out additional loans against the house since our separation? I resigned myself to not knowing much at all, as the Data Protection Act would prevent me from learning more.

Now breathing well, laser focused and pissed off to high hell because Steve never had the decency to tell me an eviction was even likely, I phoned Nationwide's legal team to glean as much information as they were able to give me. As it always pays to engage with charm, I set about building a rapport with Lucia. Obviously, Lucia was limited in what she could divulge because of Data Protection and was unable to counsel me legally because I was not her client, but I was still able to end the call knowing more than I had at the beginning. These things are always worth a try. The worst she could have said was nothing, but she did give me valuable information to help guide me forwards, which I would not otherwise have had unless I'd asked. You must always try, regardless of how wafer thin your chances appear to be, because appearances can be deceptive.

My next vital priority was to ring an emergency housing advice agency, based in the borough council offices, where I made an appointment to see Mr Smith within the hour. The humiliation of having to do this meant I had to force myself out of my comfort zone. It would have been so much easier not to go and reveal my family's complete disintegration, and ex-husband-to-be's midlife crisis spasm to an absolute stranger, but burying my head in the sand wasn't going to afford me a result, was it? So, I gritted my teeth, put my ego into a Ziplock bag and just got on with it. At this point I simply couldn't afford an ego. Looking at my children's tiny beds, the place where they slept, trusting me to look after and protect them was the final kick up the arse I needed to focus on what was truly important [*them, always them*], and to get me out of the door.

Mr Smith was a saint. An angel in Chinos and Hush Puppies, sent to reassure and guide me wisely. An angel I might add, that I would never have met if I hadn't forced myself out of the house and my comfort zone. He started by telling me how qualified and experienced he was in his field of expertise, and that I should trust his wisdom and guidance. He then drew me four or five circles next to each other in a line, each circle representing one part of the process Steve had now initiated by not paying the mortgage. He also advised me what I should be doing during each of those stages to safeguard the children and I.

One of the first things I needed to do was to apply for social housing, so I collected the relevant forms from the council agents before I left and took them home to make a start. I returned the forms, fully completed and supported by the required documentary evidence before I collected the children from school. I was lock-on, I had to be, no other bugger was going to save us. In fact, I had two of the people I had loved the most now actively conspiring against me. I had to be fully focused, because nothing was more important than trying to find a new roof for my babies to sleep under. This was not the time for procrastination. I knew now that I would have to eventually bid for a house, that time was of the essence and farting about feeling sorry for myself was a luxury I could ill afford, and which may even have resulted in a missed opportunity. I filled out those forms with tears of outrage dripping off the end of my nose and chin, but they only spurred me on to come out on top even more: *This ain't over. UNTIL. I WIN!*

I was informed quite quickly that we were entitled to social housing, primarily because we were being involuntarily evicted. However, as the repossession and eviction process can take several months to complete, we were only rated a Priority C; entitled but not urgent. This did little to allay my mother's panic, especially when I found myself looking into the photographed eyes of my children all throughout the house.

These beautiful souls came into this world only because Steve and I had invited them. They are innocent, trusting and loving and deserve only the best, but here was their father making them homeless, and hadn't had the decency to tell me, or to explain. I suddenly felt guilty for choosing this man to father them, but I had truly believed him to be an exceptional man... then. Now all he was, was an exceptional piece of shit.

The Kindness Of Janet

Where the children's father was actively pursuing an agenda against us, brand new friends who'd known us for five minutes were stepping into the breach. I met Janet via my friendship and collaboration with Sylvia and Fred, as she is similarly wired and spiritually inclined. We hit it off straight away with our devout devotion to sarcastic humour and love of the English language. Whilst Sylvia and Fred would earnestly be trying to teach us new wisdom, the pair of us would be laughing and joking like a couple of schoolgirls at the back of the classroom. Thankfully, Sylvia and Fred's senses of humour are just as robust as ours, so we raised the roof together.

I had known Janet for only eight months when our eviction and Priority C rating threatened us with the real possibility of Christmas in a hostel for the homeless. Without pausing to blink, Janet announced: *"Bugger that, you'll move into mine!"* before explaining how she would move in with a friend over Christmas, before embarking upon a scheduled holiday to New Zealand for nine weeks. I'm rarely speechless, but this rendered me mute. I struggled to comprehend why she would do such a thing for those she'd known for such a sort amount of time. The answer of course is inherent kindness and generosity of spirit.

Do you remember me telling you about Napoleon Hill's maxim within the book Think & Grow Rich, which asserts that for everything we lose, we will receive something of equal or greater value? Well this was that. By choosing to betray me, Helen had merely created space in my life for Janet to inhabit. It was like losing a penny and finding a tenner.

Janet and the kids got on like a house on fire too, as she would treat us to divine bacon sandwiches, before the kids went paddling in a nearby brook, or running around like wild things in the park. She made the children laugh by pretending to hog a whole tray of thirty jam doughnuts at her catered firework party, or by deliberately agitating my OCD by repositioning furniture and ornaments around our home.

You see, I agree with Monica Geller from Friends: if it's not a right angle, it's a wrong angle, and nothing delighted Janet and the kids more than making my OCD itch. Then she would walk into our home with the Pie Face game, complete with a big tin of whipped cream, to squeals of delight from the kids, and wild-eyed horror from me. Janet lifted the children's lives and gifted them joy in the gloom. It was really the kind of job their Auntie Teresa used to do, and could still have been doing, but it seems she had her money to count.

Mr & Mrs Scrooge McDuck

When we were truly skint, and I had to rely on Tesco Reward Card vouchers to buy the children's school uniform, birthday and Christmas presents, or our Christmas dinner ingredients, Janet would turn up with a huge hamper of "*...things you probably won't buy for yourself*". The warm-heartedness of this would make me cry whilst unpacking it after she left. These hampers truly brought the Christmas spirit into our otherwise Dickensian Christmases. We weren't exactly huddled around a candle to keep warm, but we weren't far off. Juxtapose this against the response I got from the seemingly wealthy, Jaguar-driving Teresa and Len, who didn't once check to see if the kids needed anything, despite knowing how cash strapped I now was.

Len even flew up for a local air show with his brother in a private light aircraft for the weekend and invited us to attend the show. I really couldn't afford the petrol to get there, or the £2 parking charge once I'd arrived, but I knew Alex would love such an event. The children hadn't had much fun or enjoyment since Steve had left, so we went. As promised, Len offered me the £2 car parking refund upon our arrival at the gate, and duly got us into the show for free.

We then walked for hours looking at the various aircraft and the stalls, where the children got to sit in Len's plane, a visiting microlight and one of the aerodrome's fire engines. The water we had brought with us was finished, and the kids were hungry and thirsty after hours on their feet, but Len didn't even offer to buy them a sandwich or a drink. When I advised we would be leaving to go home for lunch, Len held aloft a carrier bag he'd been carrying and said: "*I've already got my lunch!*" referring to a roll he'd purchased before we got there. Okay, duly noted.

A month or so later, whilst making Teresa and Len aware of our worsening financial situation, during a routine telephone conversation, Len suggested we go to the local food bank to supplement our grocery shopping. Despair sank like a rock in my stomach. Let me be clear, I wasn't asking for money, merely explaining how bad things had gotten financially, but it felt like Len was cutting me off at the pass before I asked for help.

I accepted Teresa and Len would side with Steve after our separation because they were family and naturally inclined to support him, come what may. I knew they had merely tolerated me during my years with Steve, and couldn't have cared less if I starved to death, but what about the children? Len's food bank suggestion completely floored me because he and Teresa had once been supremely thoughtful and generous towards the children; towards us all. How could he – they – go from so caring to so completely careless so quickly and heartlessly?

Lauren made a good point. If they truly believed any money they had lent or given would have been spent on wine, rugby players and song, a) they never knew me at all, and b) why not complete an online grocery shop and have it delivered? This way they could ensure the children got what they wanted and needed, but no. In this moment it appeared to me that Teresa and Len's past generosity had only been a superficial show to make themselves feel good and/or to impress onlookers.

They now seemed to be all about the flash and personal glorification, and to hell with the substance; to hell with my children's lives and wellbeing. When the chips were down, Teresa and Len kept their wealth to themselves, and were willing to have their own niece and nephew fed via a food bank. Noted. Thank God for the kindness of Janet, but tell me, who would you rather have in your orbit? Who would you rather have in your life: the unconditional kindness of Janet, or the self-interested clan of Mr & Mrs Scrooge McDuck? Yes, I agree with you, but I still had to give the McDucks a little more rope to save or hang themselves with, before I could close them down for good, and in good conscience.

Purposefully, I didn't let this issue stop us meeting up when Teresa and Len visited Mallie. I didn't want to severe all contact between the children and their father's family. At least not just yet and if I didn't have to. I had to give them another chance to rehabilitate themselves; or not, as it sadly transpired. Their lack of care or concern once we were evicted, compounded by Len's food bank suggestion, became the game changer and the straw that broke the camel's back for me. This part of the story must unfold in due course though, so please continue to bear with me; I'll come back to this shortly.

Turmoil

One week after receiving the initial eviction notice, I got a letter advising me how Steve was due to attend the county court on 25 November 2015, to either try and save the house with an arrear's repayment plan, or to witness the repossession proceedings; I knew not which. I wasted no time in making this letter help further my cause. In life, don't just strike whilst the iron is hot, make the iron hot by striking. You create your own luck and opportunities through action – not by sitting around and complaining or worrying.

Despite it now being half term, and having two children in tow, I was down to the council offices within the hour. Frantic this letter meant I would be issued with a 30-day Notice to Quit on 25 November 2015, I was genuinely terrified as I pleaded for more urgent housing assistance from the council. The two children sat angelically in seating about eight feet behind me, as I was unable to stem the flood of emotion bubbling up from my throat, choking my voice as I feared I had failed them. I'd gone way past the point of caring about a public display of emotion, as there were bigger issues to contend with. The council representative tried her hardest not to voice how appalled she was with our predicament, but her face said it all. Hers and mine both.

I have no clear memory of what happened, or how it happened, because it's all a kind of grey swampy hot mess in my mind, but I do remember feeling slightly more relieved at having been moved up to Priority B: entitled and urgent. In all honesty we were never going to be a Priority A, as this category is quite rightly reserved for our e.g.: armed services veterans and long-term hospital patients with no homes to go to. Now all I had to do was hope and pray a suitable house, in the new area I wanted to move us into, would become available on the council's property search forum, so I could bid for it.

You Can't Afford Petulance

The system worked on a Thursday to Tuesday cycle. New properties would go up on the website on a Thursday, and I would have until the close of Tuesday to bid for a maximum of two houses per week. To bid, I simply had to register my interest in the property by pressing a button, but the council's algorithm calculated a multitude of factors to determine who was rightfully most entitled to each. The first few weeks of checking the website left me reeling and disheartened by the condition of the few properties available. For example, some houses were coated in flaky grey stucco, with decrepit sofas or hollowed out cars in the front garden, accompanied by overflowing neighbouring bins.

Another hurdle I hadn't been prepared for was the number of people who had already bid on each property ahead of me. Being first in line didn't guarantee anyone a house, but I was shocked with how many people were bidding for houses like the grey flaky stucco offering. What hope did I possibly have of getting anything remotely decent? All seemed lost and hopeless. This led me to explore privately renting again, but even with my Auntie Alison stepping up and agreeing to be my guarantor, there was no way I could afford this option. Social housing really was the only way I had to house my babies immediately.

One Thursday, I dropped the kids off at school and completed the grocery shopping with a heavy heart and thumping head. I was fraught with worry because the 25 November (Steve's court date) was only about ten days away, which realistically meant I had forty days before we were homeless and seeking refuge in either a hostel, or Janet's home. This is not what I had worked my arse off for 24 years for. This isn't the life I had imagined for myself, or for the children I chose to bring into this world. In all the time I had been fraught about homelessness, Steve had secured his new family a new home to live in, but still hadn't had the decency to tell me what had happened to ours. I positively boiled with contempt and rage.

I did the grocery shopping unhurriedly because what was the point of anything? Every step felt like it was uphill through treacle. I drove home and unloaded the shopping first into the house, and then into the cupboards, which made it lunchtime by the time I'd finished. I ate lunch and drank a cup of tea, still completely unable to find any reasonable hope in our situation. I couldn't believe Steve was allowing us to swing in the wind like this. He may hate me, I got that, but what about the children? Was his hatred for me really stronger than his love for the children? How does that even work? I accepted how some of my actions had pushed him away and had helped to end our marriage, but I had done nothing to warrant this. And neither had the children, except to repeatedly reject Helen of course.

After lunch I just sat, listless, directionless, not really knowing what to do for the best. If in doubt do nowt and all that. As I sat there, wallowing in my worrisome self-pity, I heard: *"Check for properties"* in my right ear. I harrumphed audibly and argued downheartedly: *"What's the point?"* I remained seated, passively protesting and despondent. *"Check for properties"* was gently suggested again, as I shook my head like a petulant toddler refusing broccoli. *"Check for properties"* for a third time, and by now I was feeling nagged and badgered. I regressed into Karan the teenager, as I stood up and stomped into my office to cantankerously switch on my laptop.

I called up the relevant website and started looking through the properties with no sense of optimism or expectation. In the first instance I was surprised by how many more properties there were to choose from this week. Many were still in a high state of disrepair as before, but now there were some entirely reasonable options too. I kept looking though, because all of these houses so far had over one hundred bids on them already. And then it happened.

In one click, quite a way into the online catalogue, there was a pretty little three-bedroom new build, complete with off road parking, a manageable garden with a large shed, and a beautiful park vista with trees for as far as the eye could see. This was perfection, because I bloody love trees! This was too good to be true, so I quickly referred to Google Earth to see exactly where the house was located, before checking crime rates and flood planes in the area; but it all came back as highly desirable. Nor had there been a zombie apocalypse recently, or a nuclear reactor fallout on the village green; bonus. Could my luck really be this good? I couldn't hit the Bid button fast enough; I might even have broken my mouse! I wanted this house. Dammit, if I had been able to secure a mortgage, I'd have bought this house because it was so pretty and perfectly well situated for where I wanted to live now; in a private little secluded spot which ensured our peace and safety.

As I was entitled to bid for two properties each week, I continued scrolling through the online catalogue and found a second little new build beauty, just as worth moving away and into as Property #1. I bid on it just in case Property #1 eluded me and, as you can imagine, I pretty much lived glued to my laptop screen until the close of Tuesday, when the week's bidding process ended. Now I had to wait, which was agony. I had no idea how long I had to wait either. I was guessing it was a long time, as there were so many houses and so many bids to process.

The following day however I got a phone call to tell me Property #1 was mine if I still wanted it. Dancing like a Muppet at a silent disco, I held myself together long enough to finish the call. Fizzing, I give them the information they wanted, plus the immense gratitude they deserved, before collapsing into a heap of relief and happy tears in the middle of the living room floor.

Then I phoned Paul, whilst texting Lauren, Hayley, Carrie and Eve with the good news. The only slight problem I had now was the fact that Property #1 was not available until 6 December, so Christmas was likely to be manic this year. I reassured myself that Steve still had to go to court and may even save the house, although this was unlikely. I wasn't convinced Steve wanted to save the house. In fact, there was every chance Steve had engineered all of this to prise open the equity funds into his/her/their money-grubbing hands.

No, I couldn't be sure of that, but nothing would have surprised me.

I caught myself on and decided whether Steve saved the house of not, we would still be moving out and away. I couldn't tolerate his influence in our lives any longer; with the uncertainty and naked malice that evidently came with him. This was my opportunity to branch out under my own recognisance, and create a new life of independence, as free and as far from Steve as I could get. Maybe I could leverage my earlier rapport with Lucia and negotiate more time to vacate, following my inevitable Notice to Quit? I needn't have worried, because it was all taken care of for me.

From out of the blue, my rapport building with Lucia was about to pay dividends. The postman arrived early afternoon, which was not unusual, and delivered a two-month extension, if I needed it. *Oh, hell yes!* I quickly drafted an acceptance letter, steeped in gratitude, and posted it that afternoon on the school run. I now had breathing space for the first time in weeks... months even. Evidently, Nationwide were highly aware of the optics of evicting a single mum with two children during the Christmas and winter season. Evidently, Nationwide were more concerned about where my children were going to live and sleep than their father was, and I will be forever grateful to them for that. All kudos to Nationwide and their legal team, with sincere and heartfelt thanks.

Dawn Rescue

Dawn and I had now known each other as friends for about eighteen months, but our friendship had been comparatively limited to chats during karate lessons, and the occasional after school coffee and natter.

Whilst undeniably relieved the children and I had somewhere to move to, I still didn't know how I was actually going to move us out. I couldn't afford a removal service and had no one available to help me lift and shift the larger, heavier items. Then one day whilst dropping Alex off at school, Dawn walked up to me at the classroom door and asked if I fancied a Costa Coffee: "*Always, but I haven't brought my purse to school*" – which although true, was also my roundabout way of saying I couldn't afford it. "*That doesn't matter, if you've got the time, I'd appreciate your help with something*", so she drove us to Costa Coffee and bought us breakfast.

We chatted about the issue Dawn was dealing with before moving onto my news about the new house. I then started to fret about how I was going to affect this relocation with only one hatchback car to my name, before Dawn announced: "*Don't worry, I'll help!*" and started detailing all the ways in which she and her family could help me make the transition. Seriously, how do I keep finding all of these angels? Like I said about Janet earlier, Helen had created room for them in my life by choosing Steve over me, and I could not be more thankful now if I tried. Yet again I'd lost a penny and found a tenner. Seriously Helen, *thanks!*

More than that though, and knowing how Steve had left our current house with a multitude of unfinished projects for us to live with, Dawn suggested we take the eviction extension time available, and the generous Dulux paint budget the housing association had given me, to create a beautiful and fully completed home for the children to move into; and she would help me decorate. This was a wonderful idea, and the children revelled in choosing their new bedroom paint colours and carpets. This helped to make moving to a new house an exciting adventure for them, rather than another emotional loss and upheaval.

As Dawn and her husband were in the middle of extensively renovating their home, they had all the tools and know-how to make our home project happen quickly. This was exciting and humbling, and I really should have paid for breakfast. Then it hit me. For all my life – by one definition or another – I have helped and rescued others. As a child I had also brought home innumerable hurt or deceased critters to nurse or bury [*much to Noel's annoyance*], and as a teenager and adult the rest is history.

Now for the first time in my life, I was being helped and rescued. Rescued by Paul, Lauren, Hayley, Carrie, Eve, Janet, my wide circle of friends and Team Karan supporters, Nationwide, Andy at the Job Centre, Auntie Alison, the borough council, Mr Smith, the housing association, and now Dawn and her family. This was karma. You must remember that you reap what you sow. If you sow shit you reap shit, but if you sow love and kindness, you reap love and kindness. It may take a while but trust the process. Please trust the process.

Dawn's generosity and friendship were beyond humbling, and I spent many hours in my head piecing together the parts of the jigsaw, to fully understand how my life was coming together really rather beautifully. I was still missing *my Steve* dreadfully, but I knew in all certainty that the man Helen was now living with, bore little or no resemblance to the man I had once loved and respected. I almost felt sorry for Helen, but quickly talked myself out of that. She had coveted Steve. She had wished for Steve to be hers, thinking she'd get what I had, but actually ending up with the dregs of what was left. Talk about a bait and switch! *Chuckle*.

Hear Me Out

Whilst I was waiting to take receipt of the keys for our new home, I was advised whilst consulting with my spiritual entourage, to do something shocking. I was advised to contact Steve and invite him to spend time with the kids. Wait, what? Yep, you heard me, but that's pretty much the reaction I had initially too. It had been fourteen months since our meeting with the mediators, which had demonstrated to Steve how strongly resolute the children and I were in our position. In the months that had passed, Steve had done nothing to try and re-establish contact with his children.

Christmas and their birthdays had come and gone – again – and he had sent them merely cards (and a little cash) professing love from all of them, knowing full well how the children felt about Helen, Oliver and Emily. With every month that had passed, my disgust and contempt for the Imposter had only solidified further. Now my Guides wanted me to do what? Seriously? This spiritual guidance lark is seriously testing, but then that's the point, isn't it: there's no growth with challenge. *Urgh!*

My War Council was called upon and almost every member reacted the same way you did, initially. But the more we discussed the merits of the case, the more we revealed the potential benefits. Of course, the exercise was fraught with danger, because it could all fail and result in two desperately hurt children again, but there were ways to mitigate those risks. This would also involve a huge climb down from my moral high horse, and a willingness to be brutally ejected from my newly established comfort zone. Sod butterflies in my stomach, we were back to the bats and pigeons, whenever I seriously contemplated contacting Steve again. This was the last thing I wanted to do or focus on now that I had a new home to prepare and move into; but there's no growth without challenge. *Ahh, shut up!*

At 8.23am on Tuesday 8 December 2015 I sent Steve the following text message. He had blocked me on WhatsApp, but not my number from his phone interestingly enough: *"Dear Steve, It's been a long time since we last spoke, I hope you're well? We both know the house will soon be repossessed. I will be taking Sofia and Alex to the park on Saturday 19 December, between 11am - 12pm, if you would like to see them before we leave the area; they would truly love to see you. I will park myself – and a flask of coffee – in the wooden shelter/seating area of the main playground and hope to see you there. Take care. Karan"*.

I sent the text and instantly felt sick. I personally never wanted to see or be in his Imposter energy again, but I had to give Real Daddy one last chance to make his peace and reconcile with his children. Maybe he thought I'd stab him in the bollocks if he came anywhere near them? God knows I'd thought about it, so he was right to be cautious, but I had also told him we were going to love him through this crisis. Perhaps he would think I was lying or trying to trick him? Unfortunately, he was likely to be judging everyone by his own (and Helen's) despicable standards, so I couldn't win.

The text was carefully worded to try and persuade Steve he was safe to accept the invitation, that I knew about the repossession, so he didn't have any monumental news items to break to me if we were to meet. I also alluded to the fact we were moving out of the area (which was entirely true), to add a sense of urgency to this opportunity. How many other chances would he get, if he passed on this one? How difficult would future contact with the children be? How far away were we moving exactly? These were all questions I was deliberately trying to plant in his mind. I knew he was either fearful or reluctant to see me, and I was fine with that, but could he strap on a pair of man-stones just long enough to rescue his weakening relationship with his children, before it was potentially too late?

[341]

Although hurt and angry, the children *still* love and miss him terribly. Maybe enough time had passed for Steve to reconsider his standpoint? Maybe now he could countenance "living two lives", or at least be willing to see them regularly and respect their anti-Helen sentiments? Maybe by seeing how much the children had grown, and how beautiful they are, would twang some god forsaken memory in his mind, and reignite his paternal need to hold and love them again? I had to try. I had to be able to say – hand on heart – that I had done everything I could possibly think of, to hold the children's relationship with their father together. I had to be able to look them squarely in the eye and tell them I had done my best to affect their wishes. If I failed it would be on him.

True to who he is was now, Steve didn't respond to this text at all; giving himself wiggle room until the last possible moment I guessed. This left me juggling the viables: a) Had he received the text? b) Had he received the text but was going to ignore it and not show up? c) Had he received the text but Helen was prohibiting the meet? d) Was he going to accept the invitation and the spirit in which it was offered? e) Was he going to accept the invitation, show up and tear me a new one? f) Was he going to show up with Helen? Urgh. The possibilities went on and on, so I caught myself on and focused on the cards I knew I had, and for all that I was responsible for... me.

Bolstered by ongoing wise counsel from my War Council, I decided I would be true to my word and take the children to the park as promised. If Steve failed to show up or arrived but then turned around and left upon seeing us in the distance, or even invited World War IV by bringing Helen, that would be his karma to carry. I was responsible for me, so I was going to do my best in this situation, because it would put me in the best possible position in the next situation. I had to be the best version of myself.

[342]

Without integrity we have nothing.

Whilst Sofia knew something was afoot and wanted the details, we decided not to tell Alex about our plan. Sofia was old enough and emotionally mature enough to understand the risks I was taking, and for the greater good I was trying to bring about. Sofia didn't want to be blindsided again (with a surprise encounter in the park), and so accepted the risk of being hurt by a potential no-show. Alex however was still far too fragile after the Sunday 16 February 2014 "*Just five more minutes Mummy*" devastation to even consider telling him. So, this is the plan Sofia and I devised.

I would take the children out for breakfast as a special treat, and to fill their little tummies in readiness for the cold December morning. Whilst having breakfast I would ask if they fancied having a visit to the park. Sofia would respond excitedly, leading Alex (in case he wasn't that interested because it was cold) into agreeing with her. I needn't have worried because Alex never passes on an opportunity to run around like a wild thing; he's my perpetually active little Duracell Drummer Bunny. We then drove to, and parked inside the park, before walking up to the area where I said we'd be. I duly sat down in the wooden shelter, opened my flask and let the kids run their legs off. It was a good idea for them to generate some body heat for whatever may have come next. If Steve failed to show, we would simply leave the park after an hour or so, with Alex none the wiser, and me having only Sofia to console.

We arrived about fifteen minutes early, just long enough for the kids to go off and play, and for me to compose myself. It was important I held my temper whether Steve arrived on his own or not, or regardless of anything he might say and do. Then my nerves kicked in. What if he didn't arrive? Whilst Alex would remain oblivious in the short term, how in the world could I save

Steve's relationship with Sofia; it would be in tatters? I started to rehearse some of the excuses I could offer her if he didn't show up, i.e.: maybe he didn't get the text, because he never did respond? Maybe he forgot, because I didn't remind him? Maybe he was unwell that day, and simply too ignorant to advise me accordingly?

I sat where I said I'd be and kept an eye on the vehicles driving into the park, as we had done. Then a few minutes after 11am [*typically*], I saw Steve walking towards me from the perimeter fence, as he'd parked in a nearby side street and had no doubt conducted a recce to see if we were there, before approaching us from his vantage point. I know it can't have been easy for him, and I was impressed with his courage and grasp of his life's priorities at last.

Neither of the children had seen him coming, and his appearance had changed a lot since they had seen him last. He walked up to me and we said hello calmly and civilly. He asked if the children knew he was coming and I confirmed that Sofia did, but Alex did not. I warned him gently there would be tears and snot bubbles, and he nodded to confirm he'd heard me, but looked like he was swallowing his own wrought emotions. I stood up slowly, so as not to spook him, and took a couple of steps towards the swings Sofia was playing on. She happened to be facing away from Steve, and it took a couple of calls for her to hear me. This roused Alex's attention too, who was behind Steve and possibly didn't recognise the back of his head. With both children looking at me I said: "*Here's your daddy*".

About 20-30 paces away, they both started walking in Steve's direction, but as he turned around to face them, they both ran at him with their arms opened wide. When they reached him, they threw their arms around him and

[344]

squeezed, as Steve kissed the tops of their heads and hugged them back. Alex started crying, disbelieving this was really happening. Sofia looked overwhelmed and like she was trying to retain some emotional control. Steve looked mostly dry eyed, but otherwise highly emotional, whilst I thought I was going to choke on the lump in my throat.

We all sat down in the wooden seating area, and everyone clammed up. No one knew what to say, so I started to lighten the mood by gently teasing the children about how big they'd gotten, and how Alex would eat us out of house and home if I let him. We talked about Alex's karate, and the children's excellent school reports, all nice and neutral stuff, but it was hard work. Steve was clearly uncomfortable and noticing the disconnect between him and his children, but this is precisely what we were trying to rectify. I offered Steve a picnic-sized cup of coffee to help warm him through, but he declined more than once, so I drank some in front of him in case he thought it poisoned or something.

I had taken a backpack filled with various balls *[leave it!]* for the children to play with, either in the playground, or on the vast expanses of grass all around. Sofia and Alex asked for a ball, so they could go and shoot hoops, and Steve was up on his feet and away with them in a hurry. He clearly didn't want to sit and talk or explain himself to iron things out. Fine by me.

It wasn't long before the kids wanted to play on the playground equipment, so Steve quickly found himself coming in handy by pushing them up and down zip wires etc. The kids were having fun, seemed happy and were otherwise at ease and relatively comfortable with him. I remained seated in the wooden shelter, drinking coffee and watching discretely for signs of upset or distress. The children eventually gravitated towards some play equipment at the outer edge of the playground, far away from me, only just within view if I stood up, but they seemed to be sitting and chatting with Steve now. All seemed well.

True to form, my coffee ran through me – and the cold weather didn't help – so I needed the loo. The nearest toilets were located about 500 yards away from where the children were talking with Steve. Was I comfortable to leave the playground for a toilet break, and leave Steve alone with the kids? I had no reason to think not, so I walked closer to them, so they heard me when I told them where I was going, but otherwise turned around and went to the loo. I wanted to demonstrate to Steve that despite whatever lies Helen may have been telling him about me (like I was having an affair and poisoning the children against him), that he actually knew me better than anyone ever had. I had every right to be pissed off with what he'd done, but I had also vowed to love him forever and never cause him harm. This was me walking that walk. No, we were never going to be a couple again, but I didn't want to hurt him. If I had wanted that, he would have known about it long before now.

I came back from the loo and took up my position in the wooden seating area again, still resolved to give Steve and the children as much private healing time as possible. I waved at the kids, so they knew I was back, but I otherwise let them enjoy their precious daddy time. After another hour or so it was time for us to go home as Sofia was due another course of antibiotics, and we were already slightly behind schedule. I explained this to Steve and invited him back for a hot chocolate, but unsurprisingly he declined.

Steve and the children hugged and said their goodbyes. I waited for Steve to say something – *anything!* – about seeing them again soon, but he didn't. I also waited for him to ask where we were moving to, but he didn't ask that either. I was beyond stunned, so had to take the bull by the horns by saying: "*If this is the last time you want to see the children, tell them now*". He said this was not what he wanted, so I continued: "*That's good, because they love you and they want you. You love them, and you want them. I have reached out to you, to try and get you back on track. The ball is now in your court. You have my mobile phone number, and you have my email address, so you're able to contact me when you're ready*".

All he said in reply to that was: "*It's been two years and a lot has changed*". Not fully understanding what he meant by that, because he clammed up immediately afterwards and wouldn't be drawn further, I reiterated that the ball was now in his court, and that the children loved him and wanted him.

Please tell me what more I could have done?

We walked back to the car, with neither the children nor I ever looking back. Obviously, I have no idea if Steve looked back, but I'm betting he did. I will never know how he repeatedly declined my invitations to spend more time with the children, but that's what he did. I had zero comprehension of who he was, and I didn't like this version either.

He felt frightened to me. He felt heavy, leaden and sorrowful. The children told me he didn't once look at his phone (to text or speak with Helen), which surprised me if I'm honest. I felt sure she'd want updates in real time, or that she'd otherwise gate-crash his time with them. That's not to say his phone wasn't vibrating its battery flat in his pocket, just that he was able to resist if it was. The kids also said his voice sounded strained and higher than usual [*barely suppressed emotion?*], and that he kept looking over at me [*in case I was running with scissors and looking for balls to stab?*]. He was otherwise

[347]

engaged and easy going, but the children didn't feel truly connected with him, which upset them. I felt like he may have been there to say his goodbyes but hoped more than anything to be wrong.

The kids and I got home, had some hot chocolate and cuddles, where I answered Alex's questions: Did I know he was going to be there? *No, but I had invited him and hoped for the best.* When will I see him again? *I honestly don't know, but he knows he need only phone or text to set something up.* And then the tears came, exactly what I feared would happen. The whole exercise could neither be claimed as a success or failure, it felt like a big, fat, glutinous *meh*.

As the days turned into months, and still no "Thanks for that" text, or follow up request to see the children, I was baffled. I had a bit of a rage at my spiritual entourage: "*You told me to invite him... but for what? WTF was that about – nothing happened?!*" I asked my supremely spiritual, wise and gifted friend for any insight she might have had into the situation, and she told me this (and I'm paraphrasing): "*The whole process was suggested so you could show the children you would do anything for them, and anything to help restore their relationship with their father. Obviously if he had optimised the opportunity you gave him, then so much the better, but if he failed to make the most of it, the children would always know that you gave them your all*". Hmm, cold comfort.

Whilst I didn't appreciate the weak outcome, I could see the sense in what my friend was telling me. From the end of November, when it was first suggested I contact Steve, through to the 8 December when I text him, to the 19 December for the meet itself, I had been suffering with huge doubt and anxiety. The whole thing had been agony for me to live through, only to be rewarded with this tepid, grey, *meh* of an outcome. It didn't feel fair. I believed the courage Sofia and I had exhibited in the run up and execution of the invitation warranted a triumphant reconciliation. Instead we felt more grief and disbelief. Oh well.

THE TIDE FINALLY TURNS

Mallie-Free

We visited Mallie on Wednesday 23 December 2015, to have dinner and to collect the children's Christmas presents. None of us enjoyed these visits as they were a study in hard work, self-control and swallowing more words than you permitted yourself to say; because it just wasn't worth it. Years ago, I devised this strategy: get in, get out and have the same number of live ~~biddies'~~ bodies as you did when you arrived. Mallie had been able to suck the will to live out of me without speaking a word. Her energy had been kryptonite to me in my younger years, before I learned how to tune her out and neutralise her... err... *ways*. I was not a fan, but I put up with her, for the sake of Steve and the children's relationship with her, for 26 years. I'd have been out for murder in less time than that!

We arrived in a flurry of fake cheerfulness, trying to make the best of the interminable hours which lay ahead. The children and I had armoured ourselves by visualising an imaginary force field around us, which would repel all of Mallie's snark and negativity. I can't speak for the kids, but the Star Wars Imperial March was deafening between my ears as I crossed the threshold. We had arrived. Let the games begin.

We were greeted with a cheery *"Hiya"* from Mallie in the kitchen, as Alex decided he wanted to change straight into the policeman's costume he'd left behind previously. He ran upstairs to get changed, eventually bringing down his civvies for me to look after on the sofa beside me. He and Sofia then went to play upstairs, leaving Mallie and I dangerously unattended. We made small talk for a couple of minutes, before Mallie was no longer able to contain herself and blurted out, without thinking through the consequences: *"It was so good of you to let Steve see the children on Saturday*". Let? Fucking *let*? Karan stepped into the arena and unsheathed her mighty truth.

Oh, what bullshit had Steve told this woman? What prissy little pussy had he pretended to be, to polish the cheap alloy halo over his head in front of his mummy? Mallie clearly had not been told – or accepted – the truth of this matter. Mallie didn't appear to know – or accept – that it was Steve who had walked out on his children, who had refused to spend time with them (without Helen and brood in tow), simply because he was not willing "to live two lives". I looked her directly in the eyes and stated calmly and surgically: "*There is no let about it. Steve has repeatedly rejected the children by hanging the phone up on them, not calling, not arriving to collect them, not wanting to live two lives, not visiting Sofia in hospital when she had the meningitis scare*".

Mallie launched. Mallie then got herself hot and emotional under the collar as she told me it was all my fault, because there was no reason Helen and I could not still be friends. Scoffing and incredulous, I asked Mallie if Len – hypothetically – ever had an affair with Teresa's childhood friend Judy, would she still expect Teresa to be friends with the adulteress? Mallie snapped: "*That would never happen*", to which I retorted: "*That's what I thought with Steve and Helen, but I was wrong*". It was clear to me now that Steve and Helen really had sold Mallie a complete pile of horse shit about how they had got together. Fine, so be it, Mallie wasn't worth the time or energy to convince otherwise. The truth will always out, and so I left it there in the spirit of rescuing what time was left of this visit.

I did however want to shed some light on the depths of Steve's descent into deadbeat daddery. Deliberately trying to destabilise Mallie's glowing opinion

[351]

of ole Golden Bollocks, I informed her succinctly that he'd had the house repossessed and was shamefully making his children homeless. Hah! What do you say to that, bitch? Mallie shot back in a beat with: *"Well he couldn't afford the mortgage!"* Wait, what? For the first time in 26 years, Mallie had silenced and outplayed me. I hadn't expected her to know this, and I most certainly didn't expect her to excuse his awful, heinous actions and selfish choices. She had known. She had fucking known! And she didn't say anything to the mother of her grandchildren? She hadn't reached out to check on where we would live, if the children would be okay, or how we would manage? Where was her love, compassion and concern for Sofia and Alex?

Yep, she had known all along, and not once did she think to phone to offer so much as a crumb of support for the children. I knew she disliked me intensely, and could not have cared less if I lived or died, but what about her grandchildren? My mind was reeling and struggling to compute her coldness, her detachment from the children and wilful ignorance in respect of the lesser Imposter Steve had become. Furthermore, if Mallie had prior knowledge of the house being repossessed, then so did Teresa, Len, Mike and Kate. Collectively, or individually, where was the outpouring of love and concern for their grandchildren, niece and nephew? What is wrong with these people?

Oh, but Mallie wasn't finished yet. Mallie was spurting out verbal diarrhoea as if her oral sphincter was malfunctioning, and she couldn't stop. She then foolishly started to disparage Sofia, who'd been playing peacefully upstairs with Alex since we arrived about ten minutes earlier. She started spitting out all the venomous accusations she'd once levied against Mike's eldest daughter, Emma, when his first marriage was in crisis, and Emma had naturally supported her mother through it. Sofia was X, Sofia was Y, Sofia was the other, and none of it good. We had to leave before I told Mallie her fortune. I had to get out of there, because I was not prepared to argue with this cretinous octogenarian.

I stood up and called for the kids to get their coats and shoes on, because we were leaving. Understandably confused, because we had only just arrived, and oblivious to the tempest brewing downstairs, the kids questioned what was going on. I was not prepared to explain right there and then, so impatiently hurried them into putting their shoes and coats on. The timer was ticking down fast on this timebomb about to go off, if I didn't get out of there soon.

The kids sensed this from my face and scrambled to their feet and towards the door. Mallie looked at me and said: "*You're not going to do this!*". I snapped my head back in her direction and with a quietly seething ferocity, I looked her dead in the eyes and stated resolutely: "*Watch me*". Mallie spluttered and reiterated that we couldn't leave, which finally unlocked: "*I have put up with you for 26 years, for the love of Steve and the children, but it's now time for you to say goodbye to your grandchildren*".

We walked the length of the long hall towards the front door, where a huge pile of Christmas presents was waiting to be loaded into my car. I was perfectly prepared to leave them behind, but Mallie insisted I take them. I don't think she fully grasped what I meant when I told her to say goodbye to her grandchildren. She never did listen. I duly loaded the presents into the car, as the children were gathering their belongings together. Just as we were ready to leave, Alex remembered his civvies were still in the living room. I told him to go and fetch them quickly, so he ran past Mallie in the hall, as Sofia and I were standing at the door, and he collected his clothes. As Alex ran back past Mallie in the hall, she grabbed him by the shoulders and shook him, saying: *"Everything's Mummy's fault, everything's Mummy's fault!"* somewhat hysterically. She shook my seven-year-old son! She shook my seven-year-old son in front of me! Enraged and barely able to contain myself, I hurried the children out of the door. Alex was in shock and crying. All I wanted to do was calm and comfort him, but my fury was about to snap its leash, and I didn't trust myself with this abysmal relic.

We drove home, with a million questions spilling out of Sofia's mind and into the dystopian silence of the car. But I couldn't speak to answer any of them. The outrage caught in my throat, as the words unsaid had devoured my voice. I wasn't sure I knew what the hell had just happened to be able to explain it to her. All I knew was that Mallie would never see her grandchildren again, because they weren't loved or safe with her. If she could shake Alex in front of me, if she could try and poison my child against his mother in front of me, then what the hell was she capable of on her own?

Alex had settled by the time we finally got home, but Sofia was brewing, also enraged by Mallie's assault on her baby brother. Like most siblings, Alex and Sofia can argue, bicker and drive each other up the wall and down again, but only they are allowed to irritate each other. If anyone else so much as looks at the other sideways, they will come rushing in to defend and protect. Sofia was furious and disgusted by what had just happened; once I'd calmed down enough to explain what she'd witnessed and heard. Alex was frightened and, unsurprisingly, never wanted to see Mallie again. Which was handy, because I was never going to allow that to happen.

We had been scheduled to return to Mallie's house on Monday 28 December 2015, the day after Mallie's birthday. Steve, Helen, Oliver and Emily were visiting on the birthday itself, so we were going to go the day after, along with Teresa and Len, and possibly their adult daughter Jess. Mallie clearly knew something was wrong because she left a couple of voicemail messages asking me what time we planned to arrive on Monday. This was a weak excuse to call and to try and clear the air, because we had already agreed upon a time, the time it had always been. I didn't respond to any of her messages because we were done, and I had no interest relitigating what had happened. There was no excuse for attacking Sofia the way that she had, and shaking Alex was simply unforgivable.

On Monday 28 December things stepped up a gear, as I knew they would. When it became clear the children and I would not be attending Mallie's birthday dinner, Teresa tried calling my mobile phone, which I ignored. We then had the following text exchange, interspersed with her repeated attempts to call me. I knew that if we spoke, Teresa would likely hand the phone to Mallie, and I wasn't about to be drawn into another battle.

[Karan]: *Hi Teresa, hope you've had a lovely Christmas? We won't be coming for dinner, so please go ahead at your convenience. Thank you for the children's Xmas presents, they love them all and Alex even tried to sleep in the jacket! Wishing you a happy, healthy and prosperous New Year - I hope it's your best one yet x"*

[Teresa]: *Hi Karan, we had a very different, relaxing Christmas thank you. What time do you think you will be over? Really looking forward to seeing you all xx*

[Karan]: *Like I said, we won't be coming over. Please enjoy your day, have a safe trip home and a happy new year x*

[Teresa]: *There are more presents here at Mum's for Sofia and Alex, and Jess would love to see you all. Is there something or has there been something going on since we last spoke? xx*

Like she didn't know. Do I look like I've just come down the Lagan in a bubble?

[Karan]: *Have a chat with your mum.*

[Teresa]: *If you don't want to come over here, can we pop over to you please? xxx*

[Karan]: *You, Len and Jess (+ Mike & Kate) are welcome this afternoon. We're out now, so please let me know what time you're thinking. Please respect my position regarding this matter, it is not my wish/intention for this issue to involve you too.*

[Teresa]: *Can we come over about 3.30pm?*

[Karan]: *Yes, that's fine.*

I knew Mallie was likely to only convey her version of events, but I didn't care. These people were nothing to me anymore, and their opinions of me mattered not. All I was trying to do now was salvage the children's relationship with as many people on that side of their family as possible, even if it meant I had to continue gritting my teeth to get through it.

At around 3.30pm I saw their car pull up outside the gate, before swinging out into the road, to reverse down the drive. This did not bode well. My hackles were up as Mallie was barely mobile on her feet, and I wanted to make sure Len wasn't parking her as close to my front door as possible. I couldn't make out who all the occupants in the car were, but there was clearly

[356]

one more than Teresa, Len and Jess. Surely, they wouldn't be so stupid as to test me and bring Mallie?

I opened the front door and stood imposingly on the threshold, specifically to block access until I knew who the fourth passenger was. Teresa and Len got out straight away, and Teresa mounted the two steps up to the door to be standing directly in front of me. I refused to move. Jess got out of the car, but the fourth occupant was being somewhat hesitant. Teresa said: *"Hello dear, how are you?"*, possibly expecting me to stand aside, but I remained in position. If this was a test, they were about to fail it. Then the remaining car door opened, and Jake (Jess' brother) got out. Teresa said: *"Is it okay if Jake comes in?"* which of course it was. I simply hadn't been aware he'd made the journey from Berkshire with them.

They spent a couple of hours or so with us, giving the children more gifts and initiating silly games to break the awkward silences. I had nothing I wanted to say to them, so just let the kids play with their relatives. It was awkward and stiff. No mention of Mallie or the incident took place. It was a civil and good-natured visit, but I was glad when they left. Little did I realise that this would be the last we would hear from them for months, just as I was about to embark upon preparing our new home and moving us in. Absolutely zero interest was shown in where we were going, how we were managing, if there was anything they could do to help, kiss my arse or nothing. The elephant in the room was wilfully and skilfully ignored. Noted.

Towards the end of February, Teresa sent me a text and asked for our new address, so she could send my birthday card. I sent back a quick reply to advise her to send anything through to the old address, as we hadn't moved yet. This was all true, and it must have perplexed them with how slow rolling our eviction had been, but as they hadn't shown any interest or concern, I chose not to offer any insight. Like I've said before, I never volunteered more information than was absolutely necessary, and so they had no idea about the Nationwide time extension we'd been offered. They asked nothing, so they knew nothing, and I have no appetite to defend or explain myself to people who are determined to believe the worst lies about me.

Then at 10.23pm on 23 March 2016 I received an uncharacteristically late-night text from Teresa, just before the Easter school holiday: "*Hi Karan, Len and I are coming for a flying visit following our visit to Harry Potter World tomorrow. We would love to see you all – do you want to come over to Mum's or shall we come over to you? xx*"

OMG, where to start unpacking this? I had advised Teresa and Len repeatedly about how skint the children and I were, only to be directed to the nearest food bank. How thoughtful and considerate of her to tell me what expensive fun they were going to be having, whilst I'm scrambling to secure food and a new home for her niece and nephew.

Secondly, was she seriously giving me less than 24 hours' notice before summoning us for an audience with them - *hello?* Some of us are skint, single-mothers of your niece and nephew, rendered homeless by your selfish, crisis-riddled brother, attempting to pack, decorate, relocate and unpack into a new home, whilst ensuring the kids attend school, do their homework, eat well, exercise regularly and otherwise survive this sustained assault on their childhood. I'm so sorry I can't drop everything to service your latest whim.

And finally, what planet was she on trying to paper over the canyon between her mother and I? Good lord, did she really anticipate high levels of success with this implausible gambit? Honestly, these people! I text back: *"Hi Teresa, so sorry but we have plans tomorrow, and all of the Easter holidays are pretty hectic to be honest. Hope you enjoy your Harry Potter thingy. Love to you both, take care xxx"*. To which she responded: *"That's a shame, it would have been a quick visit on Friday xx"* which did not persuade me otherwise. Besides, this last sentence was a statement not a question, I didn't have anything to add and so went to bed. Never forget, silence itself can be a powerful answer.

Decorating Is A Point Of View

Everything I had said was true. I got the keys to the house on 22 December 2015, but planned to decorate the place before we moved in. The kids picked out their paint colours and carpets, and I ordered them some new beds and bedroom furniture, along with some new kitchen appliances I needed. This was all funded by a rather lovely surprise cheque from my late father's bank.

Apparently, they had conducted a full review of his account prior to shutting it down after his death and had run a routine PPI check on it. Now here I was with a cheque for thousands of pounds in my hot little disbelieving hands because he'd had five PPI's pay out. Seriously my luck has never been so good since Steve left me! It was like a bath plug had been pulled which sucked away all the negativity around us.

As Paul had had his PIP backdated, paid out, and was otherwise financially secure and comfortable, he graciously let me keep the half I was honour bound to share with him. He had been just this side of fraught, worrying about how I was going to furnish our new home before Dad delivered us from this concern from beyond the grave. Carrie came and helped me on Decorating Day #1 (5 January 2016, when the kids went back to school after Christmas), before telling me she was pregnant and subsequently forbidden from helping any further. When I asked her why she hadn't told me of her pregnancy beforehand, she stated: *"Because you wouldn't have let me help"*. Damn right! I'd have made her a cup of tea and told her to put her feet up – or sent her home of course, but this is the measure of who she is. That didn't stop her taking the kids out for days during the half term holiday, sparing them from the boredom of watching me paint in a cold, empty shell of a house. Carrie wasn't allowed to decorate or lift anything (as far as I was concerned), but she still did all that she could to continue helping; for which the kids and I were truly grateful.

Dawn had a prior engagement on Decorating Day #1, but oh boy did she make up for it when she got going. We spent almost every day (when I wasn't seeing clients or working on the business), painting and preparing the new house between 5 January and 1 May 2016, when we eventually moved in. We primarily worked on school days, but Dawn and her husband worked over a couple of weekends painting ceilings, to help move things along. In turn, I continued to work throughout the February and Easter school holidays, which is why I was too busy to meet up with Teresa, following her Harry Potter World trip. Not that she thought to ask how we were getting on. Perhaps she was afraid I might ask for help? But I never did or would.

Dawn was an absolute godsend and helped to reveal how much I'm truly capable of. For instance, who knew I am absolutely amazing at cutting in and glossing doors without drips? I didn't! Admittedly I would urge you to buy a lovely Harris paintbrush, but with a lovely Harris paint brush, the cutting in I was able to achieve around my light switches, power sockets, door frames and coving is legendary; even if I do say so myself. This I would not have learned about myself until the only way to get it done was to do it. The same can be said for the furniture Dawn and I put together, simply by following the instructions carefully and patiently. We've also put up shelves, Venetian blinds, towel rails and saucepan racks, we did it all. We took the view that if a man can do this, how hard can it be?

Then there was Janet who turned up, not feeling at all well, and base coated my ludicrously large downstairs bathroom [*which Sofia jokingly refers to as the dance studio*] just because she promised she would. These fabulous women walked through the fire with me, when "family" busied themselves looking elsewhere or counting their money. Dawn and I moved the majority of the contents from the old house to new house, before Lee helped with a couple of guys to lift and shift the big stuff on moving day.

Now I had to juggle the costs of two homes temporarily. Whilst I was not paying rent to Steve on our family home, I was still liable for council tax until we moved out. Where the new house was concerned, I was liable for both rent and council tax, from the moment I took possession of the keys. All of this expenditure helped to drain my Dad's PPI windfall pretty quickly, but then Paul stepped in. He knew how important it was for me to provide the children with a completely finished house, personalised to their tastes and entirely lovely to move into.

Paul understood my frustration of living in my "make do marriage" for 24 years, and never enjoying a fully finished house. I chose to optimise the eviction time extension, was thankful for Paul's financial generosity and Dawn's insane act of friendship, to give the children the best I could. If ever two children deserved the best parenting I could ever wring out of myself, Sofia and Alex were they. Delivering my best for these children has been the making of me.

Don't get me wrong, the only reason our old house was never entirely finished was because Steve was working his nuts off building a business and providing for his family. I understood it then, and I understand it now. That being said however, I cannot stress how maddening it was to see the beautiful results he could achieve for his clients, but not for our family home. This was now my opportunity to stop the rot. This was now my opportunity to become more than I had previously been and to create what I had always dreamed of. Steve never did fulfil my dreams in this respect, I did.

By the time the house was finished however I had one enormous, grotesque question leering at me: if I had been capable of decorating the new house, why hadn't I redecorated the old house, and taken some of the pressure and expectation off of the fiendishly hard-working Steve? I felt like I'd been impaled and run through the guts when I demanded this answer from myself. Why hadn't I done more? My War Council agreed this was a valid question, but they also slapped some sense into me. Prior to my Helen-blindness, I was running a home, a business, a husband and responsible for two very young children. It was now unreasonable of me to have expected more from myself in the past, as I had been pulling more than my fair share of the weight. Hmm, okay.

Shanked

With the decorating complete, the carpets and flooring down, the appliances in, the furniture built and positioned, Dawn and I worked like maniacs to get the old house emptied into the new house. Yes, Lee and his mates had helped to take care of moving the large bulky stuff, but Dawn and I moved the million boxes [*I counted!*] of stuff, and we made dozens of time-consuming trips. I shudder to think of the miles we racked up between us. Thankfully Dawn had a large MPV at the time, so together with my mid-sized hatchback, things could have been a lot worse. Things can always be a lot worse, which is why we must be thankful for all that we have, when we have it. There is a profound proverb I quote often: *I once complained of having no shoes, until I met a man with no feet.* Hmm, quickly wedgies you out of self-pity, doesn't it?

We had set the goal of moving into the new house on Sunday 1 May 2016 (over the May Day Bank Holiday weekend), primarily because it was the start of a new month re: housing benefit and council tax relief. This we did, and the kids revelled in the adventure. There were no tears or regret about moving out of the old house, which I thought there might have been, due its association with their errant daddy. They still talk about how excited they were to move somewhere new and fresh, so again, things could have been a lot worse.

Then, if Dawn couldn't have been a better friend already, she and her husband dashed out on moving day to collect a cache of pizza goodies, so I didn't have to worry about destroying something for dinner in my new oven. Yes, really. Yes, I know she's a gift. Yes, I have told her so, but am quickly shushed because she doesn't crave attention and adulation, like you know who.

Whilst we were all moved into and sleeping in the new house, we still had a lot of possessions in the old house left to recover; we'd lived there for over twenty years don't forget. Dawn and I continued to shift another million [*nods*] boxes during our first week in, and were hot, sweaty messes at the end of every day. We could not have worked any harder and were successfully keeping a multitude of plates spinning simultaneously. I was also obliged to inform the council that I had moved out of the old house, which I did directly after the bank holiday on Tuesday 3 May 2016.

Imagine my surprise then on Saturday 7 May, when I still had about a third of the old house contents left to clear, to receive a phone call from my friend and neighbour from across the road, Shelly. Shelly rang to tell me that Steve, Helen and a locksmith were forcibly gaining access to the old house (as I'd changed the locks when he moved out), even though I had clearly not finished moving.

This, only five months after inviting him to the park, in good faith, to see the children before we left the area. I was shocked, hurt and infuriated. If he had just waited another day or so, until I'd processed everything, I'd have gladly given him the damn keys. Thinking about it though, I quickly pieced together why Steve was choosing to shank me in this way, even after my December act of kindness and attempted parental reconciliation. The answer of course was money.

As I had notified the council of our relocation, Steve (as the legal owner) was now responsible for the property's council tax, and he clearly was not prepared to pay for this and allow me continued access to our belongings. It wasn't just my stuff he was denying me either, as a great many of the children's toys and prized possessions were denied to them also. So childish and petulant of him. So needlessly mean and spiteful. I do hope he felt proud of himself. I do hope he felt like a big man and smug in his ability to oust me from the house once and for all. I do hope he can imagine what his gentle, honourable and compassionate father thought of his choices and behaviour.

Shelly also told me how Helen made a point of standing on the threshold of the front door, up high because of the steps into the house, appearing to survey all that she had conquered. I chuckled because she had conquered an empty relic of a marriage she had helped to annihilate, which was soon to be repossessed. This repossession would negatively affect Steve's credit rating for a minimum of six years and would forever be a tightening noose around their future dreams and goals. This was the very definition of a hollow victory, and the daft bint hadn't realised it yet. Her karma was deepening and darkening with every unforced error she was willingly stepping into; and all I had to do was wait for it to play out.

I can only hope Steve did the decent thing with the (sentimental) items of value we were forced to leave behind. I know I still had some possessions belonging to Mum, Dad and Nanna to pick up, which may now be truly gone forever; perhaps even burnt in a fire bin for all I know. I can't possibly overestimate the influence Helen has on Steve's thinking now, nor the malevolence he carries in his heart for me.

One thing I can confirm right here and now though, as a direct message to Steve and his family is this: all the (sentimental) valuables, photographs and heirlooms of your father's, and other deceased loved ones you have cherished, will remain safe in my care, before I hand them down to the children at the appropriate time. I choose to honour the love you have for your father and loved ones and will respect their possessions accordingly. You may have destroyed my past, but I am mortally sorry you are not worth looking down upon. I will let you shoulder the karmic consequences for this alone; be lucky.

Artemis' Boulder

The house was repossessed at 12.20pm on 20 June 2016, and I sat alone in our new home and cried. The eternal optimist in me had hoped Steve would wake up and rescue his life's work in the nick of time, but old school friends Lee and Shelly watched the process unfold from across the road, and solemnly confirmed he did not. Steve arrived and handed over the keys to whoever, letting our past successes slip from between his fingers on a keyring, and for what? I couldn't surmount the grief I felt for the needless waste our years together now represented, for the mountain of work we'd done together and for the countless sacrifices we'd made. Now here we were, middle-aged and back at square one with nothing. I didn't know how at the time, but I vowed the years I now considered a waste, had to count for something. I then suddenly had the following blog article burst out of me.

Artemis had been pushing an enormous boulder up the side of a mountain for a great many years; decades to be precise. Not only was the boulder massive and heavy, it was also stubborn and awkward to manoeuvre, but Artemis persevered anyway.

The closer to the top of the mountain Artemis got, the heavier the boulder and the steeper the mountainside became, but Artemis persevered anyway. What drove Artemis to persevere? Well, Artemis was determined to reach the pinnacle, because it was what she and the boulder had agreed upon decades ago. It was a shared goal, so Artemis continued to push onwards, despite the pain and challenges it cost her to make it happen.

The problem came however when, almost at the top, the boulder didn't want to go - or to be - at the top anymore. The boulder explained that he was tired from having been pushed all that way, over so many years, and was now resentful because he thought the view would be different. Disappointed with the view and resentful from having been pushed to the place he had initially wanted to go; the boulder made the decision to slide back down the mountainside - carelessly *and remorselessly destroying all of the intricate footholds that had been created on the way up. Those who had cheered and supported the boulder's ascent, were now crushed and aghast by his wilful descent.*

Artemis was taken down the mountainside too, powerless to prevent the wanton and needless destruction of their progress and ambition. The boulder was resolute in his determination to roll back as far away from the summit - and everything *that had been achieved - because he feared the great heights once available to him.*

And so, the day came when the boulder and Artemis lay at the foot of the mountain, staring up at the carnage and debris. The boulder now, as he had always done, sat motionless and waiting to be pushed up a new mountainside, hoping the view would be better next time - little realising the view is only ever what you create it to be.

Artemis, now released from the debilitating and oppressive weight and magnitude of the boulder, chose to stand up and dust herself down, before beginning her fresh ascent up a new and picturesque mountainside. Now stronger and entirely unfettered, Artemis created new footholds, *found new and powerful leverage points, and a clearer path to the top. And the view? Well, that will be whatever Artemis has envisioned it to be; watch this space!*

I know there will be zero points for subtlety, but the words fell out of my head, like so much of my writing does, and I had to give them light and life. This is precisely how I felt, following the repossession of our former marital and family home. Steve's actions felt wholly sacrilegious to me. Oh well, at least it wasn't my credit rating taking the direct hit and scuppering my progress for six years.

Equity

The house was put on the market and sold in August 2016. By this time, I was knee deep into the school summer holidays, and starting to think about Alex's eighth birthday. The kids returned to school at the beginning of September and I shifted up a gear, getting everything ready for Alex's birthday on the coming Saturday. On the Thursday beforehand however, I received an interesting phone call from Lucia at Nationwide's legal team.

Lucia confirmed that Steve had racked up a business debt with The Bank, which had necessitated them putting a charge on the house. This meant that when the house was sold, The Bank had to be paid before Steve could enjoy the balance of the equity. I was already aware of this, as the Land Registry had sent me the updated title deeds, which detailed the charge. I was furious with how Steve was selfishly squandering the children's safety, security and future inheritance for his own ends, but there was nothing I could do about it.

Lucia asked if I had any objection to Nationwide settling the debt with The Bank. Somewhat bewilderedly, I asked Lucia what legal right I had to oppose The Bank being paid off first, and she agreed I had no legal standing whatsoever in this respect. I therefore couldn't understand why she had taken the time to call me, it all seemed so pointless. Lucia still pressed me for an answer and, without any legal authority to prevent such a thing, I verbally consented to The Bank being paid their debt.

The following day, whilst still up to my eyes in birthday preparations, I received an email from a colleague of Lucia's, asking me to confirm in writing what I'd verbally consented to during the telephone conversation. Busy, and on an immovable deadline, I promised myself I'd respond on Monday, when the birthday boy had been thoroughly celebrated.

Monday rolled around, the children were deposited into school and I got home to enjoy a cup of tea and some much needed quiet. The weekend had been long and filled with continuous excitement and noise, and this INFJ needed an energetic recharge. Whilst sitting quietly I remembered the email response I needed to get off to Lucia's colleague, and picked up my phone to compose the brief message. After about three or four words into the email I heard: *"How have you suddenly the authority to approve this?"* in my right ear. The question stopped me dead in my tracks. They had a point. I had addressed this very question on Friday, and it had been agreed I had no authority to approve or disapprove anything, so why do they now want it confirmed in writing? At the very least this warranted a phone call.

I called Lucia and asked the question again. Lucia wasn't entirely sure why I had been asked to confirm my authorisation in writing but asked if I was happy to do so. Now suspicious, I asked if it would be okay to decline putting anything in writing, not because I objected to The Bank having their debt repaid, but because I had a better chance of securing my share of the equity if The Bank were still in the legal mix with me; it would slow Steve's roll.

Rightly or wrongly, I calculated that if The Bank were paid off, there would be nothing to stop Steve scooping up the remaining equity for himself and legging it. I didn't trust him to share any of it with me. His was the only name on the title deed, he would argue it was his house, and the innumerable mortgage payments I'd made over the years, and the children I'd borne him be damned. Furthermore, if he had scooped all of the money, I couldn't have afforded to challenge him legally, whilst he could have afforded to legally defend himself. It was now well documented how horribly self-interested Steve had become.

Lucia confirmed it made no odds to either her or her firm if I consented in writing or not. Once I decided not to approve The Bank's debt repayments, in favour of seeking a judge's ruling on what was fair and equitable, Lucia confirmed that 100% of the equity balance would be sent over to the Royal Courts of Justice in London for safe-keeping, because Nationwide has a policy of not sitting on residual equity. I now had to apply to the RCOJ for my share.

I'm not legally trained and had no idea how to approach such a thing. So, following the simple principle of one foot in front of the other, one step at a time, with charm, respect and politeness all the way, I reasoned I should start by phoning the Royal Courts of Justice, for which Lucia had given me a phone number. How hard could it be? Granted, the people I spoke with were laser focused and busy and became somewhat impatient with my endless questions, but it was the only way I was going to learn what to do. I felt like David going up against Goliath, but I couldn't afford a solicitor to do it for me. The relevant paperwork was sent out to me, with instructions on what to do next given to me verbally. I exuded genuine relief and gratitude for the help I was offered, and duly got on with what needed to be done.

Okay next... I had to show I was in the process of divorcing Steve. Whilst the divorce process would take months, I at least needed a case number to quote within all future court documents. I couldn't afford a solicitor for this either, so I Googled *"How To Get Divorced Without Hiring A Solicitor"* and simply followed the advice from a website I called up. I requested the appropriate forms, applied for the fee waiver because I was on the appropriate benefits, and duly got the ball rolling. I eventually submitted the completed forms, was successful in my application to have the fees waived, and now waited to see if Steve would contest a divorce. I know, how could he contest it when he was the one to leave me, but I couldn't predict which way he would bounce on this, or anything else for that matter.

I thought he may have contested the divorce on the grounds of us not having a custody or access agreement in place for the children, but we'd attempted mediation and they had said they couldn't help us. To try and head him off at this pass, I made it clear he'd committed adultery, together with all the ways in which he'd rendered himself a biological fact only where the children were concerned. There was now a mountain of evidence against him, if he tried to counter my claim, and he'd be a fool to even try, but who knew what went on between his ears these days?

Pleasingly, the divorce petition came back signed quickly and without drama or contest. Steve had agreed to the divorce and didn't defend a single point I'd made about his deadbeat daddery. For sure The Imposter has no shame. The only thing he contested was my insistence he pay for the divorce, which seemed only fair considering he left me. He had wanted out of the marriage, so he could bloody well pay for it, but he cited affordability as a reason not to. We would have to see what the eventual divorce judge thought about that.

Now I had my divorce case number, and Steve's uncontested application back, I got busy creating a dossier detailing why I felt entitled to 50% of the residual equity from the house. This was a mammoth task as I had to try and predict, as best I could, all the questions I thought would be asked of me; should I ever be called in to defend my claim. My Imaginary Judge was working overtime. With zero legal training [*and watching old episodes of Boston Legal doesn't count*], all I could do was my best.

This work took me several weeks (between clients, kids and chores) to complete, and had no fewer than 25 appendices of supplementary evidence to support every claim I made. It was a weighty tome to be sure, and I was proud of it. I thought I might have had to sell a kidney to send it recorded delivery, but it was thankfully sent without surgery. All I could do now was sit back and wait for the judge's ruling. This was late November 2016.

As for the divorce, I put that on hold and pinned it all to a noticeboard. As the Applicant I controlled the speed in which the process took place. Hayley taught me this and guided me through the associated perils and pitfalls. Steve, as the Respondent, could only respond to what I served him with and when; he had no control over what happened. I couldn't afford to be divorced from Steve until the equity issue was resolved, so I pressed pause and waited. Do you see how and why strategic patience is an essential art to perfect? You simply cannot afford to *not* learn and deploy this indispensable skill. And you'll obviously need the strategy chops to go with it, to make it count for something. Patience without a plan is just waiting. A plan without patience is doomed.

On Monday 30 January 2017 I checked my bank balances over a cup of tea, first thing in the morning. With one click of a button my eyes shot out on stalks, exactly as they do in cartoons. My heart started pounding as my disbelieving mind scrambled to find an error or misunderstanding in what I was seeing. Perhaps a misplaced decimal point? Perhaps eye strain or newly acquired numerical dyslexia? Was I over-tired? Drunk? High? No, of course not, because it was only 6am. Actually, there was only one logical explanation for what I was seeing; the Royal Courts of Justice had ruled in my favour and approved the release of 50% of the equity, as requested. I promptly burst into tears from the immense relief.

I wanted to spend the day celebrating the end of years of poverty, struggle and seven bells of hardship, but I had clients to meet and a ton of work to complete. I would have to celebrate later, just as I'd had to cry later, almost three and a half years earlier when my life blew up. I sent out a joyous text to Paul and my War Council lovelies, before transferring every pound Paul had ever given me towards the realisation of our dream. My War Council responses were as happy and as congratulatory as you'd expect them to be. These platinum grade angels had been with me every step of the way through the fire, and now they would stay with me every step of the way through my walk in the park. Loyalty is returned.

Anyone and everyone will ride with you in the limo. What you want however are the nutters who coalesced around you, wouldn't let go and lovingly took the bus with you in your darkest days. In that 6am moment I took a mental inventory of everyone who'd helped us, everyone who'd turned away from us, and everyone who'd try to do us down. Now would come their reckoning in the form of my silence and distance.

Oh

I had assumed that when the Royal Courts of Justice were considering my application for 50% of the equity, they were considering the entirety of the case too. I assumed they would be ruling on The Bank's claim, and Steve's entitlement at the same time. Like I've said, I'm not legally trained, but this seemed like a logical conclusion to come to. I waited for the inevitable fallout from Steve, who I expected to be enraged with my success at securing 50%, but the silence was deafening. This puzzled me. Maybe he was reconciled with me securing my fair share? Maybe his malevolence towards me was mellowing? I honestly didn't know what to think, but I sure as hell wasn't going to contact him and poke the bear, so I just got on with my life. Only happier.

Promptly, in February 2017 I restarted the divorce proceedings, submitting my application for a decree nisi, which was subsequently granted in April 2017. Now all I had to do was to wait for six weeks, before applying for the decree absolute.

On the first day of the Easter school holiday a loud thud emanated from my doormat. A hefty A4 envelope had landed, decorated with the postal franking marks of a legal firm based up north. Intrigued, I opened the envelope immediately, only to learn The Bank were suing Steve and I – WTF? How in God's name had Steve's business debt become my responsibility? The documentation made clear The Bank was seeking satisfaction of the debt Steve had accrued but didn't make clear how I was part of any of it.

I spoke with my solicitor over the phone, who said they could review the documents the following day to then advise me of my position, but this would cost more than £700. Yes, I now had the funds to pay this, but I didn't know if those funds were at risk of repayment. I didn't want to make any unnecessary expenditures, which could eventually leave me in debt. There's no doubt about it, I was worried. I sat still and quiet, trying to collect my thoughts when I was told: *"Phone the man"* in my right ear. Eh, which man? *"Phone the man"*. The penny eventually dropped. I was to phone the solicitor who'd bought the suit against me, whose name was Spencer. The worst he could say was "You're not my client and I can't talk to you" – and I'd have been no worse off than I already was. To be honest I assumed he was going to turn me away, but assumptions are not facts, so I got busy diving into the facts, rather than paddling in the doubt. It was worth a shot.

Bedecked again in my big girl pants, I phoned Spencer. Remembering how it always pays to engage with charm, I asked him how I came to be named on the lawsuit, calmly and respectfully. Spencer was pretty charming himself and explained that he had been told I opposed The Bank being repaid their debt, but obviously had nothing in writing to prove such a claim.

As I had secured the HR1: Notice of Matrimonial Interest on the property (which was detailed on the title deed above and prior to The Bank's charge), Spencer also assumed this had been at the root of my opposition; but he was working on misinformation and too much assumption. I explained what had happened, and the discussions I'd had with Lucia and her colleague, which Spencer understood. So far so good.

Then Spencer referred to the equity – 100% of the equity – still sitting with the Royal Courts of Justice. Wait, what? Spencer was under the illusion the whole amount had remained untouched. How? Hadn't he applied for the debt amount immediately, as and when I had applied for my 50%? This didn't make any sense. I interrupted Spencer to ask him if I could shed some light on the situation for him, and he politely agreed. I then went on to explain how I had applied for, and been granted, 50% of the equity. Spencer went quiet.

Spencer went *very* quiet.

Once he'd gathered his thoughts and computed the ramifications of what I'd just told him, he asked when those funds had been released to me, so I told him. More silence. I really didn't understand what the problem was, or why the remainder of the funds hadn't been meted out when mine had been. Spencer continued to splutter, pause and think, and I didn't know what I'd said to cause this response from him. Why was this news to him? Finally, he expressed his complete amazement that I'd "had the balls" to approach the Royal Courts of Justice (no less) and to just ask for my 50%. *Err... okay?* It had merely felt like the next logical step to me, but whatever.

Apparently, this was a big deal to Spencer. Apparently, the Royal Courts of Justice are prohibitively intimidating to many solicitors, so he was having a hard time digesting how little ole me had just wandered up to them and simply asked for what I wanted. Not only that I'd had the temerity to ask for it, but that it had been granted too. What the hell had I said to persuade the judge? Spencer asked me how I had done it, so I told him about the dossier.

All the dossier was, was a compilation of the evidence I had, and had been collecting, against Steve and Helen since Day #1 of our separation. Very simple and stealthy really, but devastatingly effective. They. Never. Saw. It. Coming. I had successfully dug the ground out from beneath their feet, by consciously not distracting them from the throes of their infatuation with each other. This is why Psycho Bitch wasn't allowed to play, as she would have made them alert and defensive.

Everything they had thrown at me, I had kept, recorded and presented back as evidence against them, to benefit us. The spite, the malice and the hatred were all taken, absorbed painfully and passively and stored quietly for future use. I had taken the lemons Steve and Helen had thrown at me, made a chocolate cake with them, and left everyone wondering how the hell I'd done it. I hadn't thought to be afraid or intimidated by the RCOJ, because all I had been seeking was advice, information and the appropriate documentation. My lay person's status, and comprehensive work product, had been treated with the greatest of respect. Evidently, my abundance of reason and evidence was enough to persuade the Royal Courts of Justice.

Spencer had gone quiet again. I was now concerned that I'd done something wrong and may have gotten myself into some kind of legal jeopardy, but Spencer assured me I hadn't. He was simply full of admiration for my relentless tenacity, and what I'd achieved with it. I was confused but went with it, and for once in my life accepted a compliment.

Spencer then wanted me to confirm what had happened to the second half of the equity, and by now I didn't even want to hazard a guess. I told him I had assumed all three parties (Steve, The Bank and I) had been satisfied on 30 January 2017, but evidently The Bank had not been, hence these legal proceedings. As neither of us could confirm if Steve had received the second half, or not, Spencer hung up and rang the RCOJ to check. A short while later he called back to confirm the remaining 50% equity was still with the RCOJ and, as there were enough funds to cover Steve's debt plus the additional interest and legal costs accrued in having to pursue it, Spencer relieved me of my legal responsibility. *Phew!*

It appears I had been the only one, out of the three parties involved, to have had the initiative and audacity to approach the Royal Courts of Justice. This fact I found hard to believe and hard to digest, particularly as Spencer should have known better, I thought. Now because of Spencer's questionable job performance, Steve was going to be liable for additional interest, court costs and legal fees. If Spencer had applied to the RCOJ straight away, as I had done, the debt could have been recovered long ago. Instead, he appears to have waited for the money to be served on a silver spoon. It certainly seems to have been a profitable delay for his legal firm that's for sure; so perhaps it wasn't a dereliction of duty at all? Perhaps it was part of his revenue generating game plan? Who knows, but Steve and Helen didn't have the gumption to challenge what had happened or why. *Oh well.*

If I had been on Team Steve at the time, I would have encouraged him to kick up a stink about the additional costs, citing Spencer's questionable job performance; but Steve didn't want me. Steve wanted Helen, who appears to have all the intellectual curiosity of a house brick. His choice of inferior life partner was now costing Steve hugely. *Bummer.*

Spencer had the enviable pleasure of advising Steve of what had happened to the first 50% of the residual equity, more than two months after its payment to me. Evidently Steve hadn't applied to the RCOJ for his money either, probably because neither he nor Helen knew how, or thought to learn how. Honestly, why were these people sitting around waiting for things to happen? But I digress. Spencer's *Breaking News* resulted in complete and spluttery disbelief from Steve, and complete and spluttery unhinged outrage from Helen. Spencer informed me how, whilst talking to Steve on the phone, Helen could be heard yelling: *"BUT THAT'S NOT FAIR!"* repeatedly in the background. Like she really wanted to talk about what had been fair, *oh please!* This news positively warmed the cockles of my heart, as I remembered this timely piece of wise advice: *Move in silence and speak only when it's time to* say **checkmate, bitch!**

Helen had known our mortgage was paid off, with only a small home improvements loan left outstanding. Helen knew Steve was a successful entrepreneur, with a lovely thriving family business and some money and assets to his name. Helen may have considered Steve an upgrade from Lee and hadn't thought twice about throwing me out of the boat to try and steal the life I'd created for my family. Little did she – little did they – realise how much work I did in front of, and behind, the scenes, until it was too late, and I was gone.

. When they erased me from their equation nothing added up or made sense anymore. I don't think Steve fully appreciated how far I'd helped propel him and the business forward. Yes, Steve had undoubtedly done the hard-physical graft and maintained a golden reputation for excellence, which in itself led to more work via recommendations; but I had provided the impetus and the inspiration to generate, support and administer it all. We had once been a perfectly poised counterbalance; where one was weaker the other was stronger, and it had worked really well. We need only look at his current profit and loss to validate this point. Now I was gone, and their boat drifted aimlessly with no obvious means of propulsion, as far as their limited vision could see. Oh, the times I've imagined Steve and Helen in the boat they threw me out of, looking quizzically at the high-performance outboard motor, but not knowing how to operate it, and so opting to paddle with their splayed hands instead.

Jumping back to the equity issue briefly, Steve duly attended court, almost 200 miles away on 6 June 2017 to witness the presiding judge award The Bank their debt plus interest, plus legal fees and court costs. He walked away with less than a quarter of what he had originally anticipated. From the court documents I was sent, it is now clear what transpired.

In July 2015, having accrued the initial £11k business debt, it looks as though Steve may have decided to withhold the mortgage payments to eventually, and deliberately, spark repossession proceedings. I had previously made clear my unwillingness to sell (in January 2015), so they may have decided to pull the house out from under us to force the issue. Ruthless, but an otherwise efficient path to the residual equity, or so they believed. They probably calculated the value of the house, and the approximate equity left once the Nationwide and Bank debts had been settled, and figured he'd be able to get away with it all, as the sole name on the title deed. Oh, that and their chronic habit of underestimating me, of course. Obviously, I don't know for certain what went on in his/her/their collective mind, but can you state for certain I'm a million miles away from this being even a remote possibility; given all that you've read?

As Steve was the sole owner, he would only have had to split the equity with me, in the event of being divorced by me; the proceedings for which I hadn't started, in 2015. Maybe he was betting on me never finding the resolve to divorce him? In reality however, I had been waiting for him to make a move on the house, before I started divorce proceedings, because if I wasn't careful and divorced him too soon – or without an adequate strategy – I could have locked myself out of any entitlement I had. I needed to wait patiently in the long grass, bide my time and let things unfold as they should. It was an intensely ants in your pants edgy time to be alive, waiting for something that's moving too painfully slowly for your liking; but the dividends are worth it my friends. You must keep your eyes on the prize at all times, and let that focus determine every single one of your decisions.

With pressure building from The Bank for the debt to be repaid, Steve had no choice but to make things happen, so he stopped paying the mortgage, and knowingly risked his children becoming homeless. He never forewarned me about what was happening, or the potential danger he'd put the children in, so I could arrange alternative housing to keep them safe. No, his malice towards me seemed so all consuming that it overrode any parental concern he ever had for his babies. This toxic level of bitterness is going to eat him from the inside out, but he should know I wish him peace.

Once again, Steve had underestimated me and hadn't counted on my initiative, temerity or murderous work ethic. This is surprising given how many years he'd benefitted from all three qualities. Yes, it was harrowing to live through. No, I wouldn't wish those experiences on anyone, or ever wish to relive them, but I now see them as a gift, because now I know who I am, and what I'm truly capable of. I have come through the storm and clawed back more than I lost. The children and I are infinitely better for having lived through it all, because there are some things only a storm can teach you. What doesn't kill you makes you stronger, and all that jazz; as Hayley would say.

With the equity issue resolved, all that remained was for me to apply for the decree absolute, which happened to be awarded on what would have been our 28th anniversary. I kid you not. It made me smile quietly inside because, every seven years we humans are regenerated. Every cell of who we are is refreshed and renewed, and here I was now clean, clear and free to embark upon my new chapters, without being impeded by Steve's dragging sack of negativity. That's Helen's responsibility to look after now. Yeah, good luck with that, buh-bye.

Act II in the Life of Karan started well, particularly when the divorce judge ruled in my favour, rendering Steve liable for all the divorce costs. This must have been particularly galling.

Steve and I have still not spoken. He still has not seen, or shown any interest in the children, despite my best efforts during mediation and the park visit. And for what it's worth, the children are happy for The Imposter to keep his distance. Should Real Daddy ever bubble to the surface again, then he should know they are waiting – forever loving the memory of who he truly is – with their abundant love and hugs. He need only knock on our door to come and claim them.

As for that side of the "family", the children and I have severed all contact because where were they when we needed them? What added value have they offered the children's lives? How have they been an enhancement to the children's (emotional) development, safety or security? If they could not be relied upon in our darkest hours, we need them not in our years of triumph and comfort. We're only taking the platinum friends, family and angels with us, on our journey forwards, because they walked through the fire beside us.

Everyone who underestimated me, who bet against us, who turned away from us in our hour of need can now stand below and watch us fly. What they did, where the children were concerned, was unforgivable. All I wanted was for them to love Sofia and Alex as much as they ever professed to, but they couldn't do it. Evidently, they were all flash and no substance. They failed their family. They know who they truly are, and they should be ashamed of themselves, but I will leave them now with my blessings for the futures they truly deserve.

The children and I are free, loving life, and have never been happier. We are blowing the doors off and smashing glass ceilings wherever we find them and revelling in the joy this brings us. Whilst it most certainly didn't feel like it at the time, The Imposter leaving and taking Helen with him, was the best thing to ever happen to us. We truly are too relieved to grieve now. Yes, we hope Steve comes back to himself one day and re-enters the children's orbit, but when and if he does, Helen will still have been permanently exorcised from our energy, like a Basuka'd verruca.

Never ever give up, because it ain't over. UNTIL. YOU. WIN!

CONCLUSION

So, there you have it, the story of this particular chapter from my life. You now understand how the children and I have been mentally, emotionally and financially brutalised by a man who said he loved us to the moon and back. You have also been a witness to my comeback. I have shown you how I came out swinging, Not Giving In and vowing throughout that: It ain't over. UNTIL. I. WIN! I did this simply by doing my best in every situation, because it put me in the best possible position in the next situation. My Imaginary Judge is nodding in agreement with this, you'll be pleased to know.

Now it's your turn to clapback at the heartbreak and injustices levied on you, but there's something else I want to share with you, particularly if you're going through comparable circumstances. Contained within the following article is an old and wise fable, which represents another life lesson I have taught my children, particularly in the depths of their despair. I have also had to keep this fable at the forefront of my own mind, to counteract the dimming of my life's light from time to time, and to help keep myself strong.

The fable is about resilience, and it is my deepest wish for you to engrave your mind with this story, and the mental images I'm hoping to conjure up for you, to help you battle on. Here goes:

Here's How To Shake It Off

So, your life is crashing to hell in a handbasket, and you have über-positive people like me encouraging you to make chocolate cake out of the lemons life is throwing at you. The problem is, these lemons aren't just being thrown at you, they're being rocket launched at your head, with a heat seeking sensor, programmed to track the scent of the blood you're sweating!

[384]

It would be natural enough for you to think: "*Well, that's easy for you to say; you don't have X, Y and Z to contend with – YOU go and make sodding chocolate cake, I have my life to fix!*" So, when you've plummeted into a hole of some kind, how exactly do you shake it off? How do you use the elements of your experiences? How do you turn the situation to your advantage and create yourself a positive outcome? Well, I have outlined how I did it in this book, but obviously each individual case will be different, so for now I must keep it broad and generalised. To help convey my advice, I'm going to tell you this old story...

Many years ago, a man's favourite donkey fell into a deep and narrow hole. The man tried in vain to rescue the donkey, but after exhausting every attempt, it just wasn't possible. The man decided to bury the donkey alive, believing it to be the most humane of all solutions available to him.

The man started to shovel heaps of earth onto the donkey, but the donkey just shook off each load and adjusted its footing accordingly. As ever more soil was thrown onto the donkey, it continued to shake off the dirt and step onto the newly thrown in soil. With every shovelful of earth, the donkey rose higher and higher in the hole, until eventually it was able to climb out altogether.

The donkey could have chosen to stand there, doing nothing and accepting its apparent fait accompli. Instead however, the donkey took every shovelful of adversity thrown at it, shook off the negative weight, which would eventually have become overwhelming, and used it to achieve the optimised outcome of rescuing itself. This was all a process though, which *had* to be played out one painfully slow shovelful at a time. This was not a magic wand waving, wiggle of the nose ta-dah panacea. This self-rescue process took time, grit, determination, patience and a reserve of faith and resilience deeper than the hole itself. But it is during times like these when we learn who we truly are, and what we're truly capable of, so don't shrivel… SHINE!

What is it they say? Oh yes: *"No pressure, no diamonds"*.

Take what life throws at you and shape it into something beautiful or triumphant. This often-arduous process will help you grow into who you're ultimately meant to be. By doing the things you think you can't, by feeling the fear and doing it anyway, you will evolve into your full potential; your very best self. The alternative is to not, and to otherwise run, hide, quit and whimper instead. Is that who you are? Is that who you're prepared to become?

You haven't come this far to only come this far. Why else are you reading this book? You are reading this book because you wanted help, hope, inspiration and empowerment. You are not ready to lie down and quit; you only need a little ignition to get you going and you'll be off. Just because you may not be able to see the win right now, doesn't mean it's not there waiting for you to collect it. I couldn't foresee my successes during the dark days of 2013 and 2014, but they were there, nonetheless. All I had to do was work diligently towards them. Now you go and do the same because, yes actually, you can!

Nine of Diamonds

For those swamped in a seemingly endless swirl of worry, anxiety and even downright panic (as I was when Steve left, when we were made homeless, and when Paul was diagnosed with Stage 4 lymphoma), I want to give you another way, a way to help reframe your thinking.

Apparently the nine of diamonds, in a standard deck of playing cards, is bad luck. I don't know why, but you can always Google it if you're interested. I'm only using this as an example though, so it doesn't really matter. Please imagine yourself shuffling a deck of playing cards and fearing the nine of diamonds showing up in what you're about to do next. Now spread the cards out in front of you, before selecting one card at random. One card out of fifty-two.

This card shuffle, spread and your worry about selecting the nine of diamonds, represents you and your dilemma. Yes, there is one chance you will pick the nine of diamonds, there is one chance the thing you're worrying about will happen, but there are also fifty-one chances (in this example) that it won't. Whilst your odds may be greater or less than this example, my broader point still stands.

The problem with worrying and fretting in this way, is that you're in danger of attracting the thing you don't want towards you. Everything is energy, and it all vibrates at differing frequencies; particularly your thoughts and feelings. The Law of Attraction teaches us that like attracts like, which is easily verified by playing with common magnets. So, when you send out negative thoughts, vibes and worries into the universe, you're attracting more of the same towards you.

The reverse is also true. If you think positive thoughts, you attract more positivity. You can't fake it though. You can't simply parrot empty positive sounding words without meaning the intention behind them. Your energy changes when you're in a positive or negative frame of mind, and the universe responds to that, not your words. So always genuinely expect to succeed in everything you do. Never say anything about yourself that you wouldn't want to be true and be careful what you breathe life into with your thoughts, words and actions.

If you're predisposed to think everything in life is a bit shit, then that's all it ever will be to you, because you'll see what you expect to see. Did you ever hear the tale of the two dogs entering a room? Dog #1 was an excitable, happy waggy little chap, who went into the room for a few minutes and came out even more excitable, happy and waggy. Dog #2 was hostile and aggressive and came out of the room even more hostile and aggressive. Why? What the hell was in that room? Ahh, but the room was full of mirrors, so whatever energy the dog sent out into the room, it got back many times over.

Dog #1 went in happy and playful and was greeted by many reflections of the same energy, which made him happier and more playful. Dog #2 experienced nothing but an apparent room full of hostile and aggressive dogs, and so his natural instincts sent him out of the room more belligerent than he went in. Of course, this is only a cheesy illustration, and profound it ain't, but it is instructive: we get what we give. What we see in others is merely a reflection of ourselves, so if you want better, you're going to have to be better.

We are however, still allowed to have our blue days, but it's worth remembering they're only as 24 hours long as a good day, and that all things must pass. You don't drown by falling in the water, you drown by staying in there, so do something! There's relief to be found in taking action and doing something – anything – to alleviate the situation you're in. What can you do about it now? Then go and do it, or diarise it for a more appropriate time, or let that shit go. Take yourself for a walk, chat with a friend, have a good long weepy slide down the shower room wall – whatever is going to affect a positive change in your world and make you feel better, do it. Dwelling on things, without affirmative action, makes those things more dwifficult [*sorry, couldn't resist*].

There may be mental health issues in play and if so, please take action by seeking professional medical assistance quickly. You are not alone; you have bugger all to be ashamed of and you can and will get better with the right advice and support. You, my lovely, have been strong for far too long, and it's about time you let the rest of us help you for a change. You are the only one of you we have, and we need you, so please take care of yourself. If you have just scoffed at that last sentence, please will you consider this: The same God who created animals, mountains, oceans and galaxies, thought we needed you too. You are divine, you are strong, and you are loved, so please take care.

Negativity however is entirely another kettle of fish and can become a habit; sometimes grown from the seeds planted in your past. This you have control over. This you can do something about either by yourself, or with the support of high calibre friends, family, coaches, and therapists. Let me give you another example. If you were to walk into my shed and I said: *"Mind the gigantic spider"*, you'd be looking for the gigantic spider until your fear or caution helped you find it. The same goes for life and negativity versus positivity.

If you're looking for the faults, the flaws and the failures you'll find 'em. Okay, bravo, now what? Does that make you happy? No, not really. Does it make you more successful? Doubt it. Does it enrich your life in any meaningful way? Probably not. So why not change to a more positive outlook, a more empowered way of thinking and interacting with what happens in your world? Why not assume a new default setting of *life is great*, to override the criminally disempowering *life's a bit shit*? If you work deliberately and mindfully towards this change, your positive energy shift will turn things around.

Inverse Paranoia

Until about ten years ago, I didn't know what Inverse Paranoia meant either, so here's the gist. As you know, paranoia is a mental condition, characterised by an extreme and unreasonable assumption that other people don't like you, are plotting against you, or are going to harm, ridicule, shame or criticise you. So rather than live a life of extreme anxiety, (wrongly) believing everyone is conspiring against you, flip it and become an Inverse Paranoid.

An Inverse Paranoid person simply chooses to believe the world in plotting for them, rather than against them. Instead of seeing every trial, tribulation and thwartation [*new word*] as a negative packed agony, an Inverse Paranoid chooses to believe the challenge is sent to empower and enrich them, whilst advancing their cause, rather than crushing it.

Most successful people are Inverse Paranoids; and by successful I don't just mean the super-rich and the highly accomplished. Successful people can be defined as those who have got their shit together, are happy, living and thriving as their best and most authentic selves. When strife inevitably hits them – because why wouldn't it, we're all here to learn in the Classroom of Life – they ask: *"Where's the lesson, where's the growth opportunity, what can I learn from this?"* It's not what happens to you, it's how you respond that makes the difference. The quality of the answers you are seeking depend entirely on the quality of the questions you ask.

Remember the chapter Lessons Repeat Until Full And Learned, where I highlighted the difference in value between the extrinsic *"Why does this keep happening to me?"* and the intrinsic *"Why do I keep allowing this to happen?"* What you learn, and how well you respond to your challenges and trials, is entirely dependent on whether you assume the *"poor me, everything has external power over me, I am powerless"* position, or the Inverse Paranoid's preferred MO of *"where are the lessons, growth and opportunity in this situation?"* Inverse Paranoid people understand their power comes from within. It is precisely this power that drives them towards finding solutions, rather than falling back and wallowing in extrinsic *poor me* control dramas; ultimately solving nothing.

Now by way of example, look at how I dove straight into contacting the Royal Courts of Justice to chase my equity, compared to Steve who waited for it to be handed to him. He took the extrinsic *"life happens to me"* position, and probably ended up poor me-ing himself to sleep because it felt like the universe was conspiring against him. In reality however, what exactly had he done to help himself, to secure his desired outcome? Nada, zip, FA.

Alternatively, I took the intrinsically inspired *"if it's meant to be it's up to me + ooh, these lovely people at the RCOJ are really trying to help me as best they can"* Inverse Paranoid approach. Bear in mind, those RCOJ professionals would not have sought me out to help me at random. It was only because I asked for what I wanted that they gave it to me; be it information, general guidance or the 50% equity itself. None of it was going to come hurtling through the ether because it wanted to. It was essential I did my bit by actively working towards attaining it, and this is precisely what is meant by *you create your own luck.* You have to do the damn work, both inside your head and out!

You see, you get to choose what you think about. You get to choose what you grant headspace to. You get to choose the shape and consistency of your life, and the people you want in it. You have way more power and autonomy than you are using. You are the sole boss of you, so if you don't like something, change it. Others may try to control you, beat you down, influence or destroy you, but they will only succeed if you let them. This is why I'm a mentor and life coach, to help others realise their innate strength. I help people to stand in their own divinity and to grow into the space they want to inhabit in the world. I help to activate what's possible, because you already have the raw materials and qualities just waiting to be ignited; but all too often, you keep getting in your own way.

Are you wondering how to reprogram years of negative thinking and self-talk? Well, it takes focused dedication over a period of time for a start. This is not something you can wave a magic wand over, so the fairy dust does the heavy lifting for you. Be honest with yourself. If it has taken you X number of years to get to where you are, it shouldn't come as a galloping shock to realise it's going to take you at least a fraction of that time to overwrite your habits.

You can start small today though by using this one simple, free and painless technique: for every negative thought you think or utter to yourself, immediately overpower it with three positive things to smother that ~~mother~~... naughty thought. With enough practice you will automatically rewrite your ingrained negative thoughts with positive, fresh ones, and your brain will eventually develop resourceful new habits, which actually empower you. With a serious willingness to self-improve, your nature will gradually become more positive and optimistic, and therefore more resilient and efficient when the life shifts hit the fan.

Elizabeth Gilbert's Big Magic

Too Relieved To Grieve was started on 24 December 2017 and completed on 18 June 2018 [*176 days excluding endless months of editing and proofreading; you bet I counted!*]. This book is all Hayley's fault, we know this. How? Because in the middle of December 2017, Hayley and I were having one of our customary Kick Up The Arse (KUTA) chats, during which she urged me [*again!*] to write a book. Exasperated [*again!*] I asked her what I should write about, and she answered: "*Your life*". Urgh, the thought of that sent an odious shudder down my spine, but I guess Hayley sensed my prevarication [*again!*]

A couple of days later a small package landed unexpectedly on my doormat. Hayley had gifted me a copy of Elizabeth Gilbert's Big Magic – which I wholeheartedly recommend (along with her fabulous podcasts) to anyone not nailed down. Inside the front cover Hayley had written: "*To Karan, If this doesn't get you to write the bloody book then nothing will! Love Hayley -x-*" I started to read the book straight away and was finished within three days; it's heady and inspirational stuff. This was now Christmas Eve 2017.

With the kids otherwise engaged and a little alone time to go into my head, an idea began to form. I began to visualise how a book about my life needn't be about the whole of my life, just this one almost-five-year chunk of awfulness, which (if written correctly) could be helpful and instructive to others going through similar angst and emotional turmoil. Elizabeth Gilbert's theory of how ideas will ask you in your quietest moments: "*Do you want to work with me?*" was actually happening to me in that moment. It truly felt big, and it most certainly felt magical. I suddenly felt alive, motivated and in the throes of my newly untethered creativity. In the moments that followed I had written the first 1200 words.

Elizabeth Gilbert urges us in Big Magic to accept an idea's invitation to collaborate quickly, because it might otherwise leave you to find someone who will. This advice spurred me into becoming the unstoppable writing maniac I needed to be to get these 125,000 words out of me and down on to paper. This advice also gave me a powerfully cathartic vision in my mind's eye, which quickly went on to transition into a full epiphany.

Sitting quietly, mentally planning my book-to-be, I suddenly envisioned a white rubber bath plug in the centre of my chest [*as you do*]. Once I had become aware of it, the plug was pulled with an accompanying pop, and a flood of clarity and emotion poured out. Now I was "seeing" Steve walking away from me again, leaving me for Helen again, but then came the beautiful truth: he had taken all the debt, chaos, frustration, stress, problems and historical hurts that continue to weigh him down, with him. As he was walking away from me towards Helen, he was dragging a big dark sack of negativity behind him, and she was waiting at her door welcoming it all into her life. I was free, and a full catharsis burst open in me like an over inflated tyre. This was when I was told my book title: *Too Relieved To Grieve.*

A catharsis, in the literal sense, is the process of releasing, and thereby providing relief from, repressed emotion. I had been strong for so long and had held myself together – mostly for the sake of the children – for just over four years at this point. I had passively resisted the hate, silently absorbed the pain, grown steadily in strength, to prevail in every battle Steve had engaged me in. I had answered every challenge with love, light and the best version of myself possible, but my inner pressure valve needed to release, and so it all came out. The result was a euphoric serenity and the clearest vision I'd ever been blessed with. Just for a moment I felt certain I knew the secrets of the universe. The clarity was divine. Something had opened.

I'm telling you this now because it is not something I ever imagined happening, despite all my overthinking in the past. When I was plumbing my depths, I never imagined I could have prevailed as comprehensively as I have. But just because I couldn't see triumph in my darkest hours, doesn't mean it wasn't there waiting for me to collect it when the time was right. This is why you *must* have faith, because your hidden triumphs are waiting for you too.

The journey I have undertaken during these past almost-six post-Bomb Drop years has changed me; for the better I might add. It would have been so easy for me to mindlessly repeat the patterns of behaviour my Mum had helped to imprint upon my psyche as a child; to have self-medicated or self-harmed in some way. But I had been mindful when my time came to learn from Mum's experiences, choices and mistakes, just as I hope you can learn from my experiences, choices and mistakes now. It is my strong belief that by self-medicating (e.g.: alcohol, drugs, overspending, sex etc) or self-harming (i.e.: anorexia, bulimia, workaholism etc), we only delay the triumphs buried deep within our life lessons.

If I had chosen to hit the bottle to numb the grief of Mum's passing, and the pain of Steve and Helen's immediate betrayal, I'd have lost however many weeks, months or years in an unhealthy foggy, fugue state, only to then have to pull myself out of an even deeper hole than I had started in. Pain tells us when there's something wrong, so don't run and hide from it like a coward. Instead lean into it, keep going and seek all that it has to teach you. When confronted by your next heartbreak or challenge, ask yourself – out loud if you need to: *Where is the lesson in this? Where can my growth and personal development be extracted from? How can this god-awful situation help me? How can I profit (and not just in the financial sense) from this? How can this situation be optimised and swung back around to my advantage? What must*

[395]

I do to prevail? Then do it, no excuses, get it done.

When you think in these empowering terms it helps to prevent you from sinking into the depths of self-pity. Self-pity is dangerously like the gingerbread house in the story of Hansel and Gretel; desperately appealing in the midst of a famine or hardship, oh how you want to go in, feel warm, safe and to gorge yourself on its sweetness, but you enter at your own risk because it is fraught with peril. Once inside the gingerbread house (self-pity), can you be sure you will ever get out? Self-pity will keep you small, living your life within only a short arm's reach of your comfort zone, dissuading you from (romantic, financial, career, personal development) adventures again. A small life is no life to be proud of.

Lean In

If you're afraid of trying or loving again, because it too could end in pain, list all the ways in which you have grown and benefitted from the challenges you've prevailed against so far. Were they not ultimately worth the temporary pain and heartbreak? I know mine were. If your future holds the potential for more pain – which of course it does in this Classroom of Life – then reframe it in your mind, as the Inverse Paranoid you are now.

Instead of your future bringing you inevitable pain and hard choices, choose to see the added strength, wisdom, experience and opportunity that will come your way via the lessons gifted to you. More strife more life, as it were.

Leaning into future love and pain costs and hurts you in the beginning, but its ultimate value to you is worth far more, because you get incrementally stronger with every heartbreak and failure. Failure is learning, that's all. It's certainly not an excuse to never try again. It's a means of trying again, only this time with more knowledge and experience to guide you – like a baby finding its balance and eventually learning to walk, having fallen over multiple times. Winston Churchill also taught us: *"Success consists of going from failure to failure without a loss of enthusiasm"*, so lean in and learn.

Expecting to walk through life without ever falling down is unrealistic, because it is in perfecting the art of standing back up and continuing along our way (only bigger, better, stronger, harder and faster) that harbours the true purpose of us being here at all; growth and advancement. Remember that at the root of all frustration and disappointment is expectation, so keep your mind focused in the moment, and carry on. Don't expect anything, just accept what flows towards you and know that you have the power and wherewithal to deal with it efficiently, because you are strong and wise.

It is a delusion of entitlement – a belief that you're entitled to an easy and trouble-free life – that will upset and demoralise you, so accept that life is simply a series of tests and challenges. Reframe your thinking, because if you change your thinking, you will change your reality. Besides, where is the guarantee on your birth certificate that you will live a charmed life, free from stress, duress, and struggle? This thing called life is not a holiday camp, it's a classroom, as we've established. When you accept this fact, and lean into the continuous lessons on offer, the happier and more successful you will be.

In my personal example laid out in this book, I have learnt that I had spent from the age of twelve living in other people's lives, helping them to realise their full potential, without ever realising my own. This was a travesty, because I had unintentionally surrendered my own life's path. Yes, I had to meet Steve, love Steve, have Steve's children and be emotionally decimated by Steve to learn how much inner strength I actually have – because I had no accurate clue beforehand.

My old perceptions about myself had to be razed to the ground, before I could learn who I truly am, and having no one but my children to look after. Mum, Steve and Helen had all been taken from me, and having to also ensure my children came out of this harrowing experience realising their full potential too, was the making of me. I'm nothing like I was before. My change game is strong and neither Steve, Helen or his family can claim to know me, because they don't, and clearly never did.

Like anything in life, you get out what you put in, so if you run and hide from life's harsher lessons, what will you gain? How will you grow? Now turn this around. What if you stand and face and endure life's harsher lessons? Damn right it'll be brutal but imagine this for me please. Imagine a 30kg dumbbell on the floor at your feet.

Now imagine (assuming you're not a über fit and super strong gym bunny), trying to pick up the weight on your first attempt and successfully completing ten bicep curls. No, it's not going to be easy or comfortable. Okay. So, the solution is to start smaller with repetitions with lighter weights, to gradually build your strength and stamina. This is the nature of life; incrementalism is the key, but you do need resistance to build strength. You and your muscles will grow with persistent consistency, determination, discipline and a plan. So will your positive new habits and outlook, but you have to keep going.

By i.e.: refusing to fall in love again, or start another business following a bankruptcy, you're essentially running away from the challenge. You're refusing to even look at the dumbbell, much less gain any strength or benefit from having a go and starting slowly and carefully again. We must grow through what we go through.

Michelangelo's David

One last thought about your life before I leave you. I'm sure you're aware of Michelangelo's great sculpture of David? If not, you should be, so please Google it - I'll wait.

David started life as a 14ft high block of marble, which Michelangelo spent years chipping away at and shaping, before becoming the exquisite work of art we can see today. Your life is that 14ft chunk of organic material, which you get to shape into anything you can imagine it to be. It is a slow, painful and arduous task. It is an intense labour of love that'll take your entire quota of years on this earth walk to complete, but it is yours alone to create, in the image you imagine.

The heartbreaks, the pitfalls, the challenges and the agonies are the chips of marble that fly off as you hammer away, but their loss from the project results in the shape you want to sculpt. Your edges are smoothed with every harsh abrasion. Every grinding assault brings you closer to who you ultimately will be, so don't hide from the superficial unpleasantness, because it's temporary – everything is temporary – and all things must pass. Seek beyond what you can see. Sit in your quiet stillness and go deeper. Feel what is happening and accept life's gifts (which are admittedly often wrapped in a scabby bandage) and be thankful for what eventually reveals itself, if you let it. Trust in the process and know that you are strong enough to not only endure it, but to master it.

It has been hypothesised that we create the blueprints for our lives in Spirit before we're born. If true, then you need to remember this one critical point:

you can solve, endure and prevail against anything this world hurls at you, because you have sent yourself the problem to solve, so there is always a solution. I'm not saying it's going to be easy, but by overcoming everything that challenges you, you will grow into the person you ultimately need to be; and I wish you every success and happiness.

Thank you for reading. I sincerely hope the retelling of my story has helped you. Please now take anything you may have learnt and pay it forward. Please help others stay or become strong in the midst of their struggles, because we all need someone.

Be strong, be great and don't stop until you win!

With much love,

Karan *x x x*

Printed in Poland
by Amazon Fulfillment
Poland Sp. z o.o., Wrocław